A theory of adaptive economic behavior

GP85 00443

A theory of
adaptive economic behavior

JOHN G. CROSS
The University of Michigan

The right of the
University of Cambridge
to print and sell
all manner of books
was granted by
Henry VIII in 1534.
The University has printed
and published continuously
since 1584.

CAMBRIDGE UNIVERSITY PRESS

Cambridge
London   New York   New Rochelle
Melbourne   Sydney

Published by the Press Syndicate of the University of Cambridge
The Pitt Building, Trumpington Street, Cambridge CB2 1RP
32 East 57th Street, New York, NY 10022, USA
10 Stamford Road, Oakleigh, Melbourne 3166, Australia

First published 1983
Reprinted 1985

Printed in Great Britain at the University Press, Cambridge

Library of Congress Cataloging in Publicaiton Data
Cross, John G.
A theory of adaptive economic behavior.
Includes index
1. Microeconomics – Psychological aspects.
2. Equilibrium (Economics) 3. Learning, Psychology of
I. Title.
HB172.C76 1983 338.5 83–7563
ISBN 0 521 25110 9

Contents

Preface

The research reported in this book was initiated during 1968-9 with the support of a Ford Foundation faculty fellowship. Initially, the work was intended to be confined to an application of the Bush-Mosteller model of reinforcement learning to the economic theory of the firm. Discussions with colleagues, however, both individually and in seminars, made it clear that the fundamental premises of psychological learning theory are very difficult for economists to accept. In fact, it has often happened that seminar presentations that have been intended to outline specific applications of learning theory have been sidetracked into issues that, to a psychologist, have not gone beyond first principles.

Whether or not these elementary principles of behavior will finally become a part of economic theory, they certainly are not generally available in the economics literature or in contemporary textbooks. Thus, unlike models developed under conventional maximization theory, any economic model that makes use of adaptive theories of behavior must be prefaced with a development and defense of the underlying paradigm.

Therefore, it was decided that a book would be the best format for presentation of research in this area. A book can provide space for discussion and analysis of a variety of relevant psychological issues that cannot be compressed effectively into journal-length introductions. Having completed this basic material, it is then possible to present quite a wide variety of applications of the underlying theory without needing to repeat or redevelop the introduction. Moreover, one can take the opportunity at the same time to demonstrate that the formal theory of adaptive behavior has a great diversity of applications and is not confined to just one or two specific problem areas.

Any study that has extended over a long period of time is indebted to the intellectual contributions of a large number of colleagues and students. Among these, special thanks are due to W. James Adams, W. H. Locke Anderson, Theodore C. Bergstrom, Lawrence E. Blume, John Fitts, Melvin J. Guyer, Robert H. Holbrook, Saul H. Hymans, John P. Laitner, John Platt, Richard C. Porter, Gardner C. Quarton, Carl P. Simon, F. M. Scherer, Guy Swanson, Sidney G. Winter, and two anonymous readers provided by the Cambridge University Press.

I would also like to thank the editorial boards of the *Quarterly Journal of Economics*, the *Journal of Economic Behavior and Organization*, the *Review of Economics and Statistics*, and the *Journal of Development Studies* for permission to make use of material from articles that have been published before.

CHAPTER 1

Introduction

All human reasoning must be placed second to direct experience. Hence they will philosophize better who give assent to propositions that depend upon manifest observations, than they who persist in opinions repugnant to the senses and supported only by probable reasons.

> Galileo Galilei
> Second letter to Mark Welser
> on sunspots

Economics is outstanding among the social sciences for the active role its practitioners play in the formulation of public policy and corporate decisions. Whether or not their advice is followed, economists are routinely consulted on matters ranging from food-stamp programs to social security, from cost control to market forecasting, from oil leasing to tax policy, and from health-care delivery to defense spending. What is surprising is that those who seek this advice would, like most reasonable people, reject out of hand the behavioral principles on which these consultants rely. The gross oversimplification of production technology, the restriction to only a few distinguishable market structures, and particularly the reliance on an idealized model of maximizing decision making are so at variance with everyday experience that if economists stressed these as vigorously as they do the conclusions based on them, the profession would be classified as a form of medieval Scholasticism instead of a modern social science. The view that has become traditional is that these apparently unrealistic "assumptions" are vindicated by the success of the models they generate, and most economists may now be placed somewhere along a continuum ranging from those who accept these premises as approximations to the truth that are adequate for the purposes at hand to those who accept them in their entirety as valid empirical propositions in their own right.

The models that are developed in this book focus on only one class of assumptions: that composed of assertions that economic agents can be represented as conscious (and efficient) maximizers of profits in the case of firms and maximizers of utility (or self-interest) in the case of consumers. We do not intend to reject the validity of this representation in

1

all cases or even in most cases; indeed, it will develop that maximization often is a good model to use, but it is our intention to add some discrimination to the theory, differentiating between circumstances under which it is a good tool and circumstances under which it is not.

The proposition that living systems do not follow optimal paths as a general rule is as old as literature itself. To the extent that human nature provides the subject matter for classical writings, for the Judeo-Christian tradition and the religious philosophy that developed from it, and for the last three hundred years of poetry and prose, we find an image of mankind in the ordinary business of life following almost anything but optimal rules of behavior. This is not to say merely that human behavior is seen to be erratic, composed, as it were, of random disturbances that are centered on rationality; one finds example after example of systematic biases away from even ordinary common sense. Indeed, it is extraordinary that the perception of humans as nonrational beings, which has become commonplace throughout two thousand years of literature, should be so thoroughly rejected in contemporary economic theory that economists regard suggestions that it be reintroduced as controversial. Particularly with respect to circumstances under which efficient decision making would require foresight, self-control, or detailed analysis of a variety of hypothetical alternatives, artists persist in asserting the deficiencies of human activity and even use these deficiencies as justification for their own endeavors. In the words of Aleksandr Solzhenitsyn in his 1970 Nobel address: "Art is capable of the following miracle: it can overcome man's characteristic weakness of learning only from his own experience, so that the experience of others is wasted on him." Unless we believe that art has already accomplished its miracle, we must take seriously this view that efficiently implemented long-run self-interest is not an unfailing characteristic of human behavior.

Even if it is true that in many cases models derived from optimization principles produce accurate descriptions of market behavior, one cannot help but feel uncomfortable with a science whose assumptions conflict with reality but whose predictions do not. If indeed it is the case that we are dealing with usable approximations, we ought to have at least an intuitive insight into what makes them usable so that we can distinguish between real-world problems for which the approximations are close and those for which the approximations are unlikely to produce satisfactory results. Holding to the intuitive level, one can readily identify circumstances under which the maximization assumption is plausible and others under which it would strain the credulity of the most committed neoclassicist. The shopper who for years has frequented the same supermarket or department store has surely acquired some facility in making efficient use of budgetary resources at that location, and although minor mistakes would from time to time be readily acknowledged, a suggestion that gross errors are being made in finding the most satisfying products for a given dollar expenditure would not be easily defended. When given a chance to gain shopping skills, most of us believe that we can spend our money well, and we would accept an optimization model as a good tool to use in describing such situations. However, economists apply the same basic behavioral paradigm to choice under dynamic circumstances and to the analysis of risk, even though this extension flies in the face of a considerable body of empirical and experimental evidence. It has even proved to be possible to formulate models of drug addiction, compulsive gambling, suicide, and violent crime in the framework of the maximization hypothesis, but our capacity to develop such models does not constitute convincing evidence that those who engage in such things are in fact carrying out optimal behavioral programs.

Analogous situations arise throughout the sciences. A frequently cited example concerns the neglect of air friction in Newtonian mechanics; when velocities are low and objects are dense, air friction is insignificant, but even though we may not be able to quantify its influence precisely, we do understand that air friction will significantly influence the acceleration of a dropped feather, and we would not be comfortable with a model that used the same equations to describe the free-fall behavior of both feathers and stones. In accordance with this analogy, most economists would like to draw the line somewhere between cases in which optimization is clearly a good rule and cases in which it is not, but because we have at best an imperfect notion of what our approximations are approximating, it is difficult to know where such a line should be placed.

When we defend the maximization paradigm by pointing to the similarity between its predictions and observed behavior, we often overlook the fact that the empirical "success" of many economic models is principally derived from accommodating adjustments in complementary hypotheses. Because individuals are presumed to maximize their own personal levels of satisfaction (which are themselves unobserved) and firms are presumed to maximize profits subject to an imperfectly specified technology, it is often possible to adapt the specification of preferences and production to bring the optimization principle into conformity with *any* observed empirical regularity. Market data are used to make inferences about the nature of preferences, expectations, and production functions through the mediating assumption of maximizing behavior, and unless these inferences are independently validated, it is impossible to uncover violations of the intermediary hypothesis. Such independent tests are rarely possible, even in principle, and consequently the "success" of the economic model is reduced to the success of a tautology, not the success of a positive science. It is sometimes argued that this is not a compelling objection to the use of optimization models: So long as people behave consistently, the descriptions generated by these models will continue to be valid, and we shall continue to be able to predict the market consequences of taxes, subsidies, and supply/demand shifts reliably. However, such an argument again fails to provide any guidance as to when such "consistent" behavior can be expected to occur and when it cannot. Moreover, it overlooks the enormous importance that is being given to the normative applications of contemporary economic theory. Traditional analyses of consumer welfare require that behavior provide an accurate reflection of individual self-interest, and this demands that maximization be a valid empirical rule, not simply a convenient framework in which to describe market data. Without the optimization principle, there is no validity to the conventional judgments regarding the welfare losses due to imperfect markets, the appropriateness of taxes and subsidies to offset externalities, or the usefulness of concepts of "consumer surplus" in defending public expenditures.

In spite of these problems, we economists frequently resort to an offensive complacency when we are confronted by challenges to the theoretical underpinnings for our work. Examples of obvious violations of optimizing behavior (individual consumers who fall victim to excessive borrowing behavior, firms which misuse accounting data and follow unprofitable business practices, or legislators who propose programs which will compound rather than resolve social problems) are frequently met not with concern that an essential tenet of our science is thereby under attack but either with ridicule directed toward the offenders for their foolishness in not pursuing their own interests or with offers of consulting assistance at a reasonable daily fee. It is as though behavior that conflicts with the essential assumptions of economics may be ignored if it proves to be easy to question the intelligence of the individuals who engage in it or to convince them that they are the victims of insufficient information or unsophisticated computational procedures. Even so, the behavior of these same victims constitutes the subject matter of our science, and it is surely time that the poor information and the inadequate analytical abilities be accounted for in the theories themselves.

Consciousness of this aspect of the problem has already led many economists to formulate theories of markets whose participants are imperfectly informed as to product quality, prices, or the future states of supply. The procedure has been to introduce uncertainty and expectations variables and to convert the imperfect information into a statistical decision problem whose solution will provide optimal behavioral rules in some expected value sense. The methodological price for this approach has been extremely high, however, for it has become necessary to assume that individuals in these markets can be represented as mathematical statisticians capable of solving specific problems that often are beyond the analytic abilities of professionals in that field. It also requires reliance on the assumption that individuals follow optimizing rules of behavior under just those dynamic and risky types of situations for which the assumption of optimization has the least empirical support. In effect, we have been able to add realism to one dimension of the problem, but only by moving even farther from reality in another direction.

This book implements quite a different approach to the behavioral underpinnings of economic theory. Rather than assuming that individuals engage in conscious optimization and planning, we assume the existence of feedback mechanisms that use historical successes and failures as guides, directing individuals into behavioral paths that, in the light of experience, have had the greatest payoffs. Over the long run, any such adaptive mechanism might be expected to produce convergence to stable behavioral patterns, and in many cases these patterns will meet the traditional criteria for optimality in the sense that slight deviations will lead to inferior outcomes from the individual's own point of view. However, this interpretation holds optimality to be an equilibrium condition rather than a property of all short-run behavior. Moreover, it introduces the possibility that a great deal of behavior is not optimal, perhaps because the dynamic convergence is not yet worked out, because the feedback is so remote in time and space as not to be associated with the proper causal action, or because the existence of uncertainty and the persistence of fluctuations in the environment make convergence impossible.

Parallels

The view that optimization can be viewed as an equilibrium condition and that practical circumstances may interfere with the achievement of equilibrium was forcefully stated over twenty years ago by Herbert A. Simon (1955, 1959), and his general viewpoint has been restated many times by such writers as Koopmans (1957), Cyert and March (1963), Winter (1964, 1971, 1975), and Day (1971). With a few exceptions, however, the implicit suggestion that models might be devised based on alternative paradigms has not been exploited. For example, although his studies suggested the relevance of a variety of psychological theories, many of which go beyond the simple feedback mechanisms that will be treated in this book, Simon did not provide fully developed models whose implications could be used as concrete alternatives to traditional optimizational procedures. To be widely accepted, any alternative hypothesis must be shown to explain at least as much as the hypothesis it is intended to replace, and the fact that most of Simon's work dealt with challenges to received doctrine, rather than with the development of alternatives, may explain why relatively little attention has been given by "mainstream" economists to his (very convincing) arguments.

The formal proposition that systems that are subject to adaptive pressures might converge to states that can be described in terms of the principles of optimization is very old and extends throughout the sciences. Perhaps the first such theory that still enjoys widespread contemporary application is Darwin's (1859) theory of evolution. This began as a dynamic theory in which the most "fit" of living organisms would reproduce at rates higher than others, so that, over time, the composition of an entire population would be found to shift in their favor. Over the very long run and under stationary environmental conditions, the population would eventually come to be composed of only the most "fit" organisms, and the theory was readily reinterpreted into a theory of "survival of the fittest." In the cultural environment of the nineteenth century, the popular notion developed that all living species were ideally formed to fit their particular "niches" in the ecosystem. Thus, Darwin's dynamic theory was deemphasized in favor of its property that in equilibrium one can describe organisms with an optimization model. A contemporary occurrence of this same interpretation is found in the emerging field of "sociobiology," in which it is argued that genetic factors may influence social and behavioral traits as well as physical traits. It is then shown that certain "altruistic" traits (behaviors that benefit others at some cost to oneself) will evolve along Darwinian lines if the altruism is directed principally toward close relatives (Hamilton, 1964, 1972). (This is because the genetic characteristics of close relatives are similar, and increased survival of one's relatives enhances the likelihood that one's own genetic type is represented in the population.) The equilibrium properties of such a model support behavior that maximizes the survival probability of certain genetic types rather than the survival of individual organisms. Proposed examples are (1) the existence of sterile bees whose behavior increases the "fitness" of an entire hive and (2) the behavior of mammals that leads to the selection of mates that are not close relatives, thus avoiding the dangers of inbreeding. In spite of the fact that this is simply an equilibrium result, sociobiologists are increasingly prone to ignore the convergence process, turning instead to optimization models to describe social behavior (Smith, 1978). Sometimes even the genes themselves are described as though they were cognitive maximizers (Dawkins, 1976).

The history of psychological-reinforcement learning theory follows a similar pattern, although psychologists seem to have retained more interest in the dynamics of this particular feedback mechanism. If we are willing to take a sufficiently abstract view, the learning process can be described in the same language used for biological theories of evolution: Behavior patterns that are most "successful" (meaning most strongly rewarded) are "reinforced," which is to say they are more likely to occur again in the future, displacing less successful patterns of behavior. In effect, it is *behaviors* that survive, and because it is the most highly rewarded that are most successful, an equilibrium may eventually occur that contains only behaviors that are optimal in the sense that they maximize reward levels. Some psychologists have followed the precedent that has been set among biologists and are employing optimization models to describe equilibrium behavior; indeed, many of them have come to use the utility-maximization models that are familiar to economists (Coombs et al., 1970). The displacement of the dynamic learning paradigm has not progressed far among psychologists, however, perhaps because the existence of the stable environment that is essential before any equilibrium can be achieved is more problematic. Not only must external conditions remain fixed, but the nature of reward must not change, no matter how often rewards are encountered. If rewards lose their effectiveness through exposure (or if "variety is the spice of life"), then equilibrium is impossible, because the conditions under which the payoff to some action is "rewarding" are themselves continually shifting. Indeed, far from accepting convergence on optimization, concern with this problem has led many psychologists to question the usefulness of the concept of "reinforcer" itself (Allison, 1981).

Disequilibrium

There is nothing improper in the careful use of optimization models to describe the equilibrium states of certain feedback mechanisms. Indeed, there are great advantages in doing so in that the mathematics appropriate to optimization theories are well developed and are much more tractable than are the mathematics that have to be used to describe the underlying dynamic processes. However, there is the danger that in concentrating on equilibrium conditions, one might come to ignore convergence entirely and fall into the habit of treating the maximization principle as though it were the underlying behavioral paradigm rather than simply a long-run asymptotic state. This is a dangerous trap, for it tempts one to apply the optimization rule to circumstances in which the equilibrium is unlikely to have been achieved, and in which such an application is therefore quite inappropriate. It also leads one to overlook important behavioral results that are characteristic of transitional states and that can be properly analyzed only in terms of the underlying dynamic mechanism. One is tempted to speculate that this is just the path that economists have been following. Traditional microeconomic comparative-statics theory treats only full-equilibrium stationary states, and the use of optimization principles for such states may well be justified. The treatment of dynamic problems (decision making over time) at first seemed almost intractable to economists because the necessary stationary state was missing, and when a theory was developed, the role of optimization was at best ambiguous. Irving Fisher (1930), who cleared the way to our modern theory, did not regard decision making as consistently optimal. His term "impatience," used to describe a seeming tendency for individuals to favor present-day gratification at the expense of future well-being, conveys a flavor of error and irrationality, a flavor that is reinforced at many points in his discussion. It was only later, when optimization was firmly established as a behavioral paradigm, that economists dropped the term "impatience" and made "time preference" into a property of utility functions, giving an aura of rationality to what Fisher saw as a short-sighted tendency to undervalue the future.

Optimization techniques can provide efficient methods for describing the equilibrium states that are achieved by various feedback mechanisms; nevertheless, it is not always clear to what entity the maximization principles should be applied. This is a problem that is familiar in economic theory: Empirical realism often suggests that consumer theory should be applied to a group (the "household"), even though it is much easier to defend the elementary assumptions of complete transitive ordering that underlie preference theory if one restricts oneself to individuals. An adequate explanation of the behavior of a firm seems to require elements from several different theories: a theory of a single profit-oriented entrepreneur, a theory of "teams" (Marshak and Radner, 1972), and a theory of the behavior of a group of self-interested managers (Williamson, 1963). And, of course, simultaneous optimization in all three of these dimensions is impossible. The same dilemma has appeared in other sciences that employ feedback mechanisms. The evolution of altruistic behavior that has been described by sociobiologists is confined to behaviors that benefit close relatives, and for this reason, almost all the proposed examples of biologically determined altruism are derived from the behavior of bees, wasps, and ants – species that for biological reasons have extraordinarily close genetic relationships. It is certainly not the survival probability of individuals that is maximized in such models, and there would be no foundation for a belief that an entire species, as a class, is ideally "fit" for its "niche" in the ecosystem, however long-standing the equilibrium may have been. Indeed, in biological examples, it is impossible to know where to apply an optimization rule without first detailing the specific feedback mechanism that is operating. "Survival of the fittest" may apply to the individual, the family, the hive, or the colony, depending on the methods of reproduction and the environmental and social conditions that govern it.

However convincing we may find the proposition that feedback mechanisms can lead to long-run optimal states, there nevertheless exist environmental circumstances under which this convergence will not take place. The largest class of such cases is associated with situations that incorporate significant elements of risk. Convergence to optimality may fail to occur simply because the environment is subject to such erratic shocks that no historically determined behavior can possibly be effective in the present. However, a much more interesting case arises if the stochastic process that is responsible for the randomness is statistically stationary, providing a long-run distribution of possible events that is quite stable. Under such circumstances, "rational" behavior is easily defined, and, indeed, the theory of optimal behavior under risk has been increasing in usefulness and sophistication ever since the first formulation of the expected-utility hypothesis by Daniel Bernouilli in 1738. The problem with using this theory to describe "equilibrium" conditions is that many of the feedback mechanisms that have been recognized to be responsible for adaptive behavior do not deal efficiently with uncertainty, so that the use of an optimization model introduces systematic errors. Psychological learning processes are well known to lead to nonoptimal behavior in this sense because they always give greater weight to recent experience than they give to the more distant past, and this prevents the kind of overall averaging that expected-utility maximization would require. There are many experiments that have been done and that bear out this conclusion. In one popular example, developed from an experiment by Grant and associates (1951), a person is confronted by a pair of signals (such as a light bulb on the left and a light bulb on the right) and is asked to guess which one is about to be turned on on each occasion of a long series of trials. Which signal is actually operated each time is determined by a random mechanism that chooses the signal on the left with some probability p and the signal on the right otherwise. Thus, the bulb on the left may come on 60 percent of the time, and that on the right will come on 40 percent of the time. The behavior that is observed is a sequence of guesses in which the subject selects sometimes one signal and sometimes the other. If we call r the frequency with which the subject chooses the signal on the left, and $1 - r$ the frequency for the signal on the right (whether or not these choices appear to be random), then, because the operation of the bulbs is random, the subject will guess correctly with a probability equal to $rp + (1-r)(1-p)$. Because this expression is equal to $r(2p-1) + (1-p)$, it is obvious that payoff-maximizing behavior would dictate a strategy of always selecting the alternative that has historically been operated with the greater frequency. That is, if p is greater than one-half, so that the bulb on the left comes on more often, the expected number of correct guesses increases as r is increased to its upper bound of one. In fact, experimental data generally reveal apparent equilibrium values of r that are closer to p than they are to the payoff-maximizing value. As in all such cases, there are many ways to rationalize this result so as to reduce its incompatibility with the utility-maximization hypothesis: We might suggest that it is more "fun" to the subject to guess the less likely outcome correctly, or we could speculate that the subject may not believe that the mechanism is genuinely random and may be engaging in an attempt to decipher the pattern. The ad hoc introduction of such considerations into the theory does reconcile the optimization model with observed behavior, but only at the great expense of postulating the existence of unobserved intervening variables. It is always possible to follow the course of inventing exogenous variables that are said to affect an outcome but that cannot be independently observed, but the cost of this introduction is destruction of the optimization model as a useful predictive tool. Whatever such variables we introduce, the straightforward view of maximization of expected payoff (or expected utility of payoff) is completely disconfirmed.

Taking another tack on the same problem, other types of stochastic experiments with random payoffs have been devised that enable us to calculate "subjective" outcome likelihoods, the idea being that if the individual believed these subjective likelihoods to be the true payoff probabilities, then expected utility maximization using these probabilities would generate the observed behavior. These subjective probabilities can then be compared with the objective (true) probabilities from which the experiment was constructed. It has been found that subjective probabilities calculated in this way are generally above the objective probabilities at low values and below them at high values (Coombs et al., 1970, pp. 128-37; Kahneman and Tversky, 1979). That is, if we were to accept expected-utility maximization as a behavioral rule, we would have to conclude that people make systematic errors in estimating objective probabilities, and of course the theory itself would give us no clue as to the genesis of these errors.

The great advantage to be gained from a feedback view of behavior determination is that it provides usable models under both risk and certainty, and under both equilibrium and disequilibrium conditions. Any convincing demonstration that equilibrium has not been achieved in some market constitutes a demonstration that models based on a maximization paradigm are not applicable. As a result, short-run adjustment problems, especially those that concern macroeconomic theory and policy, are often wholly intractable in terms of traditional analysis, and the models that have been developed to deal with them seem arbitrary and unrealistic in the extreme. Experientially motivated theories of behavior do not suffer from this disability because they are well defined under conditions of disequilibrium. Moreover, they possess an even greater methodological virtue in that the same fundamental models apply to both equilibrium and disequilibrium circumstances. Thus, it is not necessary to alter the theory in any substantive way when one shifts attention from the long run to the short run, from risk to certainty, or from decisions that operate only in the present to those that also involve the future.

Personality and cognition

In treating optimization as a possible equilibrium state for certain feedback processes, we are attempting a reconciliation of two extreme views of the determinants of behavior. Whereas the maximization principle posits a fully developed capacity for calculation and deliberate application of that ability to the entire range of human behavior, most feedback processes are passive and mechanical in operation, permitting no cognitive influences over the patterns that emerge. Most of us would be more comfortable if we could take some middle ground. Important as passive feedback processes certainly are, most of us do engage in conscious planning, simulating by conjecture the consequences of alternative behavioral paths under conditions of uncertainty or over time. Everyone does some retirement planning (although some do much more than others), gamblers do consider the odds in placing their bets, and even biological evolution may be affected by occasional deliberate eugenic influences. In comparison with the idealized methods of optimization, these methods are certainly deficient, so that the final behavior that emerges will be a mixture of a purely mechanical adjustment process and imperfect cognitive decision making. What proportions would characterize this mixture is unknown, although the evidence already cited does not favor a dominant role for the cognitive elements. The problem of finding appropriate weights for these two ingredients is made more difficult by the fact that the use of planning models and conjectural simulation may itself be learned from experience. Anyone who has experienced success in planning will be encouraged to repeat the planning process in the future, whereas those whose plans have failed may turn away from cognitive decision making altogether. Because random elements in the environment may play an important part in determining whether or not any plan meets with success, we expect to find a population to be characterized by a distribution of willingness to use cognitive methods: Whether an individual relies on meteorology or astrology to plan a picnic may depend on when it has rained in the past. Some of the most striking differences among people are to be found in this regard: Those who consciously and carefully attempt to direct their lives through intellectual reflection are easily distinguished from those who act as though their futures were determined wholly by mysterious external forces. With respect to planning for the future, Irving Fisher, as we have already noted, was inclined to differentiate these into the farsighted and the foolish, but we would prefer the less value-laden view that those who have happened to be successful in their plans, whether from superior capacity for planning or from simple good luck, will be found to use cognitive methods more than those whose earlier attempts have been less successful. This distinction is the subject of an extensive psychological literature as well. Seligman (1975), especially, provided a dramatic analysis of the extent to which human willingness to use planning or to attempt to control the future is dependent on (happenstance) elements in experience.

Having said all this, we must acknowledge that the simple models to be developed in this book will not deal directly with the extent to which planning and intellectual control play a part in decision making. In the event that cognitive decision making tends toward the same behavior as the equilibrium of a feedback mechanism, then the introduction of these considerations will have the effect of accelerating the convergence process and will not change the substance of the models in any way. This is the view we shall generally take toward planning processes throughout this work.

There are many psychological theories of behavior that rely on personality variables and cognitive processes of one sort or another to supplement or even replace the automatic feedback process of reinforcement learning. Models that employ such concepts as motivation, aspiration level, dissonance reduction, drive, need for achievement, fear, culturization, and social orientation all can be used to obtain apparent insight into the determinants of human behavior. The difficulty with many of these is that, at least at the present state of the art, they employ exogenous variables that are not directly observable and that are not easily recognized in a market context. These theories of behavior sometimes rest so heavily on personality variables that one cannot derive any sort of aggregated market theory without first specifying the composition of personalities within it. There are circumstances under which the use of such variables might be very helpful. A market dominated by one firm may have features that are in large part reflections of the personality of the chief executive officer of that firm. It may be that personality and cultural differences between French and American consumers, or between rich and poor consumers, generate important differences between markets that are composed of different proportions of these groups. In most cases, however, the use of models with these nonmarket exogenous variables would reintroduce the sort of ad hoc analysis that is so objectionable in existing economic maximization theories. Because we plan to concentrate on the traditional questions of the responses of markets to shifts in supply, tax levels, and the like, a model that would suggest that consumers will react in certain ways simply because those reactions are dictated by their personalities would not be very useful, and for this reason we shall confine ourselves to models that do not involve such a dependence.

Summary

We must acknowledge that the attitudes that we have expressed in this chapter are by no means original. The suggestion that a "natural-selection" feedback mechanism can be used to support the use of optimization models is quite common. Friedman (1953) used it as an argument in support of his proposition that economic agents act as if they were maximizers, Winter (1964, 1971) developed from it a rigorous model of the behavior of firms, and recently two volumes of studies have been published with the biological analogy as a central theme (Day and Groves, 1975; Nelson and Winter, 1982). Moreover, there is little evidence that economists sustained the view that optimization might be an adequate foundation for all of economic theory before it was demonstrated by Samuelson (1948) and others that such an assumption would open the door to a valuable and systematic formalization of economic theory that in turn would produce a great number of elegant and powerful insights. Even since then, severe reservations have been expressed by such economists as Simon (1955, 1959), Cyert and March (1963), Day (1971), Nelson and Winter (1973, 1982), Nelson (1974), and Winter (1975), and these reservations have provided the central issue for interminable debates on questions of economic methodology. With the exceptions of the work of Nelson and Winter, however, none of these nontraditional views (if that is what they are) has led to the formalization of rigorous, predictive models that are capable of being compared side by side with standard neoclassical theory. The literature has had a consistently descriptive tone, and its authors have been inclined to stress the deficiencies of optimization theory rather than the positive usefulness of any formal alternatives. The general reader might well conclude that to accept these arguments would be to throw out the baby with the bath water, because it would require that we abandon not only maximization but also the entire body of rigorous quantitative analysis that has gone with it.

This book is specifically intended to demonstrate that the abandonment of the maximization hypothesis as an elementary behavioral hypothesis does not entail the abandonment of rigorous analysis, and for this reason we shall consider a variety of quite different economic problems from the perspective of an experientially motivated model of behavior. Some of these applications prove to be rather technical, but this is part of our plan of demonstrating that it is possible to construct formal models from the general perspective of feedback or adaptive systems and to compare their implications with those of existing theory. Finally, we reiterate that it is not a prerequisite to the use of feedback models that we consider human beings to be the intellectual equivalents of laboratory mice. We shall use as much psychological material as is practicable in a general theory. Indeed, the model we shall use is partly a psychological one, but the psychology is intended to apply to people who possess cognitive powers, and for this reason we shall attempt to retain an awareness of the role of cognition in the processes and assumptions as we develop them. We shall also refer occasionally to biological models, partly because they are excellent analogies to use in describing any feedback process, partly because the biological selection mechanism has so often been considered to be applicable to economics (particularly in the case of the firm), and partly because the developing field of sociobiology is centered on the assertion that behavior, including economic behavior, may actually be, in part, a matter of biological selection, and we wish it to be clear that our own theory is consistent with this possibility.

CHAPTER 2

Models of convergence

The model we shall employ was developed originally from a psychological learning paradigm, although its formal structure can be applied equally well to almost any behavioral feedback process if the variables are suitably interpreted. There is only one condition that is absolutely essential to any application of the model, and that is that the dependent behavioral variable be defined as a probability or a probability vector rather than as a definite action. Indeed, it is because statistical distributions so often provide the best empirical descriptions of behavior that the use of feedback models has become widespread. In the case of biological and sociobiological theory, probability models are standard fare: Genetic models all describe random-draw processes that focus on the likelihood that an individual will have certain physical or behavioral traits, given the gene frequencies that characterize the population of that individual's own ancestors. Psychological models also conventionally use probabilities as dependent variables, a use that has evolved from long experience with laboratory evidence indicating that even under carefully controlled circumstances one cannot predict voluntary choice behavior with certainty. This may, of course, be a reflection only of our own limited understanding of human nature. Some might argue that every choice does have a deterministic foundation and that our failure to make perfect predictions is a reflection of our ignorance of the essential exogenous variables rather than the result of any fundamental randomness in the behavior under study. Even from this point of view, however, it must be acknowledged that, given our present state of knowledge and our inability to observe thought processes directly, the statistical distribution functions are still the best that we can do, as outsiders, to describe the behavior that we observe.

Among social scientists, economists appear to be unique in their insistence that choice behavior can be fully described in terms of a few simple variables once the (possibly unknowable) character of "tastes" is established. Even among economists, however, obvious conflicts between the deterministic model and actual experience have become inescapable, and there have been many recent attempts to broaden the theory in a way that will reduce these conflicts. These amendments all preserve the essential

15

determinism of the theory. A popular procedure, for example, is to introduce a proposition that one's choice behavior depends on one's expectations for the future. Because expectations are only inferences drawn from experience, it becomes possible to develop models in which individuals with different personal histories make dissimilar choices even under identical circumstances. Such arguments maintain the premise that individual behavior is fully determined, but by permitting statistical variations to appear among individuals with different backgrounds, they preserve variability in behavior. In fact, we could define our own model in a way that would be consistent with this view, continuing to use a probabilistic dependent variable. Besides avoiding conflict with traditional theory, this would be an attractive procedure in that it certainly would capture a part of what actually occurs in practice. Nevertheless, although we accept its relevance, we would prefer not to confine our interpretation to such a narrow view. It would require us to restrict application of the model to entire markets rather than to individuals, because the interpretation would then be that the feedback mechanism describes aggregate changes in expectations rather than a summation of random influences over the behavior of a single individual. The evidence is by now overwhelming that the conventional models of individual behavior are themselves too restrictive, and if we were to confine the model in this way, we would preclude some interesting applications to both consumer behavior and the theory of the firm. It would sidestep the question of allocative efficiency as well: Whether or not the market is successful in meeting consumer wants depends on consumers' success in making their interests manifest in the marketplace, and this question can be addressed only if our model is formulated in individual terms.

Choice

In treating the decision-making process, economic models have traditionally focused on the values of specific outcome variables, such as the production level of a firm, the quantity of investment, or the number of bananas consumed by one household. It is often evident from direct observation that these quantities are determined in practice from the application of relatively simple (even naive) decision rules. The supermarket shopper may use simple rules of thumb to regulate the generic composition of a market basket (the proportions of meats, vegetables, grain products, etc.), and the decision whether one of the meat items appears as hamburger, hot dogs, or salami is of lesser significance and may be made on the basis of purely spur-of-the-moment, trivial considerations. There is also a great deal of empirical evidence that decision making within firms is more easily characterized as the application of rules of thumb rather than as the implementation of sophisticated outcome-oriented optimization techniques. Cyert and March (1963) provided extensive documentation for the central role played by simple rules in managerial decision making, and Clarkson (1963) was able to duplicate actual investment-portfolio decisions with great accuracy using only a few simple ratio tests. Baumol and Quandt (1964) observed that the application of simple decision rules may actually be cheap enough to justify the loss of return that arises from less-than-ideal outcomes. Thus, simple rules of thumb may be a preferred mode of behavior. The weakness in all of these demonstrations lies not in any unrealism in the descriptions themselves but in the fact that these authors have not provided a bridge between the specific market situations in which decision makers find themselves and the decision rules that are to guide their activities. It is one thing to observe that choice making in practice seems to be governed by simple and inexpensive decision rules; it is quite another to show how those rules that are in use have come to be selected in preference to all of the other simple rules that could have come to be used instead.

The possibility arises that if we view behavior as a synthesis of experience, then rules of behavior can be treated as the outcome of a learning process just as well as can specific outcome choices. The portfolio manager may not "learn" to invest X dollars in municipal bonds, but to invest x proportion of any portfolio in municipal bonds. He may even learn to apply some mathematically complex decision rule whose formal derivation is beyond his competence but that can be applied through the use of readily available computer programs. Indeed, the enormous intellectual capabilities of mankind make the acquisition of decision-making rules almost inevitable. Even laboratory rats are able to negotiate mazes using previously untested routes, and many psychologists believe that rats form cognitive "maps" that enable them to use shortcuts and detours effectively (Olton, 1979). The nature of this behavior is a matter of considerable controversy, and it is not at all clear just what behavioral mechanisms are involved in these experiments; nevertheless, it is clear that laboratory animals can acquire and implement patterns of behavior that go well beyond simple memorization – turn right, then left, then right again. The capacities of human decision makers to acquire patterns of behavior and to guide their decisions by abstracted rules are so great that simple outcome-oriented descriptions would surely be excessively naive. In refusing to believe that people use optimization techniques to guide their actions, one certainly does not need to deny that they recognize regularities in their environments, or that learned responses do not include the use of elaborate and sophisticated guides for action. For this reason, a "choice" in our model is intended to be interpretable as a rule as well as a production level or a number of bananas to be consumed. Depending on the area of application, a "choice" may be a commodity vector (such as a conventional market basket), it may be a list of proportions that describe the composition of an asset portfolio, factor proportions in production, or planned production levels, or it may consist of an elaborate set of decision rules that exploit some purported insight into the "true" nature of the world.

Decision rules in practice can range from the foolishly naive to a level of sophistication that is so great as to tax the capacity of modern technology. In the last chapter we stressed the view that the selection from among this set cannot be made on the basis of logic (or on the basis of some optimization paradigm), but is made empirically on the basis of experience. Just as people with different backgrounds may come to make different choices, we must acknowledge that people with different backgrounds may come to employ different decision rules. It is well established that firms are not identical in the extent to which they use sophisticated decision techniques (Earley, 1956), and of course it is the variability in management decision-making systems that creates so many consulting opportunities for professional economists.

Many economists prefer models that describe a continuum of choices, particularly because an assumption of continuity lends itself to the use of calculus in formulating the theory of optimal choice. Given the vast number of quantity and quality alternatives available in markets, this is probably not a bad approximation. Nevertheless, discreteness is in fact a property of almost all objective-choice situations, and the number of alternatives in some cases really is quite small. Many economic commodities are large and indivisible, and even general economic market situations are characterized by the fact that both commodities and money are defined in terms of indivisible basic units. Because all choice sets are bounded in some way (by consumer budgets, or simply by physical limitations on consumption), the number of choice possibilities may be extremely large, but it is always finite.

Throughout this work, we shall designate a choice with the notation A_i, whether we mean that choice to be a specific outcome or a decision rule. The alternative A_i is drawn from the vector $A \equiv A_1, \ldots, A_n$. We implement our assumption that choice probabilities are the appropriate dependent variables by defining a probability vector $\Phi \equiv \phi_1, \ldots, \phi_n$, where each ϕ_i is the likelihood that the alternative A_i will be chosen. Naturally, $\Sigma \phi_i = 1$. The feedback process begins with some specified initial value for this probability vector. When some action is selected from the vector A, it produces consequences that then lead to the modification of Φ to some new value. Ordinarily, if A_i is chosen and is found to have a high payoff, then the element ϕ_i is increased. In biological models, if the genotype A_i is successful, then the frequency of the corresponding gene is found to be higher in subsequent generations. In a psychological-reinforcement learning situation, if the choice A_i is well rewarded, the individual is more likely to choose A_i in the future. Conversely, if the choice A_i is a failure (the organism dies, or an individual is somehow punished as a consequence of A_i), then the element ϕ_i may be reduced. Formally, we shall use Φ_t to represent the value of the vector Φ during a period t and then assume that experience during t will modify Φ_t to some new value Φ_{t+1}, where if it was the choice A_i that was made during t, the difference $\phi_{i,t+1} - \phi_{i,t}$ is some positive monotonic function of the degree of success that was encountered during the period.

Memory

An important question concerns the extent to which history plays a role in mediating changes in behavior. According to our theory, every action that has been taken in the past has led to consequences that in turn have modified the elements of Φ until it has achieved its current value. One might therefore consider this vector to be a sort of summary statistic that incorporates all of an individual's experience. Actions that have repeatedly encountered success will be reflected by relatively large values for corresponding elements of Φ. Actions that have led to failures, or perhaps have never been tried, will be identified by small values of their corresponding elements. When we consider the extent to which new experience will affect behavior, we shall naturally want to take the value of Φ into account, and for this reason the responses of every individual to new environmental stimuli are functions of that individual's own history. If we were to seek a descriptive interpretation for this model, we might associate Φ with "memory," and, indeed, given the complexity of experience, this may be the only practical means for making the concept of memory mathematically tractable in a formal model.

At issue is whether or not we should go beyond this use and insist that even more information be made relevant; for example, we might seek to include as an independent variable the character of the path followed by Φ in achieving its present state. Most biological and behaviorist psychological theories do not require such a generalization. Genetic feedback models are confined exclusively to the gene frequencies that characterize a population at a given time. What these frequencies were 300 generations ago is irrelevant, as is the sequence of intermediate values that were encountered as the population traversed those 300 generations. Psychological-reinforcement learning models are constructed similarly, and it is argued that the feedback process depends on current behavioral variables, not on the path that brought the individual to its present state.

When we move from purely behavioral systems to models that acknowledge cognitive elements (i.e., models that introduce "thinking"), this path independence is a more difficult assumption to justify. As we have noted before, most cognitive psychological theories presume the existence of some number of (often unobservable) personality and expectations variables that have their manifestations in the objective-choice probabilities. These independent variables are so complex and the list of proposed factors so long that we will have to admit the possibility that there are several different configurations of these variables that could produce the same values for Φ, but would still lead to different responses to future environmental stimuli. If this were the case, the vector Φ alone would not be an adequate variable for describing the dependence of behavior on the past. In order to construct a complete model, we would have to add new dimensions to it, and the historical path followed by Φ might be a candidate for such a role. We reject this procedure for several reasons. First, given the potential number and variety of cognitive variables, there is no evident limit to the number of dimensions that would have to be added. Any finite selection would be subject to the objection that some important dimension has been left out. Second, given the empirical difficulty in measuring most of these proposed variables, we could never go beyond the introduction of proxies that would themselves only imperfectly reflect the process we mean to represent, and certainly the path followed by Φ could not be defended as an especially good proxy. Finally, Φ is in fact an excellent summary statistic for the purposes of our model, even in the presence of cognitive variables. Cognitive theories can hardly fail to predict that any action or policy that has met with success in the past will tend to be repeated, for whatever reason, and this fact is qualitatively reflected in an increased value for a corresponding element in Φ. Cognitive considerations may influence the quantitative effect of such successes on Φ, but the qualitative effect seems to be universally acceptable, and it is this direction of effect on which feedback models ultimately rest.

Formally, we shall express the feedback process as a set of changes in each of the elements of Φ. Thus, if an action denoted by the index I is chosen during t, and if a payoff Θ_I is experienced during t, then each element $\phi_{j,t}$ will be altered according to some function

$$\phi_{j,t+1} - \phi_{j,t} = L^j(\Phi_t, I, \Theta) \tag{2.1}$$

We have described choice as the selection of one from a set of n discrete alternatives: Thus, I, which is an index of the choice actually taken, cannot be treated as a continuous variable. Indeed, one might think of equation (2.1) as a set of n different functions, each corresponding to a particular choice, and as an alternative notation, I could be used as a subscript to indicate which choice, and hence which function, is relevant. The notational form of equation (2.1) was chosen simply because it seems to be easier to read. The situation is quite different in the cases of Θ and the elements of Φ. Choice probabilities are by nature continuous variables (bounded, of course, by 0 and 1). Payoff magnitude, Θ, is also a continuous variable in principle, and although in practice the existence of n discrete choices may mean that one can experience only n discrete payoffs, nevertheless, these n actual payoffs are only points on a continuum. This being the case, it is a great convenience to treat $L^j(\Phi_t, i, \Theta)$ as a continuously differentiable function in Φ_t and Θ; there is no apparent conflict with good sense in doing so, and it enables us to employ calculus techniques for the analysis. However, one must be cautious not to extend the assumed continuity to choice itself, for in that dimension it would be entirely inappropriate. Using equation (2.1), it is often convenient to express the principle that larger payoffs encourage the actions that brought them about by specifying a positive sign for the derivative of $L^i(\Phi_t, i, \Theta)$ when $I = i$:

$$\frac{\partial}{\partial \Theta} L^i(\Phi_t, i, \Theta) > 0 \tag{2.2}$$

Independence

One naturally expects that actions or rules of action that have been successful in the past will be found to occur more frequently in the future and that actions that are followed by failure will occur less often. The effects of success or failure on the choice likelihoods of alternative behaviors are not so clear, however, if there are more than two alternatives. Because the choice probabilities must sum to one, success with A_i will induce the sum $\sum_{j \neq i} \phi_j$ to fall, and failure with A_i will induce that sum to rise, but we do not know a priori how the individual components of this sum are affected. A simple procedure would be to assume that if A_i is chosen and is a success, then $\phi_{j,t+1} < \phi_{j,t}$ for all $j \neq i$. That is, if A_i is successful, then each of its alternatives will become less likely than before. This is certainly the case in genetic models, as well as in simple learning, but it is nevertheless a restrictive assumption if one admits cognitive elements into decision making. Thought processes in general make possible phenomena that psychologists call "stimulus generalization," wherein choice situations that are very "similar" will produce similar behaviors, and "response generalization," wherein an action that is successful may lead to increased selection probabilities for a number of behaviors that, although not identical, are similar to the successful one. Response generalization may even apply to behaviors that have never been tried before; if some behavior is qualitatively similar to a previously successful action, it may emerge with a positive probability through generalization. Thus, it is possible that behaviors that have never occurred before can be "learned." If one discovers enjoyment in an Agatha Christie novel, it is possible that one will respond with an increased probability of buying not only Agatha Christie novels but also Dorothy Sayers novels. Evidence that this process exists in reinforcement learning situations is extensive, and of course it appeals strongly to an introspective view of how choices are made among alternatives that have never precisely arisen before.

Unfortunately, direct application of this principle would require that we investigate the specific qualities of actions that lend themselves to the determination of "similarity," and this enterprise would take us far from our main purpose of describing feedback processes themselves. Moreover, there is substantial risk that it would force us to reintroduce personality variables, for actions that seem similar to one individual may not seem so to another.

A conservative treatment of the problem would be to move in the direction of treating actions as though they were conceptually independent of one another, so that nothing could be "learned" (in the cognitive sense) from experience with A_i about the relative payoffs to all of the alternative choices. This view would be captured by an assumption that names of actions are irrelevant and that the *normalized* distribution of likelihoods of the alternatives to the actual choice A_i is unaffected by the experience with A_i. This amounts to an independence assumption. The normalization would proceed by defining a vector Φ'_i that is composed of elements

$$\phi'_{j,t} = \frac{\phi_{j,t}}{1 - \phi_{i,t}} \quad \text{for all } j \neq i \tag{2.3}$$

and then stating that $\phi'_{j,t+1}$ (similarly defined) is independent of the magnitude of the payoff to the choice A_i; that is, $\phi'_{j,t+1} = \phi'_{j,t}$ for all $j \neq i$. This is a particularly convenient assumption because it enables us to write down the values of $\phi_{j,t+1} - \phi_{j,t}$ for all $j \neq i$ in terms of the function $L^i(\Phi_t, i, \Theta_i)$. Using (2.1) and (2.3), we obtain $L^j(\Phi_t, i, \Theta_i)$ directly:

$$L^j(\Phi_t, i, \Theta_i) = \frac{-\phi_{j,t}}{1 - \phi_{i,t}} L^i(\Phi_t, i, \Theta_i) \tag{2.4}$$

We shall use (2.4) as our specification of independence of actions. In fact, this assumption is used routinely in behaviorist learning models. It also characterizes simple genetic selection models in which traits are determined by genes found at specific chromosome locations rather than by interactions among genes in several locations.

Models with cognitive elements should not be restricted by an assumption of independence, but we do not want to develop our theory as though possible changes in the ϕ_j values are entirely unconstrained whenever the choice A_i is encountered. Arbitrary and erroneous associations among alternative actions could lead to all kinds of revisions in the ordering of choice likelihoods that in turn could lead to endless cycling in behavior – not the sort of response we would expect from the introduction of cognition into behavior determination. At the same time, we do not want to require so much detail regarding the associations among alternative choices as to get bogged down in the specification of choices and the differentiation of personality variables. A useful compromise would seem to be to admit cognition to the extent that it might improve the likelihoods of choices with large payoffs. That is, if $\Theta_1 > \Theta_2$, meaning that the choice of A_1 yields a higher payoff than A_2, we shall not permit experience with some A_i (where $i \neq 1, 2$) to lead to a reduction in the ratio ϕ_1/ϕ_2 (which would mean an increase in the relative likelihood of the "wrong" choice). We assume, in effect, that although individuals often make mistakes by choosing inferior actions, they do not make the mistake of permitting their own intelligence to combine with experience in a way that increases the relative likelihood of inferior actions. This assumption is written

$$\Theta_j > \Theta_k \Rightarrow \frac{L^j(\Phi_t, i, \Theta_i)}{\phi_{j,t}} \geqslant \frac{L^k(\Phi_t, i, \Theta_i)}{\phi_{k,t}} \quad \text{for all } j, k \neq i$$

or

$$\Theta_j > \Theta_k \Rightarrow \frac{\phi_{j,t+1}}{\phi_{j,t}} \geqslant \frac{\phi_{k,t+1}}{\phi_{k,t}} \tag{2.5}$$

Condition (2.5) is a less restrictive statement than is (2.4), although the independence assumption is contained in (2.5) as a special case.

Boundaries

It is important to recognize that except for the possibility of learning through generalization, no behavioral mechanism that relies on experience alone is capable of expanding the set of possible choices. If $\phi_{j,t}$ happens to be zero, then we shall not encounter the case $\phi_{j,t+r} > 0$ for any value of r, because the probability that A_j will be chosen and found to be successful is zero. It is conventional for feedback theories that exist in the behavioral and natural sciences to incorporate belief in the existence of random shocks that can bring about any choice, so that even though the shocks may occur rarely, no alternative ever has exactly zero probability attached to it. A common example is the biological device of mutation – the spontaneous emergence of a new trait, perhaps because of the influence of some exogenous cosmic force. Alternatively, one may observe that new situations generate such a broad range of responses that virtually every choice has some possibility of occurrence. Learning experiments always encounter some "noise" at first, and in fact that noise is frequently useful in initiating sequences of learning that involve manipulations that are unfamiliar to subjects. The pigeon that has never before pecked at a colored disk will nevertheless do so by chance if enough time for random exploring is permitted. If that happenstance behavior is rewarded, its likelihood is increased, and from then on the new behavior may be systematically reinforced until it occurs with great regularity. If one introduces the relevance of imperfect information, this sort of noise may even occur in models of decision making that include conscious maximization: A sudden rainstorm may drive a man into a doorway that proves to be the entrance to an art gallery. If the man subsequently becomes an avid collector, we may argue that a chance event enabled him to discover a utility-generating commodity whose existence he had never appreciated before. On the other side of the coin, no action can ever occur with perfect certainty, no matter how regularly it has been rewarded, because these same exogenous random disturbances will occasionally produce deviant behavior. With these facts in mind, we shall place bounds on the probability vector Φ such that at any time t we have $0 < \phi_{j,t} < 1$ for all i, and this implies

$$0 < \phi_{j,t} + L^j(\Phi_t, I, \Theta) < 1 \quad \text{for all } j \tag{2.6}$$

Condition (2.6) implies only that $\phi_{j,t} + L^j(\Phi_t, I, \Theta)$ has asymptotic bounds, not that the asymptotes are necessarily exactly zero and one. However, none of the arguments just given is meant to imply that any choice will always have a significant positive probability, no matter how unsuccessful it proves to be, and thus we do intend zero to be the proper lower asymptote. That is, an indefinite stream of choices of A_j that always encounter disastrous consequences will lead to a sequence of values of ϕ_j that does not converge above $\phi_j = 0$. Formal specification of this condition must wait until we have been more precise about the meaning of Θ.

Beyond these restrictions, the statement that Φ is governed by a feedback process leaves room for a great variety of specific mechanisms. Pure logic by itself provides no reason for confining oneself to any one mathematical model, although in many cases empirical evidence does provide some indication of the sort of formulation that ought to be used. The most developed example is that of genetic selection, which follows a rigid set of rules. Genes are found in pairs, and each element in a pair represents a random sample drawn from a gene pair in a parent. The outward traits of the individual carrying these genes are determined by a dominance relationship between the two genes and possibly by interaction with genetic factors elsewhere on an individual's chromosomes. If these traits are beneficial, then the likelihood that these two genes are found in the population from which subsequent generations will draw their own gene samples is increased. Logically, this is not the only form that could be taken by a biological selection system. Genes could occur in triples, for example, if a reproductive system were to develop under which every individual had three parents (and in which there were three sexes instead of two), and in fact there are some variations on the basic theme: Male Hymenoptera (bees, wasps, ants) carry single chromosomes rather than pairs, so that the "sample" drawn from a male simply reproduces his genetic makeup. In every case, however, it is possible to write down, with precision, the specific mathematics of the feedback mechanism.

In the case of reinforcement learning, there has been a similar tendency to represent the feedback in terms of well-specified analytic models, but the empirical evidence is not adequate to support this effort. In the last thirty years we have seen the development of a great variety of different formulations, but none of these has proved to have entirely satisfactory algebraic properties. In fact, all of them have the same formal characteristics with respect to directions of change, curvature, endpoints, and the like, and these properties are sufficient for the description of a general model. Apparently, however, research has been diverted from this very useful goal into an ambitious attempt to emulate the genetic theory and find one single analytic system that can be used to describe all learning behavior. It is to be feared that the failure of this effort has led some researchers to abandon quantitative learning research altogether and thus has slowed the develoment of a very general and useful formal theory of behavior.

Payoff

We have been proceeding as though the definitions and units of measurement of Θ were readily available. When, in later chapters, we come to apply our model to specific problems, we shall find that the specification of this variable is often determined by the area of application, and the properties of Θ will arise in a straightforward fashion. In the case of the theory of the firm, for example, we can treat profits as the primary concern of managers and simply use that variable in place of Θ in the functions $L^j(\Phi_l, I, \Theta)$.

When we consider the case of consumers, however, or if we are concerned that the interests of managers are not perfectly aligned with profits, we must turn to some concept of consumer utility for the definition of Φ. This reintroduces the danger that our model will prove to depend on exogenous variables that are unobservable, so that any behavior at all is potentially consistent with the theory. Economists are often very free with casual assurances that it is acceptable to use the preference function as an exogenous determinant of behavior, because one can always "go to the psychologists" to get the appropriate specification. This amounts to an assertion that the quantitative specification of the utility function is a problem that economists can legitimately ignore on the grounds that it is a central issue in someone else's professional field. Psychologists, unfortunately, have failed to come up to expectations in this regard, and, indeed, much psychological work, both in theory and at the experimental level, is subject to the same criticism that it rests on assumptions of preference orderings that have no independent empirical bases. Studies of reinforcement learning, for example, presume that we know what constitutes a reward, and empirical work on learning often comes dangerously close to the circular proposition that a "reward" is something that induces reinforcement learning. Experimental psychologists usually skirt this problem by confining their payoffs to goods that serve fundamental biological needs and then applying them under conditions of deprivation; such payoffs are so obviously rewarding as to divert attention from the potential circularity of the model. The basics of sex, food to the hungry, shelter to the exposed, and affection for the unloved provide the means to this end. Moreover, these payoffs usually are treated one at a time; so there is no problem of deciding whether a unit of food or a unit of affection is the more forceful determinant of behavior.

The inadequacy of this concept of "reinforcer" has been apparent to psychologists for some time. In response, a number of models have been devised in which one interprets experimental conditions in terms of the constraints they impose on behavior (Timberlake and Allison, 1974;

Allison, 1981). Comparison of unconstrained behavior with that under constraint then provides the experimental data. All of these models have a strongly economic flavor, and, in effect, their authors are turning to ordinalist utility models to provide an alternative to the cruder presumption that any biological need under conditions of deprivation constitutes a "reinforcer." From the point of view of scientific rigor, this is a great step forward, and of course economists may be pleased to find that the analytic models that are familiar to them are proving to be useful in other fields as well, but the existence of such a trend makes it clear that the psychology profession is not yet in a position to provide significant new insights into the character of preferences under any but the simplest kinds of situations.

Unfortunately, when psychologists do provide information on the nature of preferences under more complicated circumstances, it often runs counter to the assumptions that economists expect the psychologists to validate. For example, although it is quite clear that some people are more strongly "future-oriented" than others, there is no support for the notions that consumers form detailed or even consistent consumption plans for the future, that the anticipation of the consumption goods in these plans produces satisfaction (even in the conventional "as if" sense), or that there is any systematic "discounting" process that converts future well-being into something comparable to current consumption utility. Studies of learning behavior suggest, for example, that if future consumption is to have strong behavioral effects, it must be reflected in tangible proxies that are encountered in the present. The future goods must be present in fact or in the form of physical representatives if they are to influence choice making. The birthday gift of an airplane ticket to Paris is a much stronger reinforcer than a verbal promise of a trip, apparently simply because it is so much more tangible.

Having no alternative, we must employ some sort of utility concept to generate the payoff variable in our feedback function, but we can take advantage of some of this psychological material to make our formulation more concrete. Even though we may not be able to specify the form of the preference function precisely, we can define it so that the variables that serve as its arguments are directly observable. That is, to the extent that future consumption is relevant to current choice behavior, it is reflected in the acquisition of certain goods (savings accounts, stockholdings, durable assets) that can be converted into consumption goods later on. Our procedure will be to put these proxies for the future into the utility function rather than the unspecified consumption they make possible. Besides corresponding much more closely to psychological patterns of behavior, this approach enjoys the intuitive appeal of the statement that people "like" to hold wealth even when it is unclear to them and to us what that wealth will be used for. It also avoids some of the worst of the expectations problems by removing the requirement that consumers be able to predict their own future tastes. Finally, it does not distort conventional optimization theory in any significant way. Qualitative descriptions of optimal *current* consumption behavior, and its dependence on prices, income, and interest rates, are unaffected by whether the utility function uses as arguments future consumption plans or simply the assets that make future consumption possible.

The preference theory that is used for the analysis of optimal choice is strictly ordinalist in character, and even when it is represented in cardinalist notation, there is no requirement that we specify an origin or that we find any natural units of utility measurement. It is understood that we must only have an index that is monotonically increasing in payoff and that preserves preference orderings. Technically, the same proves to be true of our feedback model: The units of measurement and the origin chosen for Θ do not alter the equilibrium and convergence properties of the model. Nevertheless, there is a natural intuitive distinction between "success" and "failure," and one would like to exploit the potential of our model for giving some relevance to this distinction. The structure of many economic problems provides a strong exogenous motivation for doing this: A new business that covers its capital costs together with the opportunity cost of its management is regarded as successful, and the degree of success is reflected in its profits. It will be natural in this case to make Θ positive and increasing in profit level. Negative profits clearly mean failure, and it will be natural to make Θ negative. A consumer who spends $5.00 to travel to a shopping area has been successful if that location yields a set of desired goods at a cost that is more than $5.00 below their cost close to home, and the corresponding value of Θ is positive. If the prices prove to be the same as those elsewhere, Θ will be negative.

Apart from such simple cases, there are still pitfalls in attempting to differentiate success from failure, because important cognitive dimensions are inevitably reintroduced. "Success" may not refer to just any positive payoff, but only to those payoffs that exceed some subjective standard. The corporation whose profits have declined may respond as though it has experienced failure even though profits are positive. An annual income of $50,000 may mean success to the taxi driver but failure to the neurosurgeon. The tendency to establish payoff targets that then become criteria for performance evaluation is widely recognized and is reflected in the variety of theories of "satisficing" behavior and "aspiration levels" that are found in both psychology and economics. We must take account of the possibility that the distinction between success and failure is in fact endogenous to experience and that it cannot be established firmly a priori. Psychological aspiration theory (Lewin et al., 1944; Siegel, 1957) suggests that achievement of a goal will lead to upward revisions, and failure to achieve a goal will lead to downward revisions in the goal itself. Although it may be that these adjustments serve only to accelerate convergence toward equilibrium states, we must recognize that the behavioral effect of any given payoff may depend on the point in experience at which it arises.

Once the distinction is established, we might expect success and failure to have symmetric qualitative effects on behavior. If A_i is seen to lead to a successful outcome, then the likelihood of its recurrence is increased at the expense of the likelihoods of the alternatives to A_i. If A_i is perceived to be a failure, then it is the alternative actions whose likelihoods increase. If there are more than two alternatives available, however, there will be an important dissimilarity between these effects. Success will tend to focus behavior on that single action that produced it, but failure, in reducing the likelihood of the relevant action, will not single out any one alternative for a corresponding encouragement, but will tend to diffuse behavior among all of the alternative possibilities. In practice, this reflects the observation that perceived failures often lead to apparent search behavior on the part of decision makers. Normally, of course, this behavior is described as a cognitive response to information that an old technique no longer "works," but it is important to note that it applies as well to passive behaviorist models.

If it should happen that the aspiration level is fixed (or that the distinction between success and failure is natural to the situation), then we need only recognize that $L^i(\Phi_t, i, \Theta)$ has the same sign as Θ itself. When this origin is treated as a variable, however, this fact must be introduced explicitly into the model in the form of a new variable, $\hat{\Theta}$, which represents the origin. In this case, the feedback function will be written $L^i(\Phi_t, i, \Theta, \hat{\Theta}_t)$, with the t subscript on $\hat{\Theta}_t$ reflecting the property that the value of this variable may change over time. The sign of $L^i(\cdot)$ now depends on the sign of $\Theta - \hat{\Theta}_t$:

$$\Theta < \hat{\Theta}_t \Rightarrow L^i(\Phi_t, i, \Theta, \hat{\Theta}_t) < 0$$

$$\Theta = \hat{\Theta}_t \Rightarrow L^i(\Phi_t, i, \Theta, \hat{\Theta}_t) = 0$$

$$\Theta > \hat{\Theta}_t \Rightarrow L^i(\Phi_t, i, \Theta, \hat{\Theta}_t) > 0 \tag{2.7}$$

A more substantive restriction arises when we impose our condition that the asymptotic lower bound of $L^i(\Phi_t, i, \Theta, \hat{\Theta}_t)$ not be above zero. That is, an indefinite string of choices, each of whose consequences is disadvantageous to A_i, will lead to a declining sequence of values of ϕ_i

that will not converge above zero. This condition is guaranteed by the following: For any $\phi_{i,t} > 0$, $\Theta \neq 0$, there exists $\epsilon > 0$ such that

$$L^i(\Phi_t, i, \Theta, \hat{\Theta}_t) > \epsilon \quad \text{for} \quad \Theta > \hat{\Theta}_t$$

$$L^i(\Phi_t, i, \Theta, \hat{\Theta}_t) < -\epsilon \quad \text{for} \quad \Theta < \hat{\Theta}_t \tag{2.8}$$

Superstition

An important, although often overlooked, property of any feedback model such as (2.1) is that there is no firm requirement that there be any "real" connection between A_i and Θ. One is tempted to treat feedback mechanisms as though the choice indexed by I "caused" Θ, but this is really a technological question that is external to the adaptive process we are describing. Examples in which systems have been modified in response to incidental associations between action and payoff are in fact quite easy to find. A common one is the biologists' description of "genetic drift": An organism with a certain genetic makeup may produce an unusually large number of offspring purely by chance, and as a result the distribution of genotypes within the population may shift slightly in that direction, even though that shift has nothing to do with any objective (i.e., noncircular) measure of fitness for survival. If a pair from some endangered species happens to be captured, placed in a zoo, and induced to produce numerous offspring, the genetic character of these two animals may come to predominate in the population, and this "adaptation" is not related to the ordinary notion of "fitness." Psychologists use similar arguments to explain "superstitious" behavior. An action followed by a large payoff is generally reinforced, whether or not there was any direct causal connection between the behavior and the reward. We presume that various gamblers' "systems" and "lucky numbers" have this property of having enjoyed chance associations with success, and these are typical of a vast array of apparently meaningless gestures and expressions in which human beings indulge. The evidence is ubiquitous that it is easy for people to pick up behaviors that have encountered incidental reinforcements and to retain them for long periods, particularly if those behaviors do not do any obvious harm.

One might suppose that the possibility that Θ is unrelated to A_i is eliminated if we admit cognitive elements into the choice process, because thought processes enable one to focus on the question of causal relationships. Even this seems to be an overoptimistic view, however. It is inconsistent with the widespread incidence of superstition within human populations, and, further, it ignores the fact that the connections between real-world actions and their consequences may be so complicated as to be well beyond anyone's capacity for comprehension. A business manager may make hundreds of decisions over the course of a year, and there is no way to determine if a favorable profit report should be attributed to all, or only a few, of these decisions. Indeed, the profits may have been the result of some exogenous shift in demand, and the manager's decisions may have been largely irrelevant. Nevertheless, the manager is encouraged to repeat his decision behavior, and his employers are encouraged to rehire him; his prestige grows, and his salary must be raised. In the short run at least, the "good" decisions are encouraged along with the "bad" decisions, and the "lucky" managers are paid as well as the "competent" ones. Of course, this is not a description of equilibrium, but only of some intermediate disequilibrium state; nevertheless, it is common enough in experience, and this experience should serve as a warning against relying too heavily on cognition to guarantee that payoffs and behavior are always accurately associated in the minds of economic agents.

Convergence to stationary equilibrium

Suppose that we are considering behavior in an entirely static and predictable environment in which each action A_i consistently produces a corresponding return valued at Θ_i. We might expect that, over time, the feedback process would finally lead to the selection, "almost always," of whichever action brings about the maximal Θ. As a general rule, however, feedback mechanisms often lead to cyclic or even divergent patterns of behavior, and more structure must be added to our elementary characterization if we are to have a stable model that reliably converges to an optimum. We are aware of only two types of procedures for achieving this end: One is to exploit the properties of "satisficing" or "aspiration levels," and the other is to add mathematical restrictions to the form of equation (2.1). Each approach has worthy advantages, and we shall consider them in sequence.

We have already observed that there is a great deal of empirical support for the belief that human decision makers define payoff goals for themselves and are inclined to attach notions of success or failure to actions whose results exceed or fall short of those goals. Unfortunately, this belief has not been carefully formalized, and a general reading in this area leaves one unclear as to just what the theory is intended to be. The interpretation that seems to apply most frequently would make utility a function not only of the payoff received but also of the extent to which that payoff achieves some stated goal (Siegel, 1957). If one is delighted to have exceeded one's target, then utility is a compound of the payoff

together with that delight. This interpretation enjoys considerable intuitive appeal, for indeed it is pleasant to find that one has done better than
one expected, and it is discouraging to fall short. However, this view
turns out to generate some ambiguity once one attempts to make use of it
in a general model. This is partly because one's evaluation of one's own
performance depends on the perceived difficulty of the task (Feather,
1961). Formally, this consideration can be incorporated into the utility
function, and thus it may involve no analytical difficulties; nevertheless,
it introduces an undesirable ambiguity into the specification of that function. A much more serious problem stems from the fact that inclusion of
aspiration levels in a utility function makes preferences endogenous to
payoff experience. Because choice is seen to be motivated by payoff
utility, this in turn introduces intransitivity into preference orderings
over the payoffs themselves. This fact is often overlooked, because
empirical research on aspirations usually has been applied only to single-
dimension problems in which individuals are treated as though they set
goals on only one aspect of their behavior. Even in a simple two-
commodity example, however, association of utility with success can
lead to peculiar dynamic behavior. Suppose that the payoff target for
good A has been set relatively low (compared with the objective difficulty
in achieving A), and that for B has been set relatively high. It will then be
easier to meet the goal for good A than that for B, and the satisfaction
obtained from achieving targets in A may divert consumption away from
the good B, even though, considering payoffs from the goods alone, B
might be the "better" choice. Of course, eventually the A target will rise
to a more realistic level, and the B target may fall; the B payoff may then
begin to draw consumption choices in the other direction, reversing the
process. Formally, there is no guarantee that this dynamic adjustment
process will converge to an optimal state, or even that it will converge at
all. Usher (1978) found some conditions under which additively sepa-
rable utility functions will provide convergence to neoclassical optima,
but in more general cases, choice behavior could as well be found to cycle
indefinitely and never touch an optimum. The problem is that if we associate utility with an achievement target for each commodity, then it
becomes possible for a change in target levels to alter the preference
ordering among commodity bundles, and this interferes with convergence. The problem is compounded if the satisfaction derived from
achievement of a goal depends on a subjective perception of the difficulty associated with the goal, because then both the goal and its perceived difficulty may be changing all the time.

If we are to have a model that converges at all, we clearly must
add enough restrictions to avoid the widespread incidence of dynamic
intransitivities. We might defend the use of such restrictions on the

further grounds that it is difficult to believe that any reasonable self-conscious decision maker would permit obvious intransitivities in preference to arise as a consequence of what are essentially changes in payoff expectations. We accomplish this by taking a somewhat less stringent view of aspiration levels, but one that is still consistent with most of the literature on the subject; that is, we associate aspiration level with a "target" level of *utility*, where the utility can itself be described with the usual transitive utility-of-payoff function. This will mean that aspirations will apply to only one dimension, so that even though "success" and "failure" may lead to different behavioral responses, they will not alter preference orderings themselves. This procedure is made possible by the ordinalist character of our utility function. Because the origin and units of measurement of utility are arbitrary, we can implement the suggestion we made earlier that we treat payoff as though the origin of the utility function is determined by the aspiration level, so that, following equation (2.7), a payoff that exceeds aspirations will be treated as a success and will encourage the associated behavior, whereas a failure will discourage the action and lead the individual to seek out alternatives.

The model in equation (2.7) states that actions that contribute to success (which now means payoff utility in excess of aspirations) will be encouraged through the feedback process, whereas actions that lead to failure (utility below aspirations) will be discouraged in favor of an entire range of alternatives. This latter case has much of the character of the process of "search and try out alternatives" that is described in the literature on "satisficing" behavior. If success is repeatedly encountered, then aspirations will rise, and our "origin" will be associated with more preferred bundles in the ordering. Conversely, repeated failure will shift $\hat{\Theta}$ down in the ordering.

Under this second interpretation of the aspiration theory, the feedback model will always converge to an optimum. For an intuitive notion of why this is so, let us first propose an extreme example in which aspiration levels are "realistic," that is, in which the aspiration level corresponds to the payoff the individual can, on average, expect to receive. This assumption approximates a situation in which goals adjust slowly enough for the decision maker to experience an average payoff nearly equal to the expected payoff. Let us define expected payoff:

$$\bar{\Theta}_t \equiv \sum_{j=1} \Theta_j \, \phi_{j,t} \tag{2.9}$$

Thus, any payoff greater than $\bar{\Theta}_t$ will be treated as a success, and any payoff below $\bar{\Theta}_t$ will be a failure. If the payoff is just equal to $\bar{\Theta}_t$, then nothing happens.

If the choice A_i that is made during t is in fact a success, then from

(2.7) we have $\phi_{i,t+1} > \phi_{i,t}$, which amounts simply to our statement that actions that are successful are more likely to occur again in the future. Condition (2.5) guarantees that the relative likelihoods of choices other than A_i do not shift in favor of inferior choices, and this implies the following:

$$\frac{1}{1-\phi_{i,t+1}} \sum_{j \neq i} \phi_{j,t+1} \Theta_j \geq \frac{1}{1-\phi_{i,t}} \sum_{j \neq i} \phi_{j,t} \Theta_j \qquad (2.10)$$

Because $\phi_{i,t+1} > \phi_{i,t}$ and $\Theta_i > \bar{\Theta}_t$, it follows from (2.10) that $\bar{\Theta}_{t+1} > \bar{\Theta}_t$.

If the choice A_i is a failure, then we have $\phi_{i,t+1} < \phi_{i,t}$, because $\Theta_i < \bar{\Theta}_t$, but (2.10) still holds, and therefore we again have $\bar{\Theta}_{t+1} > \bar{\Theta}_t$. Thus, the expected payoff grows monotonically in every case except that in which aspirations are precisely satisfied, and because this case occurs with probability less than one, the expected payoff must grow toward its asymptotic upper bound of $\max\{\Theta_i\}$.

This simple demonstration is made possible by the assumption of a close association between aspirations and expected payoff; such an assumption guarantees that any action that is regarded as a success does indeed produce above-average payoffs, so that an increase in its likelihood will increase the expected payoff. Similarly, the decrease in likelihood of an action that is seen to be a failure will reduce the occurrence of a choice that actually is inferior.

If we drop the identification of aspiration level with expected payoff, it will no longer be the case that $\hat{\Theta}$ is necessarily increasing over time. For example, new business enterprises are frequently established in an atmosphere of optimism, which is to say that aspirations are high and may even be so unrealistic as to exceed any payoff that is potentially available. A "good" choice or even an optimal choice may then be regarded as a failure because payoffs fall short of expectations, with the result that inferior choices are made more likely than before, and expected payoff falls. In time, the aspiration level will decline, and good choices will come to be seen to be successes, but in the interim, disappointment may actually drive behavior in the wrong direction.

Optimal choice is still an equilibrium property of the aspiration model, so long as we meet the general requirement that aspirations adapt to experience without "overshooting." That is, aspirations move toward the payoff levels that are encountered, but not precisely to them (which would suggest that history was totally irrelevant) or beyond them:

$$\Theta_t > \hat{\Theta}_t \Rightarrow \Theta_t > \hat{\Theta}_{t+1} > \hat{\Theta}_t$$

$$\Theta_t = \hat{\Theta}_t \Rightarrow \hat{\Theta}_{t+1} = \hat{\Theta}_t$$

$$\Theta_t < \hat{\Theta}_t \Rightarrow \Theta_t < \hat{\Theta}_{t+1} < \hat{\Theta}_t \qquad (2.11)$$

Conditions (2.11) are an incomplete statement of existing aspiration theories, because they do not specify an asymptote. Suppose that the individual encounters a long string of identical payoff values, all equal to Θ^*. One would expect $\hat{\Theta}$ to move to Θ^* as the asymptote rather than to some intermediate position, and so we must add a condition that

$$\Theta_t = \Theta^* \quad \text{for all } t \Rightarrow \lim_{t \to \infty} \hat{\Theta}_t = \Theta^* \tag{2.12}$$

It is convenient to index actions in a way that reflects preference ordering: $\Theta_1 < \Theta_2 < \cdots < \Theta_n$. This notation ensures that A_1 is the "worst" choice, that A_n is the "best," and that A_i is always better than A_j if $i > j$. Condition (2.6) guarantees that $\phi_1 < 1$; hence, from time to time, the individual will encounter payoffs, or strings of payoffs, larger than Θ_1. Conditions (2.11) and (2.12) provide that whatever the initial value of $\hat{\Theta}$ may be, it will eventually rise at least to $\hat{\Theta} = \Theta_1$ (the strings of payoffs larger than Θ_1 will draw $\hat{\Theta}$ above Θ_1, and there are no payoffs small enough to draw $\hat{\Theta}$ below Θ_1). Suppose that we have the case of $\hat{\Theta}$ just equal to Θ_1. As soon as some choice other than A_1 is made [an event that is guaranteed by condition (2.6)], condition (2.11) implies that we have $\hat{\Theta} > \Theta_1$. Indeed, the strict inequalities in (2.11) ensure that if a choice other than A_1 is made at time t^*, then $\hat{\Theta}_t > \Theta_1$ for all $t > t^*$. Thus, whenever A_1 is chosen (after t^*), it is seen to be a failure, and, from (2.7), $\phi_{1,t+1} < \phi_{1,t}$. Condition (2.5) guarantees that at the same time, $\phi_{n,t+1} > \phi_{n,t}$, where the index n refers to the best choice. If instead of A_1 it is A_n that is chosen during some t, then $\phi_{n,t+1} > \phi_{n,t}$, and, again using (2.5), $\phi_{1,t+1} < \phi_{1,t}$. If some alternative A_i is chosen during t, where $i \neq 1, n$, then we know from (2.5) that $\phi_{n,t+1}/\phi_{1,t+1} \geqslant \phi_{n,t}/\phi_{1,t}$. Thus, at any $t > t^*$, and no matter what choice is actually made, we have $\phi_{n,t+1}/\phi_{1,t+1} \geqslant \phi_{n,t}/\phi_{1,t}$, with the strict inequality holding with probability no less than $\phi_{1,t} + \phi_{n,t} > 0$. Because the feedback function has asymptotic limits at zero and one, a monotonically increasing ratio of ϕ_n/ϕ_1 requires that ϕ_1 approach zero (ϕ_n approaching one implies ϕ_1 approaching zero, because the sum of all the probabilities is one). With ϕ_1 going to zero, realized payoffs will come to exceed Θ_1 with probability one, and we can now repeat the argument with regard to the choice A_2. That is, condition (2.6) provides that $\sum_{i>2} \phi_i > 0$, and experience with such choices will eventually generate a value of $\hat{\Theta} > \Theta_2$. We can then use condition (2.5) to ensure that whatever choices are made, the ratio ϕ_n/ϕ_2 will rise monotonically, with the strict inequality occurring with a probability no less than $\phi_2 + \phi_n > 0$. We note that whenever A_2 is chosen and found to be inferior to aspirations, the value of ϕ_1 may increase; nevertheless, condition (2.5) implies that even in this case the ratio ϕ_n/ϕ_1 will not decline. Because this ratio does rise whenever either A_1 or A_n is chosen, the monotonic increase is always preserved. Thus, with probability one, the values of both ϕ_1 and ϕ_2 decline to zero, and the argument can be repeated with respect to the choice A_3. Each choice in turn may be eliminated by this procedure until we arrive at the asymptotic equilibrium: With probability one, $\phi_n \to 1$, and because A_n is the optimal choice, we have our desired result.

Proportional models

There are many cases in which one cannot make use of an adjusting aspiration level to achieve convergence. This occurs whenever the distinction between success and failure is so natural to the situation that it is implausible that the origin of the utility function should shift significantly over time. A trip to a department store to buy a particular brand of appliance is successful if the appliance is in stock and a failure if it is not, and in any such context, a theory that stresses changing aspiration targets will not be particularly appropriate. If there is a natural and fixed origin for the utility function, however, the convergence proof given in the last section does not apply, and, in fact, convergence may not occur unless we impose further restrictions on the properties of the model.

As it happens, there is a natural way, originally formulated by Bush and Mosteller (1955), to formulate the feedback mechanism so as to preserve the convergence property when we cannot resort to shifts in $\hat{\Theta}$. As a preliminary step, let us define $E[\phi_{j,t+1}]$ to be the expected value of ϕ_j in period $t+1$. This is the sum of the values of $\phi_{j,t+1}$ that are induced by the payoffs to the various possible choices A_i during period t times the probabilities of these choices. From equation (2.1), this expectation is given by

$$E[\phi_{j,t+1}] = \sum_{i=1}^{n} \phi_{i,t} L^j(\Phi_t, i, \Theta_i, \hat{\Theta}_t) + \phi_{j,t} \qquad (2.13)$$

It is often the case that specific forms for the feedback function, when substituted into (2.13), enable us to show the existence of an alternative A_k for which $E[\phi_{k,t+1}] > \phi_{k,t}$ for any $\phi_{k,t} < 1$, and this convergence in probability guarantees that eventually the alternative A_k will be chosen with probability one. Let us define the set S to contain all those actions whose returns are seen to be successful, and the set F to be its complement:

$$S \equiv \{i \mid \Theta_i > \hat{\Theta}_t\}$$
$$F \equiv \{i \mid \Theta_i \leqslant \hat{\Theta}_t\} \qquad (2.14)$$

The nature of the problem of convergence in (2.13) is made more clear if we consider the process in a case for which $\hat{\Theta}_t$ is constant (e.g., at $\hat{\Theta}_t = 0$

for all t) and for which the set S is not empty. This is a convenient example, because it is easy to prove that then $\sum_{i \in F} \phi_i$ converges to zero. If an element A_j in S is chosen at time t, its likelihood increases: $\phi_{j,t+1} > \phi_{j,t}$. Although $\sum_{i \neq j} \phi_i$ necessarily falls as a consequence, we cannot state that the likelihood of each alternative to A_j falls: There may be some perceived associations among possible choices that make some actions more likely because of what the individual has "learned" from experience with A_j. Nevertheless, condition (2.5) guarantees that these increases are biased toward higher-payoff alternatives, and because ϕ_j certainly increases, we have

$$\frac{\sum_{i \in F} \phi_{i,t+1}}{\sum_{i \in F} \phi_{i,t}} < \frac{\sum_{i \in S} \phi_{i,t+1}}{\sum_{i \in S} \phi_{i,t}} \tag{2.15}$$

Because we have $\sum_{i \neq j} \phi_{i,t+1} < \sum_{i \neq j} \phi_{i,t}$, equation (2.15) implies $\sum_{i \in F} \phi_{i,t+1} < \sum_{i \in F} \phi_{i,t}$. If an element A_k in F is chosen, either nothing happens, because $\Theta_k = 0$ (which happens with probability less than one), or $\phi_{k,t+1} < \phi_{k,t}$, because $\Theta_k < 0$. In the latter event, $\sum_{i \in S} \phi_{i,t+1} > \sum_{i \in S} \phi_{i,t}$ [using condition (2.5)], and this also implies $\sum_{i \in F} \phi_{i,t+1} < \sum_{i \in F} \phi_{i,t}$. Thus, the sum $\sum_{i \in F} \phi_i$ is monotonically decreasing, with no asymptote above zero, so that in the long run this sum is zero with probability one.

Eventually it becomes possible to restrict our attention to only those actions that produce positive payoffs. We note that whenever some choice A_j is made, where $j \in S$, we have $\phi_{i,t+1} > \phi_{j,t}$. Clearly, the potential for cycling behavior is high: Because no element in Φ is precisely zero, any element in S might be chosen, and, depending on the magnitude of $L^j(\Phi_t, j, \Theta_j)$, that choice might be made very likely the next time around. Cycling would be prevented, therefore, only if (a) we were to increase the value of $\hat{\Theta}$, thereby adding new choices to the set F (the case treated in the last section), or (b) there were quantitative restrictions imposed on the feedback function.

A useful formulation of the model may be motivated by an appeal to the natural boundaries on probabilities [expressed in condition (2.6)], from which we know that $0 < L^j(\Phi_t, j, \Theta_j, \hat{\Theta}_t) < 1 - \phi_j$ for any $j \in S$. If we think of the interval $[0, 1 - \phi_j]$ as the range of possible values for $L^j(\cdot)$, then it is natural to extend the principle that these values are increasing in Θ_j to a condition that the fraction of the interval $[0, 1 - \phi_j]$ that is represented by the value of $L^j(\cdot)$ is increasing in Θ_j; that is, to make the ratio $L^j(\Phi_t, j, \Theta_j, \hat{\Theta}_t)/(1 - \phi_j)$ an increasing function of Θ_j:

$$\frac{L^j(\Phi_t, j, \Theta_j, \hat{\Theta}_t)}{1 - \phi_j} = \alpha(\Theta_j - \hat{\Theta}_t) \tag{2.16}$$

Here, $\alpha(\Theta_j - \hat{\Theta}_t)$ is some monotonically increasing function of $(\Theta_j - \hat{\Theta}_t)$. This function is necessarily bounded by zero and one. Because Θ_j is itself only some monotonically increasing function of payoff, it is mathematically clumsy to take the trouble to write another monotonically increasing function of that, and so in those cases for which $\hat{\Theta}$ is fixed, we shall simply use the symbol α_j to represent the value of $\alpha(\Theta_j - \hat{\Theta}_t)$.

A symmetric argument can be made for the case of choices in F. If $\Theta_j < \hat{\Theta}_t$, then the interval $[-\phi_{j,t}, 0]$ provides the range of possible values for $L^j(\Phi_t, j, \Theta_j, \hat{\Theta}_t)$, and it is again natural to extend the fact that $L^j(\cdot)$ increases in Θ_j to an assumption that the fraction of this (negative) range that is represented by the value of the feedback function is decreasing in Θ_j. This assumption produces

$$\frac{-L^j(\Phi_t, j, \Theta_j, \hat{\Theta}_t)}{\phi_{j,t}} = \beta(\hat{\Theta}_t - \Theta_j) \tag{2.17}$$

If $\hat{\Theta}$ is constant, then we can again use the shorthand β_j to represent the value of $\beta(\hat{\Theta}_t - \Theta_j)$, and, of course, β_j is increasing in the argument $(\hat{\Theta}_t - \Theta_j)$. Whether or not the two functions $\alpha(\cdot)$ and $\beta(\cdot)$ are identical, that is, whether or not the proportionate feedback is symmetric around $\hat{\Theta}$, is not of immediate concern here.

Suppose $\hat{\Theta}$ is fixed, and A_k is the best of the alternatives in S, so that $\Theta_k = \max_i\{\Theta_i\}$. Then, whenever some alternative A_i is chosen, where $i \neq k$ and $i \in S$, we use (2.16) to show that $L^i(\Phi_t, i, \Theta_i, \hat{\Theta}_t) = \alpha_i(1 - \phi_{i,t})$, and we can use condition (2.5) to show that

$$L^k(\Phi_t, i, \Theta_i, \hat{\Theta}) \geqslant -\phi_{k,t}\alpha_i \tag{2.18}$$

Similarly, whenever some alternative A_j is chosen, where $j \neq k$ and $j \in F$, we have, from equation (2.17) and condition (2.5), that

$$L^k(\Phi_t, j, \Theta_j, \hat{\Theta}) > \phi_{k,t}\frac{\phi_{j,t}\beta_j}{1 - \phi_{j,t}} \tag{2.19}$$

Substituting (2.16), (2.18), and (2.19) into (2.13), we obtain

$$E[\phi_{k,t+1}] - \phi_{k,t} \geqslant \phi_{k,t}\left[\alpha_k - \sum_{i \in S}\phi_{i,t}\alpha_i + \sum_{j \in F}\frac{\phi_{j,t}^2\beta_j}{1 - \phi_{j,t}}\right] \tag{2.20}$$

Because $\sum_{i \in S}\phi_{i,t}\alpha_i$ is a weighted average of all the α_i values for choices in S, and α_k is maximal in that set, the right-hand side of (2.20) is strictly positive, and we can conclude that for any $\phi_k < 1$, the expected value of ϕ_k rises monotonically over time. Because the feedback function has no asymptote other than one, ϕ_k is converging to one with probability one, and we can conclude that the feedback process has the desired property that it will indeed converge to the optimal choice.

For this proof, we have assumed that there is a unique payoff-maximizing choice. If there are two or more choices that produce the same (maximal) payoff level, then the proof is easily modified to show that it is the sum of the probabilities of these maximizing choices that converges to one.

Primarily as a matter of curiosity, we might ask how this model would operate if the set S were empty, so that every possible choice would lead to a perceived failure. As a practical psychological matter, situations in which all actions lead to failure can lead to behavioral consequences that may not fit easily into the framework of our analysis. Seligman (1975), for example, has noted that there is a tendency for persistent failure to bring about an apparent condition of "helplessness," in which an individual fails to engage in any kind of active choice making whatever. Such behavior may be consistent with our theory: Presumably, the alternative "do nothing" is always available, and if its payoff is nonnegative, then this would actually be an optimal response if the set S were empty. If "helplessness" is learned under such circumstances, then there is no conflict with the theory. If it should appear that helplessness can be acquired under conditions in which doing nothing is clearly inferior to some alternative (even if that alternative is not "successful"), then this behavior would be difficult to reconcile with our model. In fact, it would seem to be unrealistic to presume that $\hat{\theta}$ could remain fixed under such circumstances, and experimental evidence strongly suggests that under conditions of unavoidable punishment, those choices that reduce the pain, so to speak, come to be regarded positively, implying that $\hat{\theta}$ does in fact fall. Nevertheless, simply as an exercise that will provide some insight into the working of the model, let us consider S to be empty and define the choice A_k to be the best alternative in the set F. Then, for any choice A_j other than A_k, we use (2.19) to describe the change in ϕ_k, and for the choice A_k itself, the change in ϕ_k is given by (2.17) directly (with the index k replacing j). Substituting these equations into (2.13), we obtain

$$E[\phi_{k,t+1}] - \phi_{k,t} \geqslant \phi_{k,t}\left[\sum_{j \neq k} \frac{\phi_{j,t}^2 \beta_j}{1 - \phi_{j,t}} - \phi_{k,t}\beta_k \right] \qquad (2.21)$$

Clearly the value $\phi_k = 1$ is not a necessary convergence point for this model, because at that value the right-hand side of (2.21) is negative. The inequality in (2.21) is not inconsistent with convergence, of course, and sufficiently cognitive behavior may still lead to permanent selection of A_k. More generally, however, the model suggests the engagement in constant search: Every choice being a failure, the individual is repeatedly driven toward other alternatives.

This final example serves to dramatize a behavioral asymmetry that will characterize any model that is based on experience rather than full-information optimization. Maximization models value all potential outcomes relative to the optimum, and so there is no qualitative distinction between those actions that might be termed successful in practice and those that would not (beyond the simple notion that any payoff less than the optimum is a failure). In the models to be described here, however, the distinction carries a great deal of weight. Successes tend to focus behavior, whereas failures tend to diffuse it, and this property will be seen to be responsible for many of the most interesting implications of experientially based models, as well as for a considerably heightened potential for empirical realism.

Behavior in the short run

We demonstrated in Chapter 2 that under relatively weak assumptions, feedback processes will provide convergence to equilibrium states that have the properties of optima. Thus, these feedback models are entirely consistent with the standard comparative-statics equilibrium theories used in economics, and the analysis of long-run responses to changes in exogenous variables can follow the usual comparative-statics pattern. This is the case for both cognitive and behaviorist models; indeed, the purpose of the last chapter was to show that traditional long-run comparative-statics theory is applicable even if individual decision makers eschew cognition entirely and react wholly passively to environmental stimuli.

The congruence between feedback and optimization theories vanishes when we turn to the analysis of short-run or disequilibrium phenomena. By their very nature, optimization models are inapplicable to disequilibrium states, and even the most elementary questions of dynamic adjustment have proved to be resistant to analysis by traditional means. Typical of this problem is the fact that we do not even have a clearly defined theory of short-run price changes in competitive markets. Although we know from comparative statics that equilibrium price in a competitive market rises if the market demand function rises (for a given upward-sloping supply function), according to a literal interpretation of the theory, the first firm to raise its price loses all of its sales as customers seek out its lower-priced competitors. The theory that provides our equilibrium model is incapable of application to transition states, and in order to deal with such problems within the maximization framework, economists have been forced either to assume instantaneous adjustment (thus, in effect, ignoring dynamics altogether) or to introduce speculative new dimensions (information lags, uncertainty, or mechanical price-setting rules) that are not part of the original theory and that are not always even consistent with the spirit of maximization itself. The attractive feature of dynamic feedback theories is that they are defined as short-run adjustment mechanisms, so that they are as readily applied to these disequilibrium problems as they are to long-run equilibrium states.

A further inducement to consider the short-run properties of the theory stems from the frequently heard allegation that equilibrium states never arise in practice. It could be argued that the system converges toward equilibrium so slowly that long before the consequences of any initial shock have been fully worked out, the economy has been subjected to a variety of new exogenous changes that have altered its course in all sorts of new directions. From the perspective provided by the feedback theory, this is to say that the vector Φ_t will always be found to contain several elements that are significantly different from zero, because external shocks are too frequent to permit development of an equilibrium Φ containing near-zero values in all places but one. Further, it suggests that the appropriate analysis of market changes should stress the one-period or two-period effects on the values in Φ_t as much as it stresses the long-term change in the equilibrium asymptote toward which the system is moving.

Short-run simulations

It is in the nature of any feedback theory to posit the existence of adjustment lags in the system. This arises as a consequence of the real-time dimension in which behavior occurs, not merely because of any institutionalized rigidities or information lags, although, of course, these can compound the effect. A practical economic implication of this view is that short-run elasticities will inevitably appear to be smaller than long-run elasticities. Economists seem to be agreed that this should be the case, but it is rare to find empirical work whose underlying theoretical formulation takes explicit account of the relevant time frame. Demand functions estimated from quarterly data, for example, should be different from demand functions estimated from annual data, and unless one believes adjustment to be very rapid, neither of these should be associated with the demand function of comparative statics. Nevertheless, the same underlying model is typically assumed for all of them, and when some concessions are made to short time frames (through the introduction of lagged independent variables), no theoretical justifications are provided for the specific forms of the equations to be estimated (beyond an occasional reference to technological or institutional rigidities).

There are exceptions to this tendency to neglect the dynamic aspects of demand theory, and occasionally economists have actually turned to purely behavioral rigidities in order to account for the observed dynamics of empirical phenomena. Notable examples are found in Houthakker and Taylor's extensive demand studies (1970), in which not only are consumption lags associated with "habits," but also the equations are formulated to include variables that are interpreted as reflecting a consumer's "psychological stock" of habits. Similar interpretations can sometimes be placed on models whose authors do not explicitly introduce such overtly behavioral considerations. For example, the permanent-income hypothesis formulated by Friedman (1957) is essentially a feedback model whose lags can be associated with a behaviorist theory of habit formation without any significant distortion. In spite of these occasional efforts to introduce feedback mechanisms into economics, the bulk of economic theory leaves very little room for them, and empirical studies of production and of demand have (apart from the Houthakker-Taylor work) rarely addressed the central question of the dynamic framework in which the market responses they are measuring are assumed to arise. The reason for this neglect is apparently that the optimization model that is almost universally used as a point of departure for empirical work provides no natural distinction between the short and long runs, and the question is therefore (perhaps inadvertently) ignored.

It is a relatively straightforward matter to construct simple algebraic versions of the feedback model and to use them in simulations in order to demonstrate the general character of the feedback process. As examples, we construct two such models, one intended to simulate consumption-function behavior and the other intended to describe dynamic demand functions. In order to construct these examples, we shall use the proportional model that was introduced in the last chapter, and, for the sake of definite numerical results, we apply the independence assumption (2.4) that permits us to replace the inequalities in the model [e.g., in equations (2.18) and (2.19)] with equalities. For the examples in this chapter, we use identical linear approximations of the functions $\alpha(\Theta_i - \hat{\Theta}_t)$ and $\beta(\hat{\Theta}_t - \Theta_i)$ and choose values for Θ_i that ensure that these linear approximations do not produce feedback magnitudes beyond the natural boundaries determined by the probability calculus [given by expression (2.6)]. The aspiration level $\hat{\Theta}_t$ is generated as a simple weighted average of experience.

In the case of consumption, the model is represented by

$$L^i(\Phi_t, i, \Theta, \hat{\Theta}_t) = \begin{cases} (\Theta_i - \hat{\Theta}_t)(1 - \phi_{i,t}) & \text{if } \Theta_i > \hat{\Theta}_t \\ (\Theta_i - \hat{\Theta}_t)\phi_{i,t} & \text{if } \Theta_i < \hat{\Theta}_t \end{cases} \tag{3.1}$$

$$\Theta_i = 2.2^{C_i^4(I - C_i)} \tag{3.2}$$

$$\hat{\Theta}_t = \hat{\Theta}_{t-1} + 0.1(\Theta_{t-1} - \hat{\Theta}_{t-1}) \tag{3.3}$$

where I is a measure of income that we shall restrict to the alternative values $I = 1.3$, 1.4, 1.5, 1.6, or 1.7, and where C is total consumption during a period, with the alternative values $C = 1.0$, 1.04, 1.08, 1.12, 1.16, 1.20, 1.24, 1.28, 1.32, or 1.36. These specific parameters have been chosen so as to produce an optimum value $C^* = 0.8I$ and so as to preserve the condition $|\Theta_i - \hat{\Theta}_t| < 1$ for all available combinations of I and C. For simplicity, we use values of $E[\phi_{i,t+1}]$ as the values for $\phi_{i,t+1}$ in each successive iteration, thus eliminating the need to compute a succession of higher-order terms. This procedure does produce errors, but analysis of specific cases has failed to reveal any errors larger than 6 percent of the estimated values of ϕ, and in most cases the errors are much smaller than this.

The simulations were generated as follows: Initial values were set at $I = 1.5$ and $\hat{\Theta}_t = 1.58$, and the vector Φ_0 was uniform, each choice being given a likelihood of 0.1. The feedback process described by equations (3.1) through (3.3) was then simulated over twenty iterations. At the end of this sequence, the variables had achieved values $\hat{\Theta} = 1.589$ and $\Phi_t = \{0.055, 0.059, 0.064, 0.105, 0.164, 0.193, 0.180, 0.088, 0.060, 0.053\}$. These values were then used as the initial conditions for all subsequent iterations. In effect, the convergence process is redirected toward a new goal in midstream. In the consumption simulation, for example, the income I was changed to some new value after these initial twenty iterations had been completed, and the subsequent pattern of response was recorded.

Figure 3.1 describes the results from this simulation, showing expected consumption levels as functions of income as well as of the time lag following a once-and-for-all change in income. The consumption behavior described in the figure matches closely the short-run/long-run pattern that is usually described in traditional theory: The very short-run consumption function ($t = 5$) displays very little responsiveness to income changes, whereas the longer-run functions ($t = 15, t = 50, t = 100$) approach more and more closely to the "equilibrium" relationship of $C = 0.8I$.

Similar simulations can be used to describe the consequences of changes in price. Suppose the household is purchasing a commodity x at a price P. For a simple example, we can employ the model described in (3.1) and (3.3), replacing the payoff function with

$$\Theta_i = 2.2^{x_i^4(I - Px_i)} \tag{3.4}$$

For this example, we use values of $x = 1.0$, 1.04, 1.08, 1.12, 1.16, 1.20, 1.24, 1.28, 1.32, and 1.36 and values of $P = 1.154$, 1.071, 1.0, 0.938, and 0.882. I is held constant at $I = 1.5$. Figure 3.2 describes the results of such a simulation using the same initial conditions described in the previous case and the same procedure of finding expected consumption of the commodity as a function of price and length of the lag after a once-and-for-all price change. Again, the model closely corresponds to what we would expect to find empirically: The very short-run demand curve displays very little responsiveness to price, whereas the longer-run functions ($t = 15, t = 50, t = 100$) approach more and more closely to the static-equilibrium demand curve.

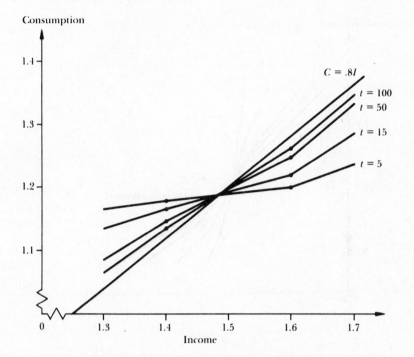

Figure 3.1. Simulated short- and long-run consumption functions.

In both of these examples the behavior of the dependent variable is similar to what we might expect from experience. There certainly are no new or surprising implications here. However, it is important to note that these patterns follow from the elementary feedback model itself, not from any auxiliary hypotheses concerning technological lags or bottlenecks, and to this extent the feedback model is quite different from traditional theory.

Short-run marginal effects

Apart from the simulation procedure, it is possible to use the formal model to derive explicit expressions for the short-period consequences of changes in exogenous variables. Just as we might seek to discover, in an equilibrium comparative-statics setting, how output levels might be altered by the imposition of a tax, we can consider the effect of a tax change on the dynamic path that is followed by the outputs of firms that are still out of equilibrium. In such a case, we do not compare the output in a period $t+1$ with the output in t and attribute that to the tax: Because the firms are not in equilibrium, output will normally change from

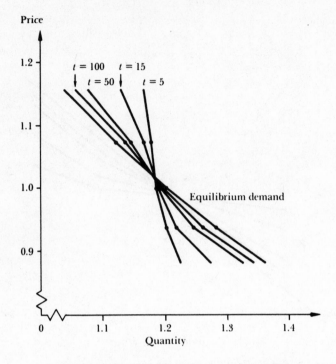

Figure 3.2. Simulated short- and long-run demand functions.

period to period whether or not the tax is levied. Instead, we must construct an expectation for output in $t+1$ in a no-tax circumstance, compare that with expected output in $t+1$ with the tax, and attribute this difference to the change in circumstance.

We are particularly interested in the question whether or not this short-run dynamic response is in any way similar to the implications of comparative-statics theory. An intuitively appealing conjecture is that if we shift the equilibrium state of an economic system in some stated direction, then every point on the path of convergence to that equilibrium will be similarly shifted, so that at least the qualitative properties of comparative-statics theory will also apply to the short run. Thus, a tax that raises equilibrium price will also lead to higher short-run prices, fixed cost changes that leave long-run output constant will also leave short-run output constant, and so on. Naturally, the case for the argument that individual decision makers act as if they are consciously maximizing well-defined objectives is greatly strengthened to the extent that short-run qualitative behavior matches equilibrium behavior, and this is the central issue to which the examples that follow are addressed.

In order to develop an explicit short-run analysis, it is necessary to take account of the influence of cognition over individuals' adaptive responses. The fact is that one's short-run response to a changed environment may depend on what one imagines oneself to have "learned" (in a cognitive sense) from some new observation. In one case, a higher price may stimulate purchases of durables because it is interpreted as a signal of a rising price trend, but in another case it may lead to deferral of purchases because it is seen to be a temporary fluctuation. A third possibility is that price increases may lead to substitutions among commodities because the substitutes may now be seen to be cheaper. Which of these is the more accurate description of a particular market may be as much a matter of history as of logic: The determination depends on the nature of the good in question as well as on the experience (and hence the personality) of the decision maker.

Any of these alternative cognitive specifications may be introduced into a feedback model; however, in keeping with the concern that the models developed here avoid dependence on idiosyncratic cognitive or personality variables, we prefer to restrict the analysis to a cognitively neutral formulation. Thus, we construct an example of short-run dynamic adjustment using the "independence" assumption given in equation (2.4). If we substitute (2.4) into (2.13), we obtain an expression for the expected value for each element of Φ_{t+1} as a function of Φ_t and Θ, and after some rearrangement this becomes

$$E[\phi_{i,t+1}] = \phi_{i,t}\left[1 + \frac{L^i(\Phi_t, i, \Theta_i, \hat{\Theta}_t)}{1 - \phi_{i,t}} - \sum_{j=1}^{n} \phi_{j,t}\frac{L^j(\Phi_t, j, \Theta_j, \hat{\Theta}_t)}{1 - \phi_{j,t}}\right] \quad (3.5)$$

Depending on circumstances, A_i is defined to be either a single choice or a vector of choice elements (such as an entire market basket of commodities, or a production vector, listing all inputs and output quantities). Suppose that we consider one of these elements, denoted by x, and define x_i to be the quantity of x that is associated with the choice A_i. Unless all the x_i's have the same value, it is normally impossible to predict the quantity of x that will be observed during either period t or period $t+1$, because the choice vector A_i is itself only stochastically determined. We can calculate expected values for x, however, by weighting each x_i with the likelihood that the associated A_i will be chosen, and summing. Thus,

$$E[x_t] \equiv \sum_{i=1}^{n} x_i \phi_{i,t}$$

$$E[x_{t+1}] \equiv \sum_{i=1}^{n} x_i E[\phi_{i,t+1}] \quad (3.6)$$

Definitions (3.6) reflect the fact that the elements of Φ_t are established (by historical realized-choice behavior), but that the elements of Φ_{t+1} are not yet determined and can be represented only by expected values. Using (3.5) to provide these expected values, we can determine $E[x_{t+1}]$:

$$E[x_{t+1}] = E[x_t] + \sum_{i=1}^{n} \{x_i - E[x_t]\}\phi_{i,t} \frac{L^i(\Phi_t, i, \Theta_i, \hat{\Theta}_t)}{1 - \phi_{i,t}} \qquad (3.7)$$

For purposes of short-run analysis, we want to know how changes in the environment that alter values of the elements of Θ will alter the expected value for x during $t+1$. Suppose that Z is some exogenous variable such as a market price, tax, or subsidy. The nature of the influence of this variable over $E[x_{t+1}]$ can be determined through differentiation of (3.7):

$$\frac{\partial E[x_{t+1}]}{\partial Z} = \sum_{i=1}^{n} (x_i - E[x_t])\phi_{i,t} \frac{L^i_\Theta(\Phi_t, i, \Theta_i, \hat{\Theta}_t)}{1 - \phi_{i,t}} \frac{\partial \Theta_i}{\partial Z} \qquad (3.8)$$

where $L^i_\Theta(\Phi_t, i, \Theta_i, \hat{\Theta}_t)$ represents the partial derivative of the feedback function with respect to Θ.

It is evident from (3.7) and (3.8) that the actual short-run effect of some exogenous change on $E[x_{t+1}]$ is dependent on the specific form of the feedback function. Because we have put very few restrictions on the general form of this function, we might be justified in arguing that the behavior of $E[x_{t+1}]$ is ambiguous, providing no support for the contention that there may be similarities between short-run dynamics and long-run comparative-statics theory. However, it is instructive to seek further for particular formulations under which this conjecture might be justified. We discussed two general forms of this function in Chapter 2, each of which will generate processes that converge to optima. The first stressed the aspiration target, $\hat{\Theta}$, using a comparison between realized payoff and $\hat{\Theta}$ to distinguish choices that were "successful" from those that were "failures." The adjustment in $\hat{\Theta}$ then provided the mechanism that guaranteed convergence to equilibrium. In the short run, however, aspirations may not change significantly, and changes in $\hat{\Theta}$ will certainly have no influence over the transition from t to $t+1$ described by (3.7) and (3.8). In order to make sensible use of the aspiration-oriented model, therefore, we would have to take a longer-term view, treating values of $E[x_{t+r}]$, where r is large enough to enable changes in aspiration to influence the direction in which behavior must move.

It is much simpler to employ the alternative (proportionate) model that is described by equations (2.16) and (2.17) in Chapter 2. This is particularly the case in that the left-hand side of equation (2.16) appears so prominently in equations (3.7) and (3.8). Because equation (2.16) is defined only for cases in which the values of Θ are nonnegative, it is convenient to make two assumptions: first, that the feedback process has operated long enough for alternatives with negative payoffs to have had their selection probabilities reduced to near zero, so that the formulation (2.17) never arises; second, that the variations in Z that are under consideration are marginal ones, so that alternatives with positive payoffs do not suddenly acquire significantly negative payoffs. Making the substitution from (2.16), equations (3.7) and (3.8) now become

$$E[x_{t+1}] = E[x_t] + \sum_{i=1}^{n} (x_i - E[x_t])\phi_{i,t}\alpha(\Theta_i - \hat{\Theta}_t) \tag{3.9}$$

$$\frac{\partial E[x_{t+1}]}{\partial Z} = \sum_{i=1}^{n} (x_i - E[x_t])\phi_{i,t}\alpha'(\Theta_i - \hat{\Theta}_t)\frac{\partial \Theta_i}{\partial Z} \tag{3.10}$$

Here, $\alpha'(\cdot)$ represents the first derivative of the function $\alpha(\Theta - \hat{\Theta}_t)$ with respect to Θ. Because we are confining ourselves to choices with positive payoffs (i.e., choices that may be regarded as "successful"), and because $\alpha(\cdot)$ is a positive monotonic function, we always have $\alpha(\Theta - \hat{\Theta}_t) > 0$ and $\alpha'(\Theta - \hat{\Theta}_t) > 0$.

Two approximations for the function $\alpha(\cdot)$ come to mind as means for generating examples of equations (3.9) and (3.10). First, we might employ a linearization: $\alpha(\Theta - \hat{\Theta}_t) = \alpha_0 + \alpha' \cdot (\Theta)$, where α' is a constant coefficient that approximates the slope of $\alpha(\Theta - \hat{\Theta}_t)$ in the vicinity of the values of Θ that are actually encountered in practice. Mathematically, this is by far the simplest form to use, because the constant parameters are unaffected by the taking of expectations. Under this assumption, equations (3.9) and (3.10) become

$$E[x_{t+1}] = E[x_t] + \alpha' \sum_{i=1}^{n} (x_i - E[x_t])\phi_{i,t}(\Theta_i - \hat{\Theta}_t) \tag{3.11}$$

$$\frac{\partial E[x_{t+1}]}{\partial Z} = \alpha' \sum_{i=1}^{n} (x_i - E[x_t])\phi_{i,t}\frac{\partial \Theta_i}{\partial Z} \tag{3.12}$$

Note that the α_0 term drops out of (3.11) because $\alpha_0 \sum_{i=1}^{n} (x_i - E[x_t])\phi_{i,t} = 0$.

Convenient as the linearized version of $\alpha(\Theta)$ may be, it is subject to a severe limitation. Because the values of this function must always fall within the unit interval, the allowable variation in payoff must be quite small. There must not be any choices with significant selection probabilities whose payoffs, when multiplied by α', will give a product as large as 1. Moreover, because $\alpha(\Theta - \hat{\Theta}_t)$ is monotone and bounded by 0 and 1, we naturally anticipate either discontinuities in its slope or severe curvature as large payoffs bring us toward some upper asymptote. When payoff variations may be large, therefore, the linear approximation will be quite unsuitable, and a more appropriate example for the function will be of some form such as $\alpha(\Theta) = 1 - e^{-b(\Theta - \hat{\Theta}_i)}$, a function that always meets the required restrictions. Using this formulation, equations (3.9) and (3.10) become

$$E[x_{t+1}] = E[x_t] - \sum_{i=1}^{n} (x_i - E[x_t])\phi_{i,t} e^{-b(\Theta_i - \hat{\Theta}_t)} \tag{3.13}$$

$$\frac{\partial E[x_{t+1}]}{\partial Z} = b \sum_{i=1}^{n} (x_i - E[x_t])\phi_{i,t} e^{-b(\Theta_i - \hat{\Theta}_t)} \frac{\partial \Theta_i}{\partial Z} \tag{3.14}$$

For our first example of short-run dynamic analysis, suppose that we apply the model to the production behavior of a firm. We define a choice, A_i, to represent a vector of input and output quantities, and Θ_i represents the corresponding profit level. If the exogenous variable under consideration is the price at which output is sold, then we can specify C_i to be the cost of the factors that are employed to produce the output x_i. C_i does not always correspond to the cost function that is usually employed in production theory; it does not presume that factors are combined in the most efficient proportions, nor even that there is no outright waste in production. We state only that the choice A_i specifies some vector of inputs and that C_i is their cost. Naturally, there are many choices that do employ factors in efficient proportions, and these produce higher profits when compared with others that generate similar output levels, but that do incorporate production inefficiencies. If P represents market price, the payoff function is $\Theta_i = Px_i - C_i$, and because P is the exogenous variable under consideration, $\partial \Theta_i / \partial Z = \partial \Theta_i / \partial P = x_i$.

Let us consider first the linearized version of the model. Substituting x_i for $\partial \Theta_i / \partial Z$ in (3.12), we obtain

$$\frac{\partial E[x_{t+1}]}{\partial Z} = \alpha' \sum_{i=1}^{n} (x_i^2 - x_i E[x_t])\phi_{i,t} = \alpha' \sigma_x^2 \tag{3.15}$$

where σ_x^2 is the variance of the distribution of possible values of x around the mean $E[x_t]$. Because σ_x^2 is always positive, and α' is positive, this implies that increases in product price will always increase expected short-run output. Because the same is true of profit-maximizing firms that are price takers, this is a case in which the qualitative properties of the dynamic model conform to those of a comparative-statics model. The quantitative short-run effect, however, depends on the magnitude of σ_x^2, a term that has no relevance to the equilibrium theory. In fact, σ_x^2 is a measure of the extent to which the firm has settled down to a consistent output decision. If the feedback has been in operation long enough to have brought about near convergence to equilibrium, then σ_x^2 will be small simply because only one element of Φ_t is significantly different from zero. Alternatively, σ_x^2 may be small even though we are far from equilibrium if it should happen that each of the A_i's with a significant selection likelihood has a value of x_i near to the mean.

The linear example used to produce equation (3.15) is only one possible case, but it is useful in that it makes clear the importance that a firm's history takes in determining responses to changes in market variables. The folklore image of the staid old firm that has been in existence for so long that it never changes its ways is well represented here as a firm with a small value for σ_x^2, whereas the younger, less settled firm may appear to be much more adaptive simply because σ_x^2 is large. Moreover, it is clear that in this model, short-run supply elasticities are not functions of factor market conditions and production technologies alone. They depend as well on the historical stability of the market and the age distribution of the firms that deal in it.

Instead of the linear example, we can consider the concave function $\alpha(\Theta) = 1 - e^{-b\Theta}$. Substituting x_i for $\partial\Theta_i/\partial Z$ in equation (3.14), we obtain

$$\frac{\partial E[x_{t+1}]}{\partial Z} = b \sum_{i=1}^{n} (x_i - E[x_t])\phi_{i,t} x_i e^{-b(\Theta_i - \hat{\Theta}_t)} \tag{3.16}$$

In the linear case, we are able to state unambiguously that increases in product price will bring about increases in output. It is clear from a comparison of (3.13) and (3.16) that this result still holds whenever $E[x_{t+1}] \leqslant E[x_t]$ (because the positive terms in the sum are multiplied by the larger values of x). However, if it is the case that current expected output is below equilibrium levels, an increase in product price may eventually decrease expected future output. The source of this result is found in the concavity of the function $1 - e^{-b(\Theta - \hat{\Theta}_t)}$. Increases in all of the values of Θ have the effect of reducing differences in the values of this function, and because it is these differences that drive the convergence to equilibrium, increases in all profits have the effect of slowing convergence. If equilibrium lies above current expected output, then expected future output will rise more slowly than it would otherwise have done. Of course, it will still be the case that $E[x_{t+1}] > E[x_t]$.

Instead of a market price, suppose that the exogenous change amounts to a change in an unavoidable fixed cost such as a tax in the form of an operating license fee. In this case, $\Theta_i = Px_i - C_i - T$, where T is fixed and is not affected by the choice of A_i. Because $\partial\Theta_i/\partial T = -1$ in this case, we obtain from the linear example (3.12)

$$\frac{\partial E[x_{t+1}]}{\partial T} = -\alpha' \sum_{i=1}^{n} (x_i - E[x_t])\phi_{i,t} = 0 \tag{3.17}$$

It is well known that one property of the comparative-statics theory is its implication that unavoidable lump-sum taxes will not affect the short-run behavior of profit-maximizing firms (because after-tax profits are maximized simultaneously with before-tax profits). In the special linear case used to obtain (3.17), we obtain the same result, and hence the two descriptions of market behavior are identical.

This correspondence between the two theories is dependent on the linear example. If we substitute $\partial\Theta_i/\partial T = -1$ into (3.14), we obtain

$$\frac{\partial E[x_{t+1}]}{\partial T} = -b \sum_{i=1}^{n} (x_i - E[x_t])\phi_{i,t}\, e^{-b(\Theta_i - \hat{\Theta}_t)}$$

$$= b\{E[x_{t+1}] - E[x_t]\} \tag{3.18}$$

Because the parameter b is positive, equation (3.18) implies that increases in fixed costs will accelerate the convergence process. This acceleration is attributable to the concavity of the function $\alpha(\cdot)$. By shifting all values of Θ downward, increases in fixed costs increase the differences in the values of $1 - e^{-b(\Theta - \hat{\Theta}_t)}$, and this increases the responsiveness of the feedback mechanism to existing profit differences.

In the case of fixed-cost variations, the validity of the contention that short-run dynamic behavior must be similar to comparative-statics behavior depends on the validity of the approximations used to produce the linearized model. If we are near to equilibrium, for example, we might argue that choices with significant selection probabilities are very similar in that the values of Θ they produce are very much alike. In this case, a linear approximation to the slope of $\alpha(\cdot)$ is a good assumption, and the traditional fixed-cost theorem holds. If we are far from equilibrium, however, variations in realized values of Θ may be large, linearity becomes a difficult assumption to defend, and the fixed-cost theorem no longer applies.

Even in the linear case, the short-run dynamic model often diverges from comparative-statics theory. For example, another comparative-statics theorem asserts that a proportional tax on profits will not affect the behavior of the firm (because after-tax profits are maximized at the same point at which before-tax profits are maximized). If Θ_i' represents before-tax profits and β is the profit tax rate, then after-tax profits are $\Theta_i = (1-\beta)\Theta_i'$. Substituting this into (3.11) yields

$$E[x_{t+1}] = E[x_t] + (1-\beta) \sum_{i=1}^{n} (x_i - E[x_t])\phi_{i,t}\alpha'(\Theta_i - \hat{\Theta}_t) \tag{3.19}$$

Comparing (3.19) with (3.11), it is evident that positive values of the profit tax rate do not affect the sign of the difference $E[x_{t+1}] - E[x_t]$.

However, the tax does change the rate at which $E[x]$ changes over time. Thus, the profit tax is neutral in that it does not change the direction in which behavior is moving, but it does have the property that it will slow convergence. This is the result we might expect intuitively: High profits taxes have the effect of reducing the significance of profit differences, and thus they reduce the strength of the motivational mechanism that drives the firm toward equilibrium.

Investigation of the profits tax in the nonlinear example reveals no determinate direction of effect. The tax lowers actual profit differences as before, thus reducing the pressures that bring about convergence, but by lowering after-tax profit levels across the board, differences in the values of the function $1 - e^{-b(\theta - \hat{\theta}_t)}$ may be increased enough to offset this effect.

None of these results are in any way implausible. Indeed, economists' gossip and folklore are filled with examples of sluggish adjustment such as this model describes, and it is surprising only that we have been content for so long to treat examples of long-standing inefficiency as entertaining examples of managerial ineptness rather than as challenges to the literal acceptance of the maximization hypothesis. The proposition that changes in certain parameters might have the effect of slowing adjustment, and thus of prolonging disequilibrium, adds a new dimension to the evaluation and analysis of the effects of taxes (or of subsidies). It suggests, for example, that high profits taxes may have the effect of desensitizing firms to changes in market conditions, permitting adjustment lags to be even greater than they would ordinarily be. This is certainly a plausible result, and it may constitute one of the most significant behavioral consequences of taxes; at the same time, it can be developed only by means of a dynamic model, and the usual comparative-statics techniques will overlook it entirely.

Similar kinds of examples may be devised for the analysis of consumer choice. In a consumer model, an alternative A_i refers to a market basket of m different commodities $x_{1i}, \ldots, x_{mi}$ that may be purchased at prices $P_i, \ldots, P_m$. We must depart from conventional theory in one important respect, however. Because purchases during a budget period are subject to a stochastic influence, the extent to which the consumer's budget is overcommitted or undercommitted is also determined by stochastic processes. Just as we argued that the firm under disequilibrium may not be combining factors efficiently, so the consumer's choices may not always be consistent with the resources that are available. The folklore image of the household that discovers to its horror that it has "run out of money" before the end of the pay period has a basis in experience. The opposite case, in which the household manages to accumulate savings (or reduce debt) over the period, is more usually attributed to the virtue of thrift, although it may be only another stochastic event drawn from the same distribution. Under these circumstances, some consumption items necessarily play the role of residuals in the budget, decreasing or increasing inversely with earlier expenditures. Cash accumulations and other forms of saving are natural candidates for this role, and it seems proper to include many durable-goods purchases in this category as well. If food and other short-run "necessities" have absorbed all of a household's income, the tendency may be to tolerate or repair old durable equipment (at least for this period) until enough money is left over for a larger expenditure for replacement. [This view is also reflected in Duesenberry's (1952) treatment of saving.] This is not to say that saving or durable-goods purchases play a passive role in consumer spending decisions; they are part of the overall consumption bundle, and they contribute to the valuation of that bundle. If we take saving alone to be the residual, then, because the price of saving equals 1, we can write the payoff function as

$$\Theta_i = U\left(x_{1i}, \ldots, x_{mi}, I - \sum_{k=1}^{m} P_{ki} x_{ki}\right) \tag{3.20}$$

where I is the consumer's (given) income.

Suppose we are interested in the effect of a change in income in period t on the expected consumption of some commodity x_k in period $t+1$. Differentiating (3.20) with respect to I and substituting into the linear model (3.12) produces

$$\frac{\partial E[x_{k,t+1}]}{\partial I} = \alpha' \sum_{i=1}^{n} (x_{ki} - E[x_{k,t}]) \phi_{i,t} U_s \tag{3.21}$$

where U_s is the partial derivative of the utility function with respect to saving.

An assumption used to simplify consumer models in a wide variety of applications states that "the marginal utility of money (income) is constant." This assumption, referring as it does to an envelope condition on long-run equilibrium states, is not readily applicable to this short-run disequilibrium model. We can make the more restrictive assumption that the marginal utility of one particular good is constant over some "relevant" range, however, and recognize that the usual assumption follows as a consequence. If that good is saving, then U_s is a constant, and we have, from (3.21), $\partial E[x_{k,t+1}]/\partial I = 0$, and this is the same result that the constant-marginal-utility-of-money assumption produces in the static consumer maximization model.

Suppose that the consumer's income is increased for a short time and then reduced to its former level. Such income will act in the short run only to increase stocks of the "residual" goods (savings or durables), and because the higher income is not sustained, the consumer will continue to purchase essentially the same bundle as before. Thus, we have a marginal propensity to consume out of transitory income that will be small or even zero. Moreover, we have reason to expect purchases of durables to absorb a substantial part of transitory-income fluctuations – a proposition that also enjoys significant empirical support (Smith, 1962; Darby, 1972).

Both of these conclusions correspond closely to conventional comparative-statics theory. As in the case of the producer model, however, differences will arise if the household is far enough from equilibrium to require that we drop the linearity assumption. The modifications that are induced by the particular nonlinear model that was used to produce (3.13) and (3.14) are the same as those already derived in the case of producers and therefore are not repeated here.

Instead of evaluating changes in income, we can use the linear model to evaluate the effect of a change in the price of some good j on the expected consumption of good k. Differentiating (3.20) with respect to P_j and substituting into (3.12) produces

$$\frac{\partial E[x_{k,t+1}]}{\partial P_j} = -\alpha' \sum_{i=1}^{n} (x_{ki} - E[x_{k,t}]) x_{ji} \phi_{i,t} U_s \qquad (3.22)$$

If again we permit U_s to be treated as a constant, then (3.22) becomes

$$\frac{\partial E[x_{k,t+1}]}{\partial P_j} = -\alpha' U_s \sigma_{kj}^2 \qquad (3.23)$$

where σ_{kj}^2 is the covariance between the consumptions of x_j and x_k at time t (or simply the variance of x_k if $j = k$). The sign of σ_{kj}^2 is opposite to the sign of the cross-elasticity of demand between commodities j and k. It is interesting to note that even in this disequilibrium model, a short-run analogue to Slutsky symmetry is preserved. Because $\sigma_{kj}^2 = \sigma_{jk}^2$, we must have $\partial E[x_{k,t+1}]/\partial P_j = \partial E[x_{j,t+1}]/\partial P_k$. The introduction of nonzero income effects (U_s not constant) will destroy this equality, just as it does in the case of ordinary optimization theory.

Even though the qualitative short-run effect of the price change matches conventional maximization theory, the quantitative effect depends on the magnitude of σ_{kj}^2, a term that reflects closeness to equilibrium and that therefore does not appear at all in the comparative-statics theory. Again, the introduction of a nonlinear model modifies these results in a way that parallels the examples of production.

A note on experimentation

From time to time we have referred to empirical material in the economics and psychology literatures in support of various characterizations of our experience-driven theory of economic behavior. It is especially worthwhile at this point to remark on experimental results that bear directly on the question of optimization versus "learning" as explanatory theories of behavior.

Laboratory experimentation has, until recently, been the exclusive domain of psychologists, and sophistication in experimental design has been increasing rapidly since B. F. Skinner (1938) first established reliable methods of operant conditioning in the early 1930s. Of particular interest to us is the development from this foundation of a set of so-called behavior-modification techniques that use the principles of reinforcement learning to change human behavior. Beginning in 1961, Theodoro Ayllon and Nathan Azrin (1966), psychologists working in an Illinois state mental hospital, devised a sophisticated method for making practical use of learning principles in patient treatment. Their procedure was to reward desired behavior on the part of patients with "tokens" that at a later time could be exchanged at specified rates for "reinforcers" (candy, movies, free time, etc.) of the patients' own choosing. This token device was seen to have two advantages over predetermined reinforcers: First, even if the payoffs were necessarily deferred until later, the tokens provided an immediate and tangible proxy that could operate effectively in the present. Second, the patients were able to exchange the tokens for any of a wide variety of goods, thus choosing for themselves the most powerful reward that was available. This token device has since been applied to a broad spectrum of problems in behavior change, ranging from classroom situations, in which children are awarded tokens for good performance (especially in mathematics), to the treatment of alcoholism and to prisons, in which inmates are rewarded for "socially acceptable" behavior.

The analogy to ordinary market economies is obvious in these experiments, and, indeed, Ayllon and Azrin described their construction as a "token economy." Nevertheless, the theoretical foundation for their work rested on a feedback model of reinforcement learning, and there is certainly no suggestion in their writing that their patients might be described as rational, maximizing decision makers. At the same time, their experimental results correspond closely to the predictions that are usually justified on the basis of the traditional optimizing model. Thus, in carefully controlled sets of circumstances, Ayllon and Azrin were able to obtain downward-sloping demand curves, upward-sloping supply curves (including the suggestion of a backward-bending supply curve), supply–demand equilibrium prices, and even the purchase of franchises (the payment of tokens in exchange for the guarantee of particular jobs). Since the publication of this work, parallel experimentation has taken place using both human and animal subjects, and consistent support has been found for the original Ayllon-Azrin results (Kagel et al., 1975; Battalio et al., 1979, 1981; Allison, 1981). Using pigeons and rats as subjects, Battalio and associates moved all the way to a purely economic interpretation and produced numerical estimates of income-compensated substitution effects.

As this experimental work has progressed, a certain ambiguity has developed as to the appropriate specification of the hypotheses that are under investigation. Whereas the original learning experiments were focused on a dynamic feedback mechanism, psychologists concerned with the proposition that learning processes will tend toward optimal ("rational") outcomes (Herrnstein, 1970; Herrnstein and Loveland, 1975) have naturally tended to focus more narrowly on outcome measures, and the more recent "economics" experiments have been presented in ways that clearly make the optimizing behavior of standard economic theory the object of interest. One is naturally led to wonder how it is that the same experiments can be said to lend support to such obviously distinguishable bodies of theory. In effect, many authors are pointing to successful dynamic learning experiments as support for the predictions of an incompatible optimization paradigm.

A potential resolution of this dilemma may be found in the models described in this chapter. If the objects of study are the usual comparative-statics properties of demand and supply functions, then both in and out of long-run equilibrium, a feedback model of behavior produces qualitative implications that are so similar to those of optimization as to make the two theories empirically indistinguishable. Thus, the alleged support for optimal-choice theory that is found in animal experiments may in fact be support for a feedback learning theory with the comparative-statics properties we have described. A proper test to differentiate these two theoretical constructions requires that we focus on areas (such as decision making under uncertainty or time preference) in which the two views will produce incompatible implications.

In addition to these behaviorist experiments, there is a growing literature concerning market experimentation in which human subjects (such as the all-purpose college sophomore) are put into experimental environments that have been explicitly patterned after real market situations; see the summary and bibliography of Smith (1981). These are of somewhat less relevance here because they focus on market outcomes rather than individual-choice behavior. One is also inclined to wonder to what extent these naive subjects can be expected to replicate the (cognitive rule-following) behavior of real-market participants who have years of experience behind them. On the other hand, these experiments consistently display the individual behavior that the models in this chapter would lead us to expect. Initial choices are erratic and usually far from optimal, but as time passes and experience accumulates, variability in choices decreases, and we observe convergence toward an equilibrium that usually is close to that described in conventional comparative-statics economic theory.

CHAPTER 4

Uncertainty

In 1921, Frank H. Knight was careful to draw a distinction between the concepts of "risk" and "uncertainty." He maintained that "risk" describes circumstances under which one can associate a known probability with each of a series of alternative states of the world. When this is true, expected-return calculations are possible, and maximization of expected payoff provides an appropriate guide for decision making. "Uncertainty," on the other hand, was a term he reserved for circumstances under which outcome probabilities are either unknown (such as the likelihood of a disaster at a nuclear power plant) or unknowable (such as personal well-being in the afterlife). In such cases, expected-return computation is impossible, and one must seek for some alternative decision rule.

The problem of decision making under uncertainty generated a considerable amount of speculation during the 1940s and 1950s, and a number of proposals evolved for the specification of behavior that might be appropriate for dealing with it. These ranged from a pessimistic "maximin" criterion (which proposes that "nature" is bent on one's destruction, so that one's best choice is that which least exposes one to potential damage) to the naive "principle of insufficient reason" (which places equal likelihoods on all distinct outcomes). A good survey has been provided by Luce and Raiffa (1957). None of these has achieved general approval, however, and in recent years Knight's distinction itself has lost currency as economists have turned to the development of Bayesian models of decision making and to an acceptance of Savage's view (1954) that one can formulate subjective probability distributions that will successfully explain behavior using the expected-utility procedure no matter what the objective circumstances may be.

The apparent failure of attempts to find acceptable normative decision criteria in the presence of Knight's "uncertainty" does not mean that the problem is without behavioral relevance. Even when outcome probabilities are knowable, the uncertainty characterization will be more accurate whenever an individual does not possess the insight and skills in analysis that are required by expected-utility procedures. Indeed, we would expect the decision modes that are used in practice to depend not only on one's intellectual abilities but also on personal background and experience. This proposition that individuals may differ in "decision style" as much as they differ in "tastes" is fundamental to the arguments that are developed in this chapter.

There certainly do exist individuals who, at least under some circumstances, are explicit in their use of expected-return calculations. Examples are provided by investors who use currently prevailing portfolio management theories to guide their investment behavior and persons who refuse to participate in lotteries and sweepstakes after calculating that the expected returns are negative. These may be exceptions to the rule, however, for it is more common to encounter individuals who deny any knowledge or even any estimate of the probabilities that are relevant to their decisions. Purchasers of tickets in state-run lotteries are usually unaware of payoff probabilities, and most of those who insure their houses against fire or their autos against collision would be hard-pressed to provide the probability distributions that expected-return calculations would require. In defense of expected-utility procedures, some might argue that the formation of subjective probabilities is unconscious and automatic, arguing in effect that it is part of the central nervous system, but marvelous as that system certainly is, expected-utility calculations would be quite out of character for a biological mechanism. A better defense rests on an observation that only a few persons need make the calculations and that the great majority of us can get by simply by following the examples set by the decisions of these other agents (Conlisk, 1980). We have a good deal of sympathy with this position, but it must be noted that "imitators" do not necessarily duplicate the decisions that would be produced by expected-utility maximization. Imitation is simply another feedback mechanism, and what decisions are produced through imitation depends on whom one happens to have observed in the past, whom they in turn may be imitating, and what consequences have been visited on all of these persons. An explicit model of imitation will be developed in Chapter 8.

Formal uncertainty models

In order to construct a formal theory, we shall suppose that there is a series of alternative possible states of the world whose relative likelihoods can be described by some distribution function. This function may or may not be known to individuals in our economy. When a choice A_i is made, the outcome, Θ_i, is now a variable whose value depends on which state of the world is actually realized. It is of no substantive concern to us whether the number of states is finite or whether the distribution describes a continuum of possible circumstances (so long as there are finite bounds on the possible values of the Θ_i's). In the first case, we define a set of M possible states $j = 1, \ldots, M$, and we use a probability vector $Q = q_1, \ldots, q_M$ whose elements describe their respective likelihoods. In the second case, we must use a continuous multidimensional density function over the values of Θ. We call this function $g(\Theta_1, \ldots, \Theta_n)$. Using the notation $\int_\Theta$ to denote integration over all the dimensions of Θ, the function $g(\Theta)$ is constrained to satisfy the condition $\int_\Theta g(\Theta) \, d\Theta = 1$. Because it seems to clarify the exposition of the theory, as well as reduce the incidence of subscripts, this second continuous representation is the one we shall use throughout our discussion. It is also convenient for us to define $g^i(\Theta)$ as the distribution of payoffs to the choice A_i. Thus, $g^i(\Theta)$ is defined to be the value of $g(\Theta)$ integrated over all dimensions other than the i dimension.

One can imagine at least three entirely different classes of behavior that can arise under these circumstances:

Actuarial behavior

A large insurance company or a large dealer in lotteries normally experiences only small fluctuations in net return per dollar of sales, because risks are pooled for a large firm, and the law of large numbers guarantees that the variance of net returns is small in proportion to sales volume. This is true even if the variance in payoff is large in proportion to any individual policy or lottery ticket. Thus, although there is always some small risk of extreme positive or negative returns, it is usually the case that the risk is so small relative to cash flow that the payoff to the choice A_i may be considered to be the expectation ξ_i, where $\xi_i \equiv \int_{-\infty}^{+\infty} \Theta_i g^i(\Theta) \, d\Theta$. In some cases, the payoff to A_i proves to be equal to ξ_i as a consequence of deliberate policy. Mutual insurance companies make rebates to policyholders where the amounts of these rebates are determined by the excess of premium revenue over benefit payments plus operating cost. In effect, any risks that are not perfectly pooled by the company are shifted back onto the general class of policyholders. Similarly, many state lottery games use printed tickets with a predetermined and fixed proportion of "winners." De facto, such firms are operating under conditions of certainty. Whether or not the risks are totally eliminated by mechanisms of this sort, we expect firms with large risk-pooling capability to come to ignore (or even be ignorant of) the variance in their profit flows, and when this happens, the theory of actuarial behavior is equivalent to the theory of behavior under certainty. The expectation ξ_i replaces Θ_i, and the models developed in the three preceding chapters can be employed without further modification.

Bayesian behavior

In this case, individuals use explicit expected-utility calculations to guide their behavior, where the required probability values are obtained either through guesses or through concrete knowledge of frequency distributions. Although it is evident that this sort of behavior can be learned, this is the sort of learning that takes place in school; that is, it is consciously cognitive in nature. There is no evidence that the probability calculus comes naturally to human beings. Indeed, both experimental evidence and anecdotal evidence suggest just the opposite. Apparent failures of the expected-utility hypothesis have been common experiences in the laboratory, with especially forceful examples being provided by Kahneman and Tversky (1979) and Grether and Plott (1979). Also see Tversky and Kahneman (1974). This evidence is not necessarily incompatible with optimization theory; models of rational behavior can be constructed without reliance on expected utility simply by treating probabilistic events as though they are separate consumption goods. Alternatively, the experiments can be viewed as rejecting only the "independence" axiom of modern utility theory. (This is the proposition that because only one state of nature is actually realized, similarities or complementarities among alternative states should never be relevant to a decision.) Machina (1982) has demonstrated that one can drop this axiom and still construct a utility theory such that expected-utility maximization is consistent with the Kahneman-Tversky experiments. This is not a particularly reassuring defense, however, because it serves to remind us of the extreme malleability of the theory of utility maximization and of the difficulty of formulating concrete experiments capable of refuting it. The independence axiom proved to be one aspect of modern utility theory that was subject to direct testing. Having failed that test, it is to be replaced by a more elaborate characterization of the form of the (essentially untestable) utility function itself. Moreover, the normative appeal of independence is still very strong, and it is difficult to accept the notion that sophisticated decision makers should be prepared to reject it as a matter of personal taste.

The intellectual ability to manipulate probability variables seems to be essential for optimal behavior in any case, and it is easy to find evidence that this ability is often missing. Many students find the formal subject to be difficult, and gamblers and stock-market speculators develop and even publicize all kinds of theories that purport to reveal underlying regularities in nature, even though elementary rules of logic are sufficient to demonstrate that these regularities do not exist. The observed concentration of lottery ticket sales among lower-income (i.e., less well educated) segments of the population supports this same view (Commission on Review of the National Policy toward Gambling, 1976). It does not seem that the application of probability theory is automatic or instinctive even among those who are familiar with it. Rather, a conscious effort is always required, so that it is actually implemented in those few areas in which its relevance and usefulness is most obvious. However sophisticated a decision maker may be, it is much easier to believe that the principle of expected utility will be applied to the purchase of insurance than it is to believe that it will be applied to decisions to jaywalk across busy streets (or not to), to climb dangerous mountains, or to smoke cigarettes.

If the probability distribution over possible states of the world is known to a decision maker, then the A_i that maximizes the value of ξ is the appropriate (Bayesian) choice. The problem becomes far more difficult, however, if the distribution is not known. In such cases, Bayesian procedures require the individual to form some estimate of the distribution, make a choice given that estimate, and then use the realized outcome as information to improve the quality of the estimate itself; for an example, see Rothschild (1974a). The statistical sophistication necessary to implement this procedure is extreme. Suppose $g^e(\Theta)$ represents the estimate of the probability distribution, and ξ_i^e is the corresponding expected value of the payoff to the choice A_i. It is not true that the optimal choice is always the one that maximizes ξ_i^e. One must also consider the value of information and the fact that apparently poor choices may make a very large contribution toward improving the quality of the estimate $g^e(\Theta)$, and this may permit greatly increased future returns. In some cases, naive maximization of ξ_i^e may lead one to overlook profitable alternative choices permanently (Rothschild, 1974b; Schmalensee, 1978). Moreover, the quality of the estimate $g^e(\Theta)$ is strongly dependent on the number of occasions on which the choice is made. If there are only a few pieces of data on which one may base the estimate, its reliability is very low; confidence intervals might be so wide as to reduce the entire procedure to an empty exercise. In short, the statistical difficulties that confront the objective of full optimization under incomplete knowledge of the underlying probability distribution are enormous, and it has proved possible to provide analytical solutions in only a few special examples. Full maximization under imperfect information is well beyond the cognitive abilities of ordinary human beings, and in most cases it is beyond the current state of the art as practiced by professional statisticians.

In summary, although Bayesian behavior certainly does occur, it is an advanced form of cognitive decision making. It can be applied fully in only limited circumstances by a few people, and although it may be employed imperfectly in many cases, it is hardly a decision style that could plausibly be used as a foundation for a general theory of behavior.

Adaptive behavior

An appealing feature of the model that was developed in the preceding chapters is the fact that it can be applied without alteration to circumstances characterized by either risk or uncertainty (in Knight's sense). We need only take into account the fact that the quantitative value of the feedback is subject to a stochastic influence. If A_i is chosen and Θ_i happens to be large and positive, then the likelihood ϕ_i of a repetition is enhanced. If Θ_i happens to be small, then ϕ_i is reduced. Thus, experience governs behavior, just as it does in the certainty model (although it is clear that the convergence properties of the system under uncertainty may be quite different from those under certainty). The probability distribution $g(\Theta)$, or its estimate, which is central to the Bayesian style, plays no cognitive role in adaptive decision making. The distribution has a positive role, of course, because it controls the experience that shapes adaptive behavior, but this does not take place at any consciously analytical level.

After the fact, individual decision makers may intentionally make it difficult for us to distinguish adaptive behavior from Bayesian behavior. We expect that however pervasive adaptive behavior may be, the powerful human motivation toward self-justification may lead to assertions that past behavior was "rational" in some formal sense, and among sophisticated individuals this will certainly include some references to the Bayesian style. (Among less sophisticated individuals, these formal arguments are often reduced to statements that amount only to superstition.) These explanations may also require the invention of one or more exogenous variables whose alleged relevance was not detailed in advance, but if it is one's own behavior that is to be described, we expect to find strong biases toward cognitive determinism, whatever the costs of these justifications may be. We use the term "decision style" to apply to either the Bayesian or the adaptive mode. "Actuarial" behavior, on the other hand, is determined primarily by one's environment, and it is consistent with either the adaptive mode or a cognitive optimization style (formal Bayesian rules would be irrelevant). In general, we shall treat actuarial behavior in the terms described in the previous chapters: An adaptive feedback process will converge eventually on a single alternative that maximizes actuarial net returns.

We expect behavior in practice to be compounded of these three basic decision patterns and the proportions among them to depend on the parameters of the situation. Increases in the length of time over which a given value of Θ_i is realized, or in the volume of transactions (number of actions taken per unit time), will tend to increase the weight on actuarial behavior as the object of the feedback process. The relative importance of Bayesian versus adaptive behavior will depend on the extent to which cognition plays a role in decision making, and this will depend in turn on the intellectual ability and background experience of the decision maker as well as on the objective character of the circumstances. Under conditions of Knight's "uncertainty," for example, normatively defensible cognitive methods are as yet unavailable, and purely adaptive behavior is perhaps the natural one to expect. At the same time, we should reiterate our point that the object of a feedback process (what is "learned," in effect) may not be a particular action but the decision style itself, and this style may be brought to bear on circumstances for which it is not appropriate. Even though there are no entirely satisfactory normative methods for dealing with pure uncertainty, previous experiences may lead individuals to continue to appeal to rules that have happened to have "worked" in the past. Thus, the principle of insufficient reason might appeal to those who have been lightly exposed to the probability calculus and whose self-esteem is heightened by the ability to apply sophisticated tools (even when that application is inappropriate), whereas the maximin criterion may come quite naturally to someone whose every picnic has encountered rain.

From what we have said already, it is evident that the term "cognition" has much broader application when we leave the certainty environment of previous chapters. In Chapter 2 we were concerned only with the possibility that experience with one choice might provide individuals with information regarding the payoffs that would be received (with certainty) from alternative choices. The counterpart under risk is the possibility that given the state of nature, individuals acquire information as to the payoffs to be received from alternative choices under that same state of nature. Clearly, this form of cognition can lead in ambiguous directions, because what is best under one state of nature may not be best under another. For this reason we shall consistently accept the independence assumption, equation (2.4), whenever we treat the adaptive decision style under conditions of risk. We have added two further cognitive dimensions: the possibility that an individual might apply formal probability calculus (properly or not) as a guide to decision making, and, given that this does occur, the possibility that a Bayesian decision maker will use experience with choice outcomes to modify the estimate $g^e(\Theta)$. In the next section we shall add still another dimension: the definition of a sensible "target" $\hat{\Theta}$. All of these different attributes produce considerable ambiguity in the use of the term "cognition," and in the following discussion it is important to keep these various meanings in mind.

Convergence in aspirations

In Chapter 2 we identified two types of formulations of a feedback process under which purely adaptive behavior would converge to optimization as an equilibrium state. The first of these models represented an aspiration level $\hat{\Theta}$, and it was demonstrated that as choices with payoffs less than $\hat{\Theta}$ were gradually eliminated, $\hat{\Theta}$ would rise over time, converging finally on the maximal payoff value. This proof cannot be duplicated if there is a probability distribution over outcome values. Suppose A_k is the optimal choice in the sense that $\xi_i < \xi_k$ for all $i \neq k$. It does not follow that we shall always find that $\Theta_i < \Theta_k$ for all $i \neq k$: There may be states of the world under which a usually inferior choice A_i is actually the best. If this is true, we cannot develop an argument that ϕ_i declines monotonically for $i \neq k$, because occasionally the unusual state will occur and ϕ_i will rise. Moreover, if the ϕ_i's do not generally converge to zero, they do not converge to any fixed value either. The value of any $\phi_{i,t+1}$ depends not only on ϕ_t but also on the particular choice that is made during t, and if several alternative choices are always possible (because their likelihoods are persistently above zero), we shall generally have as many different possible values for $\phi_{i,t+1}$ as there are different likely choices.

In order to provide a formal development of this mechanism, we must be more explicit as to the meaning of the aspiration level $\hat{\Theta}_t$. Because $\hat{\Theta}$ represents a goal or "target" payoff value, it is readily apparent that under risky circumstances different people may employ different criteria for distinguishing success from failure. At the most naive level, $\hat{\Theta}_t$ may be a weighted summation of past experience, just as it was in our certainty models. This would be the most appropriate formulation if the individual were unaware of the risk inherent in the world, or if, knowing of the risk, he had no idea of how to deal with it. It is not a particularly effective procedure from an optimization standpoint, because it admits the possibility that under adverse conditions optimal choices might be treated as failures, because they have not done as well as poor choices did during good times, whereas during good times relatively poor choices might be reinforced because the payoff was better than expected. Business firms may be encouraged by high earnings without taking proper account of the fact that they occur only during economic booms, and this will lead to inappropriate encouragement of certain decisions or certain decision makers. Similar examples are provided by individuals who use their own incomes as indicators of their personal worth without properly accounting for the nature of the labor markets in which they find themselves.

One step up from the naive decision maker is one who distinguishes success from failure partially with respect to the observed performances of others. In this case, $\hat{\Theta}_t$ is a payoff average across the society. Above-average returns will be rated as "successes," and below-average returns as "failures." Because this is clearly a cognitive procedure, $\hat{\Theta}_t$ might be more appropriately termed a "criterion" than a "goal." Examples of such criteria are common. Investment funds and individual stocks are often rated relative to the performance of some stock index, rather than relative to any absolute standard, so that a fund that loses value may nevertheless be seen to be successful if an index such as the Dow-Jones has declined more. As a practical matter, an ideal criterion is unachievable, because $\hat{\Theta}_t$ can never be perfectly measured. This is partly the case because payoffs to others are rarely entirely observable. In some cases, awareness of human nature would lead one to expect others to misrepresent their own returns deliberately. (One suspects that successful stock investments are much more often described by one's friends than are the failures.) In other cases, differences in consumer tastes produce different valuations for any given observed payoff experience. There is little evidence that individuals can be considered to be adept at making accurate inferences as to the rewards that they themselves will gain from the experiences of others, and yet such inferences are necessary if one is to acquire a criterion $\hat{\Theta}_t$ that is relevant to oneself. Finally, the sample of choice–payoff pairs that may be observed by one individual is by no means equivalent to the entire set of payoffs; it is generally confined to returns received by acquaintances and to media representations, and this sample may provide quite biased information. All of these considerations add "noise" to any observation of $\hat{\Theta}_t$, and often so little confidence can be placed in such an estimate that it will hardly be superior to the "naive" target with which we started.

At a still higher level, a sophisticated individual may be quite unaware of the density function $g(\Theta)$, but still "know" the entire payoff vector for the state that is realized during t. This level of awareness goes beyond any that we have considered heretofore, and in most multiple-choice situations we shall continue to consider an assumption of such knowledge to be quite unrealistic. At the same time, there are certain "binary-choice" situations under which that assumption is natural. If a coin is flipped, the call "tails" may or may not be successful; nevertheless, which choice would have been successful is known as soon as the coin falls. The childhood "stone, paper, scissors" game has the same property that the choice payoffs can be ranked by a player as soon as the state of nature (the opponent's choice) is known. This is a special class of situations, one that has received some empirical study, and examples will be more extensively discussed in Chapters 5 and 6.

One might object that the feedback view of behavior determination is weakened if we do not know a priori which of these specifications is appropriate. Our reply is that these differences in cognitive sophistication are matters of everyday experience. Plausible examples of each are easily identified, and they provide some of the most obvious variations in empirical human behavior. Optimization theory has traditionally admitted differences among individuals only to the extent that they may have differences in tastes, and yet differences in awareness, sophistication, cognition, and decision style are evident to all of us, and forcefully so in the case of anyone who has been priviledged to stand at the front of a classroom. The ability to accommodate differences in procedures as well as differences in tastes is a virtue in a theory of human behavior, so long as the variety of models that are generated is not hopelessly large.

The special case of full payoff information that is characteristic of certain binary-choice situations is deferred to later chapters. Here we concentrate on the "naive" and "average-payoff" definitions for $\hat{\Theta}_t$. We have already noted that, in general, convergence to a single choice is impossible under uncertainty. Under the naive formulation of aspirations, this is the case even if there is a choice A_k that is optimal in the very strong sense that its payoff is maximal under every possible state of nature. For a formal demonstration of this, let us define Φ_k to be the value of the vector Φ when $\phi_k = 1$ (i.e., Φ_k is a string of zeros except for a 1 in the kth place). Then if Φ were to converge to Φ_k, we would find $\hat{\Theta}$, which is a summation of previous experience, converging in probability toward ξ_k. If there is any variability in Θ_k across states of nature, however, it follows that Θ_k is often less than $\hat{\Theta}$, and because the choice A_k will then be seen to be a failure, the vector Φ will move away from Φ_k, and Φ_k cannot be a stable point of convergence.

Such a strong result does not apply if $\hat{\Theta}_t$ is the average return obtained by all individuals at time t (or, more accurately, the average return adjusted for differences between the preferences of all other individuals and those of the decision maker in question). In that case, if $\Theta_k \geqslant \Theta_i$ for all i in all possible states of nature, then no matter what choices are made by others, we shall always have $\Theta_k \geqslant \hat{\Theta}_t$, and we can use the arguments of Chapter 2 to demonstrate that Φ will converge to Φ_k. However, if there are states of nature for which A_k is not optimal, the convergence property is again lost: If all individuals but one have choice-probability vectors equal to Φ_k, and that one individual chooses A_j at a time when $\Theta_j > \Theta_k$, then $\Theta_k < \hat{\Theta}_t$ for all consumers but that one, and they are induced to move away from Φ_k. The one who chose A_j is encouraged in his choice, and he, too, moves farther away from Φ_k. Thus, Φ_k is not a stable convergence point.

It is also clear that there is no single value of Φ that can serve as a convergence point. So long as several alternative choices remain possible, and these have differing payoffs that themselves depend on the state of nature, the transition from Φ_t to Φ_{t+1} will obey stochastic rules that provide many possible alternative values for Φ_{t+1}, and it is likely that none of these is equal to Φ_t. Associated with each of these values of Φ_{t+1} will be some $\hat{\Theta}_{t+1}$, for the failure of Φ to converge to one value implies that $\hat{\Theta}$ will also vary perpetually.

In spite of the static indeterminacy in Φ and $\hat{\Theta}$, there is an important sense in which the feedback process is convergent. Suppose that we were to carry out the choice–feedback process over an infinite number of trials, or, what is nearly the same thing, consider a very large population composed of identical individuals. We would then observe some distribution of values of Φ and $\hat{\Theta}$ across these populations. A very useful property of the feedback mechanism is that if $g(\Theta)$ is stationary, the distribution of values of Φ will generally converge to one that is both unique and stable. Proof of this property requires more formal specification than we have given so far of the feedback function and of the circumstances to which it applies, but an example of the proof as it applies to most of the cases treated here is given in the Appendix to Chapter 6. In general, proofs of these properties rely on the fact that when there is no unique point of convergence, condition (2.6) prevents any subset of choices from coming to be chosen with certainty as a consequence of historical accident. Thus, it is always the case that any "good" choice will at some time be discovered and will acquire a positive likelihood, and although this likelihood will vary over time, it will never reach zero.[1] As a consequence of this property, we can associate a weight with any pair that specifies its likelihood relative to alternative pairs. Making our conceptual populations large enough, we can define a continuous joint density function $\Gamma(\Phi, \hat{\Theta})$ to describe these weights.

The existence and uniqueness of $\Gamma(\Phi, \hat{\Theta})$ may be intuitively plausible from the discussion already. Here we shall confine ourselves to two examples that are of interest. In these examples there are only two choices: The payoff to the first, Θ_1, has a fixed value, and the payoff to the second, Θ_2, varies according to the density function $g(\Theta_2)$. For our first example, we consider the "naive" decision maker for whom $\hat{\Theta}$ is determined by a weighted sum of recent experience. Suppose the feedback function takes the proportional form given by equations (2.16) and (2.17) in Chapter 2, and use the specific updating rule given by equation (3.3) in Chapter 3. In this case, it is a straightforward matter to use random-number tables in a computer simulation to generate approximations to the function $\Gamma(\Phi, \hat{\Theta})$. That is, given current values of ϕ_1 and $\hat{\Theta}$, the random table is used to determine which choice is to be made during t and what the payoff Θ_2 is to be. Then equations (2.16), (2.17), and (3.3) are used to obtain new values for ϕ_1 and $\hat{\Theta}$. After several thousand iterations, the obtained values of ϕ_1 and $\hat{\Theta}$ approximate the smooth density function $\Gamma(\Phi, \hat{\Theta})$. Figure 4.1 contains some examples of the distribution of values of ϕ_1 for the case in which the feedback functions are linear and symmetric around $\hat{\Theta}_t$ with slope k:

$$\alpha(\Theta_i - \hat{\Theta}_t) = k(\Theta_i - \hat{\Theta}_t)$$

$$\beta(\hat{\Theta}_t - \Theta_i) = k(\hat{\Theta}_t - \Theta_i) \tag{4.1}$$

The density function $g(\Theta_2)$ used for these examples is uniform over $[0, 1]$. The value for k used in this example is $k = 0.2$, and values for Θ_1 are 0.2, 0.35, 0.5, 0.65, and 0.8.

For the second example, we suppose that there is a large population of identical individuals and that it is easy to acquire a correct criterion $\hat{\Theta}$ that equals the average payoff. In this case, $\hat{\Theta}$ depends only on the distribution of values of ϕ_1 and the realized state of nature. Therefore,

---

[1] Formally, there is an ergodic set of values of Φ that is unique. Condition (2.6) guarantees that no small set of values of Φ can acquire large probability weights after a long series of trials (meeting the hypothesis of Doeblin) and that it will always be possible to make a transition from one set of equilibrium values of Φ to another (hence the uniqueness) (Doob, 1953, pp. 192–214).

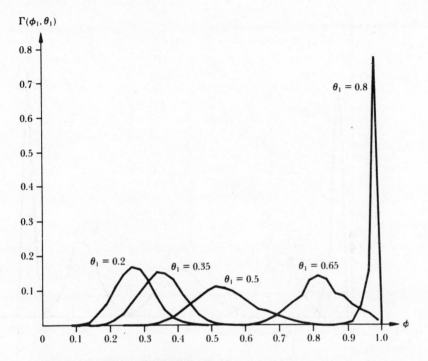

Figure 4.1. Naive model: ϕ distribution.

we can represent $\Gamma(\Phi, \hat{\Theta})$ with the simple density function $\gamma(\phi_1)$ and the condition

$$\hat{\Theta} = \Theta_1 \int_0^1 \phi_1 \gamma(\phi_1) \, d\phi_1 + \Theta_2 \int_0^1 (1 - \phi_1) \gamma(\phi_1) \, d\phi_1 \qquad (4.2)$$

We again let the feedback function take the proportional form given by (2.16) and (2.17) and perform a computer simulation of $\gamma(\phi_1)$ in a fashion similar to that used in the first example. Figure 4.2 describes simulation results for the same parameter values as were used for the first example.

It is clear from the examples used to construct Figures 4.1 and 4.2 that general feedback processes will emphasize "better" choices under uncertainty even though we cannot identify a single alternative toward which behavior will always converge. The examples also support our natural expectation that the more sophisticated target criterion leads to greater sensitivity to differences in expected payoffs, particularly when the certain payoff value is below the mean of the distribution of payoff values for the alternative choices.

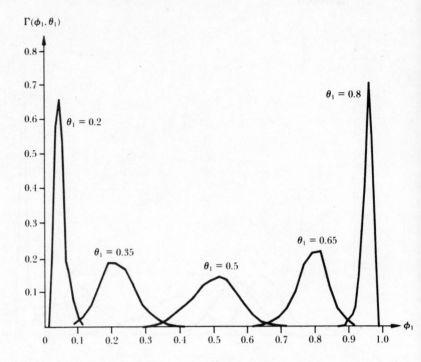

Figure 4.2. Population criterion model: ϕ distribution.

Although the distribution $\Gamma(\Phi, \hat{\Theta})$ is the best formal characterization of the nature of the feedback process under risk, it is a very clumsy one. Even in the case of simple proportional models, analytic solutions for $\Gamma(\Phi, \hat{\Theta})$ are generally unobtainable, and simulation methods such as those used to obtain the data represented in Figure 4.1 are the only means available for describing the convergence properties of the model. This makes "comparative-statics" analysis very difficult: If we wish to investigate the consequences of a change in some parameter value on long-run behavior, we must run two simulations side by side and compare the resulting choice likelihoods either visually or in terms of simple statistical properties. It is worthwhile to seek for some approximation that will simplify our representation of the theory.

It is common both in psychological learning models and in biological adaptation models to simplify representations of distributions such as $\Gamma(\Phi, \hat{\Theta})$ by using expectations operators in place of the distributions themselves (Bush and Mosteller, 1955). In Chapter 3 we obtained an expression for the expected value of any element $E[\phi_{i,t+1}]$ as a function of Φ_t and the payoff vector Θ: equation (3.5). Under conditions of risk, the same procedure can be applied, with the exception that $E[\phi_{i,t+1}]$ is now the sum of a series of such expressions, each dependent on a different vector Θ, and each weighted by the likelihood that the given Θ is the one produced by the state of nature:

$$E[\phi_{i,t+1}] = \phi_{i,t} + \frac{\phi_{i,t}}{1 - \phi_{i,t}} \int_{-\infty}^{\infty} L^i(\Phi_t, i, \Theta, \hat{\Theta}_t) g^i(\Theta) \, d\Theta$$

$$- \phi_{i,t} \sum_{j=1}^{n} \frac{\phi_{j,t}}{1 - \phi_{j,t}} \int_{-\infty}^{\infty} L^j(\Phi_t, j, \Theta, \hat{\Theta}_t) g^j(\Theta) \, d\Theta \qquad (4.3)$$

Whatever model we use for the feedback function, and however we assume $\hat{\Theta}_t$ to be generated, we can use (4.3) and these models to obtain expected values for each element in Φ and for $\hat{\Theta}_{t+1}$. Moreover, because the functions $L(\cdot)$ and $g(\cdot)$ are continuous, and because each element of Φ is always found in the closed interval $[0,1]$, one can appeal to a simple Brouwer fixed-point argument to show that there always exist stationary values for Φ and $\hat{\Theta}$ generated by (4.3) (Intriligator, 1971). We shall designate such points with the symbols Φ^* and $\hat{\Theta}^*$. That is, if we use Φ^* and $\hat{\Theta}^*$ in the feedback and aspiration-level models, equation (4.3) will produce expected values for the elements of Φ and for $\hat{\Theta}$ that are identical with the elements of Φ^* and $\hat{\Theta}^*$, respectively. Thus, Φ^* and $\hat{\Theta}^*$ provide approximations to the mean of $\Gamma(\Phi, \hat{\Theta})$ in the sense that if we start with these "average" values, the expected outcomes will again take those same "average" values.

The accuracy of an approximation such as this naturally depends on the functional character of the feedback function and on the breadth and skewness of the density function $\Gamma(\Phi, \hat{\Theta})$. Moreover, the fact that Φ and $\hat{\Theta}$ are jointly distributed means that in some cases Φ^* and $\hat{\Theta}^*$ are difficult to obtain analytically without taking the further step of treating Φ as though its distribution is independent of $\hat{\Theta}$. Even with this additional approximation, however, simple examples using the proportional feedback model produce values of Φ^* and $\hat{\Theta}^*$ that are not far from the means of simulated distributions $\Gamma(\Phi, \hat{\Theta})$. Suppose we consider the "naive" case in which $\hat{\Theta}$ represents the weighted sum of the payoff experience of one individual. If we pretend that the distribution of Φ in $\Gamma(\Phi, \hat{\Theta})$ does not depend on $\hat{\Theta}$, then the expected value of $\hat{\Theta}$ will be the sum of the Θ_i's weighted by the associated ϕ_i's summed over all the states of nature. Hence, at our approximation to the fixed point,

$$\hat{\Theta}^* = \sum_{i=1}^{n} \phi_i^* \xi_i \qquad (4.4)$$

At the fixed point, we have $E[\phi_{i,t+1}] = \phi_i^*$, and hence the two right-hand expressions in (4.3) must sum to zero:

$$\int_{-\infty}^{\infty} L^i(\Phi^*, i, \Theta, \hat{\Theta}^*) g^i(\Theta) d\Theta$$

$$= (1 - \phi_i^*) \sum_{j=1}^{n} \frac{\phi_j^*}{1 - \phi_j^*} \int_{-\infty}^{\infty} L^j(\Phi^*, j, \Theta, \hat{\Theta}^*) g^j(\Theta) d\Theta \qquad (4.5)$$

Using (2.16) and (2.17), which are the feedback equations for the proportional model, we can write condition (4.5) as

$$\int_{\hat{\Theta}^*}^{\infty} \alpha(\Theta - \hat{\Theta}^*) g^i(\Theta) d\Theta - \frac{\phi_i^*}{1 - \phi_i^*} \int_{-\infty}^{\infty} \beta(\hat{\Theta}^* - \Theta) g^i(\Theta) d\Theta$$

$$= \sum_{j=1}^{n} \phi_j^* \left[\int_{\hat{\Theta}^*}^{\infty} \alpha(\Theta - \hat{\Theta}^*) g^j(\Theta) d\Theta - \frac{\phi_j^*}{1 - \phi_j^*} \int_{-\infty}^{\infty} \beta(\hat{\Theta}^* - \Theta) g^j(\Theta) d\Theta \right]$$

$$(4.6)$$

Simultaneous solution of equations (4.4) and (4.6) will provide the desired values of Φ^* and $\hat{\Theta}^*$. For example, the density functions represented in Figure 4.1 were obtained from a two-alternative model in which the value of Θ_1 was fixed and Θ_2 was distributed uniformly over $[0,1]$. The feedback functions were linear and symmetric around $\hat{\Theta}$, with slopes k. Substituting these conditions into (4.4) and using the condition $\phi_1^* + \phi_2^* = 1$, we obtain

$$\hat{\Theta}^* = \frac{1}{2} + \phi_1^* \left(\Theta_1 - \frac{1}{2} \right) \qquad (4.7)$$

Using (4.6), (4.7), and the fact that the distribution of values for Θ_2 is uniform over $[0,1]$, we can derive equations for ϕ_1^*:

$$4(2\Theta_1 - 1)\phi_1^* - [1 + \phi_1^*(2\Theta_1 - 1)]^2 (2\phi_1^* - 1) = 0 \quad \text{if } \Theta_1 > \frac{1}{2}$$

$$8(2\Theta_1 - 1)\phi_1^{*2} - [1 + \phi_1^*(2\Theta_1 - 1)]^2 (2\phi_1^* - 1) = 0 \quad \text{if } \Theta_1 < \frac{1}{2} \qquad (4.8)$$

Table 4.1 permits a comparison of values of ϕ_1^* obtained from (4.8) and the means of the simulated distributions that are shown in Figure 4.1. For each value of Θ_1 in the first column, the entry in the second column is $\bar{\phi}_1$, the mean of the simulated distribution, and the third column contains ϕ_1^*. It is clear that, at least for the case of this proportional model, the fixed point ϕ_1^* is a good approximation for $\bar{\phi}_1$.

We can describe the case in which the individual constructs a target criterion, using the population-wide average payoff given the state of

Table 4.1. *Mean choice likelihoods,*
$\bar{\phi}$, *and fixed-point likelihoods,* ϕ^*,
for the "naive" model

Θ_1	$\bar{\phi}$	ϕ^*
0.2	0.27156	0.26395
0.35	0.35091	0.33432
0.5	0.54196	0.5
0.65	0.8226	0.81596
0.8	0.9839	0.9644

Table 4.2. *Mean choice likelihoods,*
$\bar{\phi}$, *and fixed-point likelihoods,* ϕ^*,
for the "population criterion"
model

Θ_1	$\bar{\phi}$	ϕ^*
0.2	0.04954	0.05882
0.35	0.21572	0.22477
0.5	0.49943	0.5
0.65	0.7873	0.77523
0.8	0.9518	0.94118

nature, in a similar fashion. In this case, the independence assumption is unnecessary, and the target is given by

$$\hat{\Theta} = \phi_1 \Theta_1 + (1 - \phi_1)\Theta_2 \tag{4.9}$$

where Θ_2 is specific to whatever state of nature occurs. Combining (4.2), (4.3), and (4.9) and using the fact that Θ_2 is distributed uniformly over $[0,1]$, we obtain

$$\phi_1^* = \Theta_1^2 [2\Theta_1^2 - 2\Theta_1 + 1]^{-1} \tag{4.10}$$

Table 4.2 permits a comparison between values of ϕ_1^* obtained from (4.10) and the means of the simulated distributions that are shown in Figure 4.2. Again, it is evident that the fixed point ϕ_1^* is a generally good approximation for $\bar{\phi}_1$.

Convergence to a unique choice under risk

There are special cases under which the feedback mechanism will generate convergence to one choice even under risky circumstances. An extreme example has already been treated: If the individual constructs $\hat{\Theta}$ from an accurate appraisal of the experience of all others in the population and if there is some alternative A_k that is optimal under every possible state of nature, then Φ will converge to Φ_k. A rather more plausible (but still extreme) case arises if (a) $\hat{\Theta}$ is fixed at some (low) value, (b) all choices A_i with significant selection likelihoods yield payoffs greater than $\hat{\Theta}$ under all states of nature, and (c) the proportional model applies. The first condition may apply if the individual does not establish performance aspirations but responds simply to absolute performance values. This might apply to a firm that is engaged in such a risky enterprise that it recognizes that neither past performance nor the experience of others will provide any useful criteria for the future, or it might apply to individuals who live so completely in the present that the cognitive process of standard setting does not occur. The second condition might arise if there are strategies available to the firm that never actually generate losses (however variable the profits might be), and if the likelihoods of strategies that may generate losses have been reduced to zero through feedback learning.

In developing the proportional model, we defined variables $\alpha_j \equiv \alpha(\Theta_j)$ to reflect the feedback effect of the payoff Θ_j. (For convenience here, we have set the fixed value of $\hat{\Theta}$ equal to zero.) Under conditions of risk, each α_j is actually a variable whose value depends on the state of the world. We shall define ν_j to be the expectation of α_j:

$$\nu_j \equiv \int_{-\infty}^{\infty} \alpha_j g^j(\Theta)\, d\Theta \tag{4.11}$$

Applying our assumptions to (4.3), we obtain an expression for the expected value of ϕ_k in period $t+1$:

$$E[\phi_{k,\,t+1}] - \phi_{k,\,t} = \nu_k - \sum_{i \in S} \phi_{i,\,t} \nu_i \tag{4.12}$$

Equation (4.12) is in fact identical to (2.20) in Chapter 2, except for the restriction of the summation to a set S of always successful choices and the replacement of the weak inequality in (2.20) by strict equality. We can repeat the arguments given in Chapter 2 to the effect that if A_k is a unique alternative with the maximal value ν_k, then $\nu_k - \sum_{i \in S} \phi_{i,\,t} \nu_i > 0$ whenever $\phi_k < 1$, and hence behavior converges to $\phi_k = 1$ with probability one.

Given the stringency of the conditions under which this example is derived, one may not accept its implication that behavior under risk will converge on a single choice as a general result. It is an interesting model, in any case, because of its similarity to expected-utility maximization; the choice that will come to dominate is the one that will maximize the expected value of a variable that, like utility, is an increasing function of payoff. The theories are not equivalent, because v_j is not equal to ξ_j, and expected-utility maximization would have us maximize the latter. As a practical matter, however, the models are indistinguishable. In the absence of any independent empirical means for utility measurement, it is impossible to measure the difference between v_j and ξ_j: Both α_j and Θ_j are monotonically increasing functions of physical payoffs, and unless we can write down the specific Θ function, we cannot tell the two apart.

Risk aversion

It is a property of the expected-utility construction that if utility is a concave function of physical payoff (if preferences satisfy diminishing marginal utility), then the alternative that maximizes expected utility may fail to maximize expected payoff itself. It is this property that is used to describe such "risk-averse" behaviors as the purchase of insurance or requirements that investments with risky payoffs have higher expected returns than "safe" (risk-free) investments. Because Θ is a utility index already, and it is the magnitude of Θ (rather than the physical-payoff magnitude) that drives the feedback process, we would generally expect that so long as Θ is a concave function of payoff, we would generally encounter risk-averse behavior in a feedback model as well.

Risk aversion is strongly present in the case of the proportional model that was described in the last section. Consistency with condition (2.6) in Chapter 2 requires that the function $\alpha(\Theta)$ be bounded from above by 1. If we presume the feedback function to be continuous and to have continuous first and second derivatives, then the positive first derivative together with the upper bound implies that for some large values of Θ we must encounter negative values of the second derivative. This property need not apply to all points on the function, nor even to every point beyond some large value of Θ; nevertheless, it is most convenient mathematically to assume that $\alpha(\Theta)$ is strictly concave throughout its domain.

We demonstrated that the proportional model with all payoffs positive will converge to a single choice that maximizes the expected value of $\alpha(\Theta)$. The concavity of $\alpha(\Theta)$ will compound the conservatism toward risk that is inherent in the concavity of Θ itself. Even if the utility function is known to be linear in payoff, so that expected-utility maximization and expected-payoff maximization will lead to identical choices, the choice that maximizes the expected value of $\alpha(\Theta)$ will be biased in the conservative direction, avoiding choices with very high and very low payoffs.

One consequence of the increased conservatism found in the proportional model is that empirical evidence of risk aversion may no longer be taken for evidence of concavity in preference functions. Risk-averse behavior is equally consistent with proportional preferences (or even mildly convex utility functions) in an environment in which all payoffs are positive and the feedback process approximates the proportional case.

When we consider more general situations, in which both positive and negative payoffs may be encountered, the role of risk aversion is considerably more ambiguous. Any concavity in the preference function itself will continue to provide a conservative bias; however, as our examples demonstrate, the condition $\xi_1 > \xi_2$ may lead to an equilibrium distribution where $\phi_1 > \phi_2$, but it will not lead to the condition $\phi_2 = 0$, which would apply under expected-utility maximization. Decreases in the risk inherent in a choice will increase its likelihood of occurring, but not as dramatically as it might in traditional optimization models.

Much more important is the fact that the reverse of risk aversion may occur in the case of losses. We can reasonably apply the concavity assumption, which amounts to concavity in $L^j(\Phi_t, j, \Theta_j, \hat{\Theta}_t)$, only when Θ_j exceeds $\hat{\Theta}$. Because the feedback function always has a lower bound of $-\phi_{j,t} < L^j(\Phi_t, j, \Theta_j, \hat{\Theta}_t)$, strict concavity is impossible for all negative values of Θ_j, and, in fact, the function $L^j(\Phi_t, j, \Theta_j, \hat{\Theta}_t)$ must acquire convex properties for small values of Θ_j. The implication is that whereas risk aversion is likely to apply to situations characterized by positive payoffs, we may observe risk preference under circumstances characterized by negative returns. Individuals may seek to protect gains with insurance, but accept great risks in order to get out of a bad place. This tendency toward risk preference may be partially neutralized by the underlying concavity of the utility function itself; nevertheless, apparent examples of the phenomenon do come to mind. It is alleged, for example, that losing bettors often attempt to cover their losses by playing "long shots" and that this behavior may significantly shift the odds at a race track in favor of the favorites late in the day. Many observers seem to believe that gambling behavior is prevalent among lower-income classes who are seeking to better their station in life. Whether or not these empirical interpretations are justified, we do have a model in which simultaneous occurrences of gambling and insurance buying are possible, and in which gambling behavior is consistent with concave utility. A detailed example of this possibility is provided in the following chapter.

Interdependence

The risk that characterizes a market may not be due solely to exogenous factors. Market participants themselves add important random elements if their own behaviors are governed by stochastic feedback mechanisms such as those described in this book. In competitive markets with large numbers of firms, the variations in firm behaviors can be pooled so that exogenous conditions are the only remaining sources of systematic risk. However, if a market is dominated by only a few large participants, stochastic variations in the behavior of any one may alter market conditions for all, and thus the distribution of possible payoff values that are available to one individual may be directly derived from the vector of choice probabilities that describes the behavior of someone else.

We consider the example of a duopolistic market. Two firms, A and B, make decisions that may involve quantities of output to be produced, types of advertising campaigns, pricing strategies, or other variables that influence profitability. The choices of firm A are governed by the usual probability vector $\Phi_t = \{\phi_{1,t}, \ldots, \phi_{n,t}\}$, and the choices of firm B are governed by a similar vector $\Psi_t = \{\psi_{1,t}, \ldots, \psi_{m,t}\}$. If firm A makes a choice A_i and firm B chooses B_j, then firm A receives a profit Π_{ij} that reflects this joint decision. Because the choice of firm B is subject to a probability vector, the payoff to firm A from any particular decision A_i is uncertain, and we must make use of the models that have been introduced earlier in this chapter.

It is clearly a matter of some significance whether or not the feedback mechanism that characterizes the behavior of one firm leads ultimately to unique choices in the face of risk. If it does, then, at least in the absence of any exogenous shocks, even an interdependent market may eventually come to an equilibrium, with each firm making a unique choice. That is, the risk might vanish in equilibrium.

For an example, we consider the proportional model described in the preceding two sections. We associate payoff with profit level and define $\nu_{i,t}$ to be the expected value of $\alpha(\Pi)$ to firm A in the event that it has chosen alternative A_i at time t. (We must introduce the t subscript here, because it is clear that the risk distribution that is imposed by firm B is not necessarily stationary.) Thus,

$$\nu_{i,t} = \sum_{j=1}^{m} \psi_{j,t} \, \alpha(\Pi_{ij}) \qquad (4.13)$$

An interesting question concerns the treatment of losses (or profit levels so low as to be considered to be failures). In the case of certainty, we could argue that choices that brought about failures would eventually acquire vanishingly small likelihoods, but it is quite possible that under conditions of risk, losses are occasionally incurred by alternatives that usually are very profitable. However, the mathematics are simplified significantly if every payoff is positive, and so we shall defer this question for a time and consider an example in which outright failures do not arise.

Our description of firm A now meets all the restrictions used to produce (4.12), and we can reproduce that equation here, replacing ν_k with equation (4.13):

$$E[\phi_{k,t+1}] - \phi_{k,t} = \sum_{j=1}^{m} \psi_{j,t} \alpha(\Pi_{kj}) - \sum_{i=1}^{n} \phi_{i,t} \sum_{j=1}^{m} \psi_{j,t} \alpha(\Pi_{ij}) \qquad (4.14)$$

A similar equation is readily obtained for the case of firm B, using $a(\pi)$ as the firm B counterpart of $\alpha(\Pi)$:

$$E[\psi_{l,t+1}] - \psi_{l,t} = \sum_{i=1}^{n} \phi_{i,t} a(\pi_{il}) - \sum_{j=1}^{m} \psi_{j,t} \sum_{i=1}^{n} \phi_{i,t} a(\pi_{ij}) \qquad (4.15)$$

In the case of an exogenous stationary risk, we argued that equations of the form of (4.14) and (4.15) imply convergence to unique choices. In this case, however, the risk elements are endogenous to the system. We might find that as some element ϕ_k converges toward unity, the payoffs to firm B are altered in a way that encourages some choice B_l, with the property that A_k is no longer optimal. If this occurs, the increase in ϕ_k will be halted, and some other alternative will gain in likelihood. A condition of persistent cycling is therefore quite likely, with the amplitude and frequency of the cycles depending on the parameters of the feedback – the payoff magnitudes and the sensitivity of the feedback function to variations in payoff.

For a static description of this dynamic process, we must turn again to our fixed-point approximation, seeking values Φ^* and Ψ^* such that $E[\phi_{i,t+1}] = \phi_{i,t}$ at $\phi_{i,t} = \phi^*$ and $E[\psi_{j,t+1}] = \psi_{j,t}$ at $\psi_{j,t} = \psi^*$ for all i,j. These values are given by the solutions to

$$\sum_{j=1}^{m} \psi_j^* \alpha(\Pi_{kj}) - \sum_{i=1}^{n} \phi_i^* \sum_{j=1}^{m} \psi_j^* \alpha(\Pi_{i,j}) = 0 \quad \text{for all } i=1,\ldots,n \qquad (4.16)$$

$$\sum_{i=1}^{n} \phi_i^* a(\pi_{il}) - \sum_{j=1}^{m} \psi_j^* \sum_{i=1}^{n} \phi_i^* a(\pi_{ij}) = 0 \quad \text{for all } j=1,\ldots,m \qquad (4.17)$$

$$\phi_i^* \geq 0; \quad \psi_j^* \geq 0 \qquad (4.18)$$

$$\sum_{i=1}^{n} \phi_i^* = 1; \quad \sum_{j=1}^{m} \psi_j^* = 1 \qquad (4.19)$$

It is a remarkable fact that these conditions are equivalent to the Nash mixed-strategy equilibrium solution for a two-person non-zero-sum game (Luce and Raiffa, 1957). That is, if we think of Φ as a mixed-strategy probability vector for "player" A and Ψ as a mixed-strategy vector for "player" B, then the expected payoff to firm A is $\sum_{i=1}^{n} \phi_i \sum_{j=1}^{m} \psi_j \alpha(\Pi_{ij})$. [Here, we are again using the fact that the function $\alpha(\Pi)$ is indistinguishable from a "utility" function.] The expected payoff to firm B is $\sum_{j=1}^{m} \psi_j \sum_{i=1}^{n} \phi_i a(\pi_{ij})$. It is readily established that the first-order conditions for maximization of these equations are given by equations (4.16) through (4.19).

We may have provided enough examples of feedback mechanisms that converge on optima for this latest result to be unsurprising. This two-party equilibrium is nevertheless remarkable because of the structural character of a Nash equilibrium. Optimal mixed strategies in a Nash equilibrium are essentially *defensive* in nature: The objective is to remove from an opponent any incentive to shift choices in directions that reduce one's own payoff. Suppose, for example, that we have found optimal mixed-strategy vectors Φ^* and Ψ^*. If Ψ^* were somehow fixed for all time, we note from equation (4.16) that firm A would be indifferent among all those choices A_k for which $\phi_k^* > 0$. That is, the expected return from the persistent selection of A_k is equal to the expected return from the mixed strategy Φ^* itself. In practice, such a persistent selection is nevertheless inferior to the mixed strategy Φ^*, because the optimal response of firm B to the choice A_k is generally not Ψ^*, and it is a property of the Nash equilibrium that the resulting deviation from Ψ^* will reduce the payoff to firm A below what it could be otherwise.

That such a sophisticated equilibrium state should be achieved by a passive (and unsophisticated) feedback mechanism certainly lends support to the applicability of optimization theory. This is particularly true in economic situations for which normative applications of the mixed-strategy device seem impractical. Mixed strategies are often described as mechanisms for *concealing* strategy choices. The proposition is that firm B uses a randomization device to prevent firm A from detecting B's selection in time to take optimal countermeasures. In a real-time economic situation, however, this restriction on A's behavior is hard to defend. There is no impediment to firm A's waiting a few minutes (or days) for firm B's choice to become known in order to react to it. Mixed strategies make sense in optimization models only if actual choices are required to be made simultaneously. For some, this limitation has reduced the mixed-strategy device to an intriguing trick whose relevance is confined to artificially constructed parlor situations, not to positive descriptions of real economic behavior. In the models developed here, however, the probability vectors are not chosen as part of optimization strategies; they are reflections of fundamental properties of behavior determination, and the logical objection no longer applies.

Of course, there are many situations in which the Nash equilibrium response does not involve mixed strategies. A good example is provided by the symmetric Cournot model of duopoly. In cases such as this, Φ^* is characterized by $\phi_i^*=0$ for $i\neq k$, $\phi_k^*=1$, where the choice A_k corresponds to the usual Cournot-Nash output level.

The possibility that interdependent feedback models might converge on Nash mixed-strategy equilibria has been noted in the biological literature (Smith, 1978). In the biological case, however, the stress is not on one individual following varied courses of action, but on related individuals possessing (equilibrium) genetic differences that induce different forms of behavior, so that the group (e.g., the "hive") is found to be following a genetically optimal mixed strategy.

The question remains whether this optimal interdependent decision result is a good approximation for feedback models in general or just an intriguing special case. For many purposes, the proportional model does appear to be a reasonable approximation for the more general feedback process. The introduction of the possibility of failure produces a more complicated, but similar, model that produces identical implications in the neighborhood of $\phi_i^*=0.5$.[2] A more serious question concerns the extent to which the fixed-point values Φ^* and Ψ^* are reasonable representations of the cycling behavior that is likely to arise in all cases that do

---

[2] In the event that some payoffs are contained in the set F, equation (4.12) becomes

$$E[\phi_{i,t+1}]-\phi_{i,t}=\phi_{i,t}\left[\nu_{i,t}-\eta_{i,t}-\sum_{k=1}^{n}\phi_{k,t}(\nu_{k,t}-\eta_{k,t})+\eta_{i,t}\frac{1-2\phi_{i,t}}{1-\phi_{i,t}}\right.$$
$$\left.-\sum\eta_{k,t}\phi_{k,t}\frac{1-2\phi_{k,t}}{1-\phi_{k,t}}\right]$$

where $\eta_{i,t}$ is defined as

$$\eta_{i,t}=\sum_{j=1}^{m}\psi_{j,t}\beta_{ij}$$

and $\alpha_{ij}>0\Rightarrow\beta_{ij}=0$; $\beta_{ij}>0\Rightarrow\alpha_{ij}=0$.

not have unique Cournot-Nash equilibrium choices. Simulation studies of this question suggest that they are reasonable approximations whenever the adjustment coefficients are small (which implies, in turn, very sluggish adjustment toward equilibrium), but that in the presence of higher adjustment rates, actual choice probabilities cycle around the vectors Φ^* and Ψ^* and often are not found at or even near those points.

CHAPTER 5

An application to state lottery games

From the perspective of optimization theory, the willingness of people to gamble has always posed something of a dilemma. The general acceptance of the expected-utility hypothesis, together with the belief that utility may be represented as a concave function of payoff, has led most economists to conclude that consumers will ordinarily avoid even actuarially fair gambles and will be willing to pay premiums for the assurance that the risks they face will be reduced. This expectation is in constant conflict with everyday evidence that people often accept actuarially unfair gambles, and this conflict has become even more dramatic in recent years as state-run lottery games have proliferated and become significant sources of revenue in several jurisdictions.

The most common response among defenders of the expected-utility model has been to adapt the specification of preferences in a way that will bring the theory into conformity with observation. Some maintain that the act of gambling provides so much enjoyment that individuals are willing to pay for it in the form of the difference between the cost of a lottery ticket and its actuarial value. Others sacrifice the property of concavity of utility functions over some limited range. Friedman and Savage (1948) suggested that there were (lower) income classes over which concavity might not hold and that members of these groups would be found to engage in gambling in an attempt to alter their economic situation. In an extreme version of this social stereotype, one colleague recently alleged to the author that in fact state lotteries were in the business of selling "hope" to the masses!

In a sense, explanations such as these are scientifically impregnable. They all enjoy a weak introspective plausibility, and there are no direct empirical means for measuring the quantitative relevance of the preference structures that they assume. There are certainly no simple empirical tests that might conclusively refute any of these hypotheses, and as a result, economists have tended toward a rather uncritical acceptance of what amounts to untested hypotheses, and gambling behavior is now often described as another (mildly interesting) case of expected-utility maximization.

It is possible to provide challenges to these explanations for gambling.

For example, if Friedman and Savage were correct in associating non-concave utility with a certain income class, then the personal distribution of income should display a gap (or at least a relatively low income frequency) over that range as a consequence of individuals' having acquired other income levels through either successful or unsuccessful gambles, and such a gap has never been observed (Bailey et al., 1980). One might go on to notice that different forms of gambling have quite different ratios of actuarial value to price, and rational consumers (even the hopeful ones who love to gamble and whose preference functions are convex) should gravitate always to the best buys among them. State lotteries, however, have been among the most rapidly expanding of lottery forms, and these have among the worst payoffs: In 1976, no state lottery in the United States paid over 50 cents on the dollar, and the largest of their prizes are subject to significant income taxes. Even this objection is not conclusive, of course, because purchases of state lottery tickets are both convenient and legal, and these advantages should enable dealers to charge a higher implicit price, although we again have no independent means for determining just what this price should be.

This is an example of the methodological problem that was described in the first chapter. Unspecified (and unspecifiable) utility functions are infinitely adaptable, and so long as we are willing to make accommodating adjustments in our characterization of preferences, almost any behavior may be cast into the framework of rational expected-utility maximization. We pay a high price when we accept the resulting tautologies as explanatory models, however, because these "theories" are so malleable in the face of empirical evidence that their predictive power must be considered to be negligible. What we plan to do in this chapter is demonstrate that feedback processes are capable of generating gambling behavior under quite general circumstances. Although convex utility functions or the excitement of betting will always contribute to the incidence of gambling, we do not need to rely on such special assumptions as these to develop a model of the gambling mechanism.

Lottery markets

In the last chapter we suggested that differences in behavior might be attributed not only to differences in tastes but also to differences in decision style that arise out of variations in experience and market position. A particularly compelling case for treating the decisions of sellers in a different manner than those of buyers arises in the case of state lotteries. One source of such asymmetry is a traditional one, in that the market structure is clearly one that favors sellers. There is no question of lottery games being sold under competitive conditions. Although it is clear that competition does exist between legal lotteries and illegal "numbers" games, this is still no more than a duopolistic market structure. Further entry is effectively blocked: States generally outlaw legal competitors for their games, and illegal operators are ruthless in their suppression of competition (at least according to their public image). It is not even clear to what extent the two remaining "firms" are in competition with one another; by engaging in readily distinguishable types of games ("legal," with winnings subject to federal income tax, and "illegal," with untaxed prizes), the two may have such well-differentiated products as to have separated their markets quite effectively. In any case, there can be no doubt as to the existence of supernormal profits. Administrative costs of state lotteries, for example, are only 10 to 15 percent of total revenue, leaving between 35 and 50 percent of gross revenue as clear profit. A legal entrant into this market could charge the same nominal price for tickets and offer over one and one-half times the prize money across the board and still earn a comfortable profit.

The second source of asymmetry is the difference in transactions volume between buyer and seller. Lottery ticket sellers encounter large enough sales for the law of large numbers to have a significant effect. Indeed, some games are specifically designed so as to produce a proportion of winners exactly equal to the actuarial value of a ticket, so that the only "risk" faced by the seller is due to the possibility that some ticket purchasers will forget or lose their tickets, some of which are winners. Clearly the actuarial mode of decision making is the relevant one for lottery sellers. In the last chapter we described this as equivalent to decision making under certainty: Even though there may be some risk involved for sellers, it is small, and the feedback mechanism will lead to a single (actuarially) optimal choice. Thus, we can expect the sellers' choice to converge to one that offers tickets of a type and price that will maximize actuarial profits.

In contrast, consumers of lottery games cannot be expected to come to employ actuarial decision rules. This expectation is reinforced by the fact that typical lottery games appear to incorporate prize structures that interfere very effectively with the recognition of actuarial cash flows. In the case of state lotteries, the payoffs usually appear as sets of prizes, some conditional on having won other prizes and some not, and with some very large prizes arising with very low frequencies. Frequent experience with small prizes provides one with no experience with the actuarial-value component contributed by the larger prizes. Sometimes consumers form lottery "clubs," which, through pooling of resources, are capable of relatively large volumes of purchases. Even these fail to generate actuarially reliable flows, however, because the prize structure includes large payoffs that occur much too infrequently to be encountered regularly by even a very large club. (If a club could achieve actuarially reliable cash flows, of course, then each member would routinely receive 40 to 50 cents return for every dollar invested, and interest in the club would be relatively short-lived.)

The effective asymmetry between buyers and sellers of lottery tickets will be reduced to the extent that consumers make conscious use of expected-value computations when confronted with gambling situations. The necessary mathematical calculations are simple once the underlying payoff structure is known, but in fact it is extraordinarily difficult for ordinary consumers to acquire this information. The state of Michigan, for example, operates a relatively successful, highly publicized lottery. Major drawings take place on live television, and winning numbers are announced daily on television and radio and in newspapers. Advertisements are placed on billboards, on television and radio, and at dealer locations. None of these "information" sources specifies payout rates, even in the most general terms. That advertisements fail to convey such essential product information may not be unusual, even for a government program, but the apparent reluctance to present these data anywhere in the public record is remarkable. For example, the Michigan state treasurer's report is available in libraries, and that document includes net revenue from the lottery, but in contrast to its description of other programs, it omits a statement of gross sales, and it is therefore impossible to infer the actuarial value of a ticket even from this source. The annual report of the Bureau of State Lottery (a document that is not available in any but the most specialized libraries) does not specify in detail the prize/probability structure of any particular lottery "game," nor does it specify the overall actuarial value of any type of ticket. This source does provide both gross-revenue and net-profit figures in its financial statement at the back, and the average actuarial ticket value may be inferred from these, but the calculations must be performed by the reader, and because this is only a gross average, sophisticated expected-utility maximization would still be impossible.

All of this obfuscation is not inadvertent. The great advantage of being on the actuarial side of this market is that through ordinary feedback processes, even sellers who are entirely ignorant of the laws of probability will eventually come to purvey a profit-maximizing lottery game. Certainly one feature of such a game is a design that minimizes consumers' abilities to engage in either actuarial or Bayesian behavior. Sellers have come to employ advertisements that conceal outcome likelihoods and overstate rather than reveal payoff values (the words "income tax" never appear in lottery advertisements, although they may boast of the magnificence of the prizes), and prize structure is sufficiently complex that actuarial behavior is impossible without enormous volume. It is by no means necessary that these properties came to be developed from conscious design: Simple feedback processes are sufficient to bring them about, and in practice, trial and error are much more in evidence than is a calculating exploitation of consumers. The reports of the Michigan Bureau of State Lottery, for example, contain no hint of sophisticated analysis in the design of lottery games; indeed, the issues that are addressed in these documents would seem to be extremely naive to anyone familiar with the laws of probability. On the other hand, these reports describe in detail the results of lottery games that amount to experiments. Games with large ticket prices, with low ticket prices, with "instant" tickets whose rub-off spots conceal their payoff status, and with different design motifs are compared and evaluated with respect to their ex post capacity to provide revenue to the state. This is the essence of a feedback learning process by which a revenue-maximizing product may come to be produced without any recourse to conscious optimization. Incidentally, the historical experience that has culminated in modern-day state lottery games appears to be quite long-standing, if one includes the experience of the illegal numbers games after which the state lotteries are explicitly patterned.

In spite of the difficulty in acquiring reliable actuarial data on state lotteries, sufficiently sophisticated consumers may still engage in Bayesian behavior. The fact that a state derives revenue from these enterprises is itself evidence that ticket payoffs are not actuarially fair, and anyone who acknowledges a preference for certainty over risk should avoid them. This simple rule breaks down, however, if a potential purchaser also derives some pleasurable excitement from the gamble (or if he is in the market to buy a little "hope"), because then it is necessary to compare the virtues of a lottery to such alternative forms of gambling as would be provided by trips to Nevada, visits to the race track, or participation in office football pools. The information necessary for rational choice under these conditions is, for all intents and purposes, unavailable.

The model

It is a relatively simple matter to model the purchase of lottery tickets in terms of a feedback mechanism. This is especially true because the distinction between "success" and "failure" is quite natural in this case. A winning ticket is a "success," a losing ticket is a "failure," and there is no need to define any aspiration level other than the natural origin at a net profit equal to zero. Following the pattern that has been set in our earlier examples, we shall simplify the feedback model by assuming the proportional version, which is defined by equations (2.16) and (2.17) in

Chapter 2. For reasons that we have already described, we expect a lottery to provide a variety of different prizes that arise with different probabilities. This adds a great deal to the mathematical complexity of an analysis, however, and so we shall confine ourselves to the description of lottery tickets that will allow only one prize.

We let ϕ_t describe the likelihood that an individual will buy a ticket at time t. We need only a one-dimensioned variable in this case, because there is only one alternative choice (not to buy), and this occurs with probability $1 - \phi_t$. A fraction q of tickets are "winners," and each of these pays the same fixed prize. In practice, prices of lottery tickets vary from game to game, ranging generally between 50 cents and \$1.00. It is convenient to normalize ticket price to \$1.00. A winning ticket pays R times its cost, or R dollars. Thus, the net return from a winning ticket is $R - 1$, where $R - 1 > 0$. We attach a payoff utility Θ_w to a winning ticket and a utility Θ_l to a ticket that loses (and whose net payoff is therefore equal to -1).

If a ticket that is purchased proves to be a winner, then the feedback mechanism produces an enhanced probability that lottery tickets will be purchased in the future. Using the proportional model given by equation (2.16), the likelihood ϕ_t will be increased to some higher value, where this new value is

$$\phi_{t+1} = \phi_t + \alpha(\Theta_w - \hat{\Theta})(1 - \phi_t) \tag{5.1}$$

If the ticket loses, the loss of 1 represents a failure, and we can use equation (2.17) to derive the new value of the buying likelihood:

$$\phi_{t+1} = \phi_t[1 - \beta(\hat{\Theta} - \Theta_l)] \tag{5.2}$$

In defining the general proportional model, we allowed the possibility that the feedback function for gains, $\alpha(\Theta - \hat{\Theta})$, might be different from the feedback function for losses, $\beta(\hat{\Theta} - \Theta)$. Because the situation is symmetric in the sense that wins and losses are measured with respect to the status quo, $\hat{\Theta}$, there seems to be no particular reason for making this assumption in this case, and therefore we shall simplify the model by assuming the same function form for both $\alpha(\Theta - \hat{\Theta})$ and $\beta(\hat{\Theta} - \Theta)$. As usual, this function has a positive slope and is bounded by 0 and 1. Moreover, we shall ignore the possibility of oscillations in the second derivative and assume the function to be strictly concave throughout its domain.

Once the price of a lottery ticket is established, the value of $\beta(\hat{\Theta} - \Theta)$ is fixed, and we shall use the expression β_l to represent this value. The value of $\alpha(\Theta - \hat{\Theta})$ depends on R, because Θ is a function of net payoff. It is convenient to use a function $\delta(R)$ to represent this dependence:

$$\delta(R) \equiv \alpha[\Theta(R - 1) - \hat{\Theta}] \tag{5.3}$$

It is of no consequence for the purposes of this model whether we consider $\hat{\Theta}$ to be the utility of the status quo and Θ to be the utility of an individual's status after buying a ticket (and discovering whether it is a winner or a loser) or whether we set $\hat{\Theta} = 0$ and consider Θ to be some incremental utility produced by the relevant payoff. In either case, we can retain the conventional argument that utility is a concave function of payoff and conclude that Θ is a concave function of R. It follows that $\delta(R)$ is a strictly concave function, because the function $\alpha(\cdot)$ is strictly concave. Because the functions $\alpha(\cdot)$ and $\beta(\cdot)$ are identical, $\delta(R) = \beta_l$ when $R = 2$. (A winning ticket has a net payoff of $+1$ and a losing ticket a loss of -1, and concave utility makes the value of $\Theta - \hat{\Theta}$ for a gain no greater than $\hat{\Theta} - \Theta$ for a loss.) Because $\delta(R)$ is monotonically increasing in R, it follows that

$$\delta(R) \leqslant \beta_l \quad \text{when } R \leqslant 2 \tag{5.4}$$

From the strict concavity of $\delta(R)$, we have

$$\delta(R) < R\beta_l \quad \text{when } R > 2 \tag{5.5}$$

Finally, if no ticket happens to be purchased at time t, we shall assume no change in buying likelihood, so that

$$\phi_{t+1} = \phi_t \quad \text{if no purchase is made during } t \tag{5.6}$$

This model is similar to the examples developed in the last chapter in that it leads to an equilibrium distribution of buying likelihoods across the population. It is easy to see that the extreme values $\phi = 0$ and $\phi = 1$ cannot serve as points of convergence for the feedback process. A value $\phi = 1$ would mean that a purchase occurs with certainty, and $1 - q$ of these purchases encounter failure, leading to future values of ϕ that are less than one. A value $\phi_t = 0$ is stable, because if one never buys a ticket, there is no opportunity for a win, but any $\phi_t > 0$ will lead to occasional purchases, and because a fraction q of these will encounter a win, the convergence toward $\phi = 0$ will be disrupted. As in the last chapter, a simulation procedure can be used to describe the equilibrium distribution $\gamma(\phi)$. An example of such a distribution is shown in Figure 5.1. For this example, we have set $\delta(R) = 0.16$, $\beta_l = 0.02$, and $q = 0.05$.

Investigation of the entire distribution $\gamma(\phi)$ is awkward even in this single-dimensioned problem, and therefore we appeal to the fixed-point approximation that was defined in the last chapter. If ϕ_t describes the value of the purchasing likelihood during period t, then the expected value of the purchasing likelihood during $t+1$ is given by the sum of (5.1), (5.2), and (5.6) weighted by the likelihoods that the preconditions for each of these equations are in fact satisfied:

$$E[\phi_{t+1}] = \phi_t[q\{\phi_t + \delta(R)(1-\phi_t)\} + (1-q)\phi_t(1-\beta_l)] + (1-\phi_t)\phi_t \tag{5.7}$$

Our approximation for the mean of $\gamma(\phi)$ is the fixed point ϕ^*: If ϕ^* is

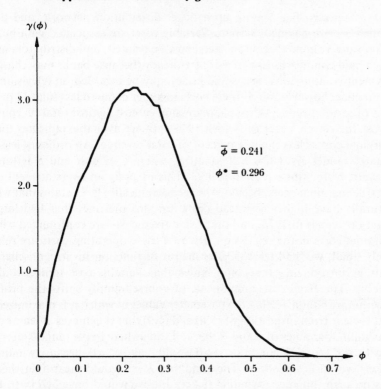

Figure 5.1. Monte Carlo simulation of $\gamma(\phi)$; $\delta(R)=0.16$; $\beta_l=0.02$; $q=0.05$.

substituted for ϕ_l on the right-hand side of (5.7), then $E[\phi_{l+1}]=\phi^*$. Solving for ϕ^*, we obtain

$$\phi^* = \frac{\delta(R)q}{\delta(R)q+\beta_l(1-q)} \tag{5.8}$$

Optimal lottery tickets

The actuarial return to lottery sellers is determined by the probability with which customers buy tickets times the expected net profit per ticket. Using ϕ^* as the average purchasing likelihood, this actuarial return is approximated by

$$\Pi \equiv \phi^*(1-Rq) = \frac{\delta(R)q(1-Rq)}{\delta(R)q+\beta_l(1-q)} \tag{5.9}$$

Lottery sellers do have costs of operating. These include the overhead costs of advertising, setting up a ticket distribution network, and designing a prize payment system. Variable costs are associated with both ticket sales volume (because tickets must be printed, and distributors are often paid commissions) and prize frequency (because banks may charge payment commissions, and some prizes may be awarded on television). In practice, however, all of these costs together come to less than 15 percent of gross revenue. A simple regression of cost against total revenues across the eleven states for which 1976 data are available indicates that marginal cost is less than 11 percent of total revenue. An ordinary least-squares model gives $C = 2.11 + 0.107S$, where C is cost and S is total revenue; r^2 for this equation is 0.93. This is surely an overstatement of the true marginal costs, because the (geographically) large states that will naturally have higher overhead costs are also the ones that had large lottery revenues in 1976, and thus some fixed costs are confounded with marginal costs in the regression. Because these operating costs are relatively small, we shall treat (5.9) as the profit function for lottery sellers, without introducing the complexities that variable-cost terms would involve. The fixed-cost component, of course, simply shifts the profit function without affecting the parameter values at which it is maximized.

It is clear from inspection of (5.8) and (5.9) that Π achieves at least one maximum for values of q and R that fall somewhere in the range $0 < q < 1$ and $1 < R < 1/q$. The condition $q = 0$ would make $\phi^* = 0$, because winning tickets would never occur. The condition $R = 1$ would mean that there was no such thing as a winning ticket, and we would have $\delta(R) = 0$. In either case, no tickets would be sold in equilibrium, and profit would be zero. If q were as large as 1, or if R were as large as $1/q$, profits would be negative. Because positive profits clearly are possible at intermediate values of q and R, we conclude that there must exist at least one point of profit maximum in the specified range.

We have argued that sellers of lottery tickets need not employ sophisticated Bayesian models in order to operate successfully. Because they are on the (relatively) risk-free side of the market, simple experience will guide them toward lotteries with optimal (profit-maximizing) parameters. Thus, our equilibrium is characterized by profit-maximizing values for R and q, and we can employ the usual first-order calculus conditions to investigate the equilibrium conditions. If we differentiate (5.9) with respect to q, set this equal to zero, and solve for q, we obtain

$$q = \frac{\left(1 + \dfrac{\delta(R) - \beta_l}{\beta_l R}\right)^{1/2} - 1}{\dfrac{\delta(R) - \beta_l}{\beta_l}} \tag{5.10}$$

The actuarial value of a one-dollar lottery ticket is qR, which we shall call W. Let us define the simplifying expression

$$v \equiv \frac{\beta_l R}{\delta(R) - \beta_l} \tag{5.11}$$

and use this together with (5.10) to obtain an expression for W:

$$W = [v^2 + v]^{1/2} - v \tag{5.12}$$

We noted that at a profit maximum, q and R must satisfy $0 < q < 1$ and $1 < R < 1/q$, and these together imply $0 < W < 1$. The second-order condition, $\partial^2 \Pi / \partial q^2 < 0$, can be invoked to guarantee that at the optimum we must use the positive root of $(v^2 + v)^{1/2}$ in defining (5.12). The second derivative of (5.9) with respect to q is given by

$$\frac{\partial^2 \Pi}{\partial q^2} = - \frac{2R\delta(R)v^2(v+1)}{\beta_l(W+v)}$$

Because $\delta(R)$, R, β_l, and v^2 are all positive, and $(v^2 + v)^{1/2} = W + v$, we can have $\partial^2 \Pi / \partial q^2 < 0$ and $(v^2 + v)^{1/2} < 0$ only if $v + 1 < 0$ or $v < -1$. From (5.11), however, this would make the conditions $R > 1$ and $\delta(R) > 0$ inconsistent. Because W must be defined as a real variable, negative values of v greater than -1 are also impossible; hence, it must be the case that $v > 0$ at the optimum. Finally, from the definition (5.11) we see that the condition $v > 0$ requires that $\delta(R) > \beta_l$; so we conclude from (5.4) that we must have $R > 2$.

If we differentiate the profit function (5.9) with respect to R and set this expression equal to zero, we obtain the other first-order condition. If we define $\delta'(R)$ to be the derivative of $\delta(R)$, and if we substitute from (5.11) and (5.12), this condition becomes

$$R\delta'(R)(1-q) = \delta(R) \tag{5.13}$$

If we know the precise forms of the utility function and the feedback function, we can use the simultaneous solution of (5.12) and (5.13) to specify the optimal values for q and R. In fact, however, we can obtain some general results without requiring any more information concerning these functions than we already have. We noted that the condition $v > 0$ implies that $\delta(R) > \beta_l$ and that this in turn gives $R > 2$, from (5.4). Using (5.5), this implies $\delta(R) < R\beta_l$, and substituting this into (5.11), we have $v > 1$. However, we note from (5.12) that $v = 1 \Rightarrow W = \sqrt{2} - 1$ and that $dW/dv > 0$ for all $v > 1$. Finally, as v increases toward $+\infty$, W converges to $W = \frac{1}{2}$. Therefore, whatever the specific solutions of (5.12) and (5.13) may be, we shall always find the value of W to be confined to a relatively narrow range:

Table 5.1. *Actuarial values and cost rates for various state lottery games in 1976*

State	Actuarial value of a $1.00 ticket ($W$)	Cost as a fraction of total revenue
Connecticut	0.462	0.119
Delaware	0.495	N.A.
Illinois	0.45	0.102
Maine	0.448	0.24
Maryland	0.433	0.133
Massachusetts	0.464	0.15
Michigan	0.45	0.1065
New Hampshire	0.473	0.146
New Jersey	0.478[a]	N.A.
New York	0.40[a]	0.15
Ohio	0.45	0.15
Pennsylvania	0.445	0.141
Rhode Island	0.458	0.194

[a] 1975 data.
Source: Commission on Review of the National Policy toward Gambling (1976), with permission.

$$0.4142 < W < 0.5 \qquad (5.14)$$

Table 5.1 contains the actuarial value of $1.00 spent on lottery tickets in each of the states that had lottery games in 1976. It may be noted that for every state but New York, W falls within the range defined by (5.14), and in New York, the exception, it is only slightly lower at 0.40. Such a close correspondence between the theory and the data is very encouraging, especially in that the predominant alternative hypothesis – expected-utility maximization – would ordinarily not support the existence of any lottery at all. Some support is also provided to the use of the proportional feedback model and the fixed-point approximation for a mean of $\gamma(\phi)$, and this is of great practical importance in that these two simplifications greatly reduce the analytic complexity required by application of the feedback theory.

Ticket prices

There is always an equilibrium in this model at $\phi = 0$: If a ticket is never purchased, there is no opportunity for a winning ticket to encourage future sales (apart from the demonstration and advertising effects that are described in Chapter 8). Even if a value $\phi = 0$ is never precisely

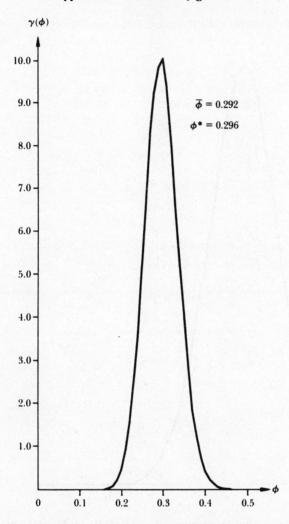

Figure 5.2. Monte Carlo simulation of $\gamma(\phi)$; $\delta(R) = 0.02$; $\beta_I = 0.0025$; $q = 0.05$.

achieved, values near zero will lead to long strings of "no-buy" choices, and sales will therefore be relatively low. If β_I is large, either because the feedback function is very sensitive to payoffs or because the payoffs and losses themselves are very large, each failure will produce a correspondingly low value for ϕ, and sales will suffer. That this effect is not offset by correspondingly high returns from success is readily demonstrated through simulations of $\gamma(\phi)$. Figures 5.2 through 5.6 display simulated distributions for values of $\delta(R)$ ranging from 0.02 to 0.64 and values of

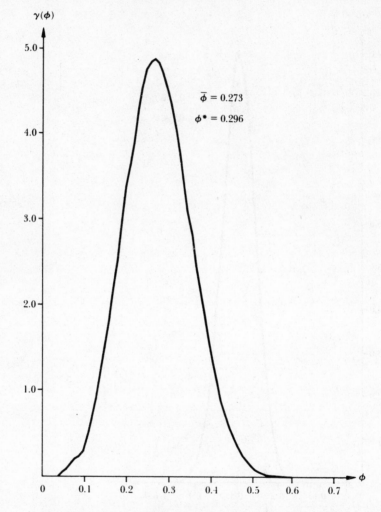

Figure 5.3. Monte Carlo simulation of $\gamma(\phi)$; $\delta(R) = 0.08$; $\beta_l = 0.01$; $q = 0.05$.

β_l ranging from 0.0025 to 0.08. In each case, $\delta(R)$ and β_l are moved in proportion so as to preserve the value of the fixed point ϕ^* at 0.296. The impact of increases in these parameters on the shape of the distribution is dramatic, and it is clear that there is a strong inverse relation between $\delta(R)$ and β_l on the one hand and the mean $\bar{\phi}$ on the other. The demand relation that the simulations produce is very closely described by $\bar{\phi} = 0.31 - 3.8\beta_l$ (where we recall β_l to be some monotonically increasing function of price).

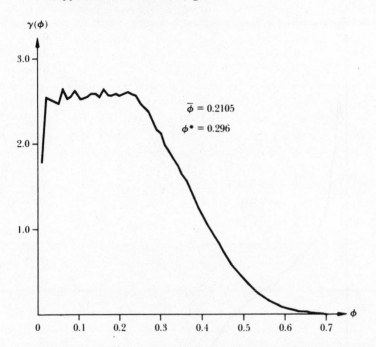

Figure 5.4. Monte Carlo simulation of $\gamma(\phi)$; $\delta(R) = 0.2$; $\beta_l = 0.025$; $q = 0.05$.

One implication of these results is that those individuals who learn rapidly (who respond strongly to both gains and losses) are much less likely to engage in lottery purchases than are those who learn more slowly. If consumers followed "rational" decision rules, then ticket purchases would be zero; thus, high learning rates drive consumers toward rationality and away from the "irrational" equilibrium described by ϕ^*. This reinforces the need for the purveyors of lottery tickets to inhibit learning in every way possible, and it lends support to the view that effective lottery sellers will interfere with information flows.[1] Another implication is that low ticket prices will be desirable in that they keep down the learning rate by minimizing the feedback term

[1] If β_l were proportional to price for small values of P, then the demand function obtained from our simulations would suggest that gross revenue would be maximized at $\beta_l \approx 0.04$, and at such a value our simulations suggest that ϕ^* might not be a very close approximation for $\bar{\phi}$. However, the demand function obtained from the simulations understates the losses that would arise from large ticket prices, because no account has been taken of the concavity of the feedback function itself: It may be easy to double β_l by doubling the (relatively small) ticket price, for example, but doubling $\delta(R)$ would require that we more than

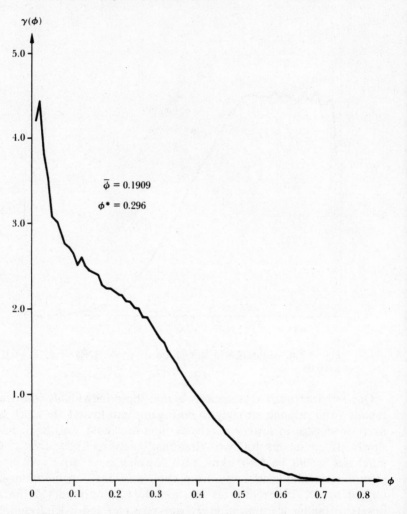

Figure 5.5. Monte Carlo simulation of $\gamma(\phi)$; $\delta(R)=0.24$; $\beta_l=0.03$; $q=0.05$.

β_l. Evidence suggests that optimal ticket price is in fact quite small. In 1975, the state of Michigan introduced a "Bicentennial" $5.00-per-ticket

double the (relatively large) value of R. Thus, proportionately large values of $\delta(R)$ and β_l would require relatively high actuarial values of each dollar's worth of tickets, and correspondingly low profitability for each dollar of sales.

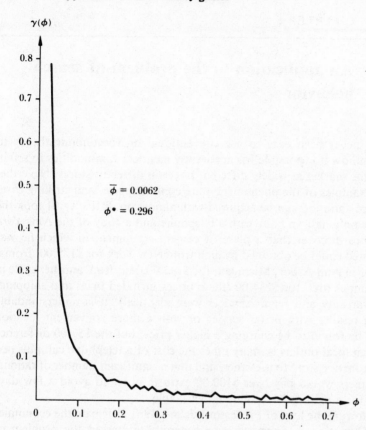

Figure 5.6. Monte Carlo simulation of $\gamma(\phi)$; $\delta(R) = 0.64$; $\beta_l = 0.08$; $q = 0.05$.

lottery game as an experiment. The performance of this lottery was dismal, generating only 10 percent of the gross sales per week as did the 50-cent games, leading the Bureau of State Lottery to conclude that "most customers prefer faster action and a lower priced ticket."

CHAPTER 6

An application to the problem of search behavior

It has never been easy to use conventional microeconomic theory to explain how it is possible for apparently identical commodities to sell in the same market at widely different prices in different stores. Nevertheless, examples of the phenomenon are commonplace, and striking cases of price variation can be acquired with almost no difficulty. It took the author only half an hour with a telephone and a copy of the *New York Times* to discover that a piece of camera equipment in which he was interested could be obtained by mail from New York for $125.00, from a retailer in Ann Arbor, Michigan, for $182.00, and from another store in the campus area for $234.00 (these prices included taxes and shipping, and warranty and repair services were identical). It is understandable that a retailer with better service or with a more convenient location might be found to be charging a higher price, but the $57.00 difference between local outlets is many times the cost of a telephone call plus taxi fare from one store to the other, and that a significant number of rational consumers would pay over $100.00 extra in order to avoid a few days delay for a mail order is quite unbelievable.

Following the lead of Professor Stigler's 1961 article on the economics of information, economists have generally addressed the problem of price variation by suggesting that consumers are uninformed as to the prices charged by various "stores" and that the presence of high search costs prevents rational consumers from uncovering all the information that would be required for full optimization. Under these assumptions, it is possible to construct models in which competitive markets can sustain a variety of different prices for the same good (Diamond, 1971; Rothschild, 1974*b*; Butters, 1977; Salop and Stiglitz, 1977; Reinganum, 1979; Wilde and Schwartz, 1979. At the same time, one can describe the sort of search criteria that might be used by rational consumers in such markets (McCall, 1970; Phelps, 1970; Whipple, 1973; Rothschild, 1974*a*; Kohn and Shavell, 1974). These search models, however, are generally Bayesian in character, and one is naturally led to wonder how consumers are to behave if they lack the analytical sophistication necessary to implement these decision rules. Moreover, if the consumer enters more than one market in the course of acquiring goods, the optimal program requires estimates of price levels and of dispersions in each market, and it is difficult to see how even relatively sophisticated consumers are to come by these estimates. Finally, the search-cost explanation for price distributions remains unconvincing for many cases. In the example of the camera equipment, even the consumer who happened to be ignorant of the information provided by newspapers could use the telephone to compare prices at the two major local retailers, and the small search cost imposed by this call could hardly support such a large price difference between the two dealers.

It is possible to consider the problem of imperfect market information in quite a different way. Instead of treating each purchase individually, assuming that consumers approach each market with an appropriately tailored optimal search strategy, we may treat search as an object of the feedback process. Thus, we would make the general willingness or unwillingness to engage in search the object of study, assuming that when an effort at search is successful (because a higher-quality or lower-priced product is discovered), it is the probability that search activities will occur again in the future that is enhanced, and, symmetrically, searches that end in failure will discourage the activity.

Everyone can identify some acquaintances who seem to devote great effort to investigating the alternatives available in a market before making a purchase, and others who seem to make no such effort at all. Traditionally, these variations have been attributed to differences in tastes (psychic search cost) and economic-opportunity costs. These differences certainly do exist. It is equally possible, however, that this is a case in which one's decision style is endogenous to happenstance circumstances. Some people have been fortunate in that their attempts at market search have generally been profitable, and they will naturally be found to engage in more search activity than will those who have not been so lucky. Across the market as a whole, what appear to be intrinsic differences in consumer decision styles may actually be acquired habits that have been developed from differences in experience, especially in cases of individuals in similar economic circumstances. This is essentially the interpretation that motivates this chapter.

When we come to compare the implications of a feedback model with those of optimal search models, we certainly expect to find similarities. In either type of model, for example, we expect that the quantity of search activity will vary inversely with search cost. Indeed, it proves to be the case that if we determine average search behavior across a market, we can obtain a quantity that is quite similar to that derived from optimizing search routines. That is, even though consumers have neither the information nor the analytical capacity to engage in optimal search procedures, and individual buyers will follow search behaviors that vary widely from the optimum, it is possible that the market as a whole will produce average search frequencies that do approximately match the predictions of optimization theory. Compared with optimization theory, however, the feedback view permits us to make a much more clear-cut distinction between the individual and the group. Whereas optimizing consumers differ only in "tastes," "adaptive" consumers differ in experience as well, and thus it becomes possible for the predictions of optimal behavior models to be disconfirmed at the individual level and still receive support at the level of society as a whole.

The framework of a model

Suppose that a consumer has investigated n different dealers, incurring a search cost, C, at each one. We mean this cost variable to include both financial cost and the personal inconvenience associated with searching, but we give it units of price in order to permit comparisons with product prices. We shall assume that the order in which n dealers were encountered is irrelevant; this amounts to a condition that a favorable offer from a dealer who was investigated early in the search sequence can be retrieved costlessly. It implies in turn that if dealers were to differ only in the prices that they charged for a given homogeneous product, then each firm i would find its expected sales, Q_i, to be a declining function of its price, P_i. In other words, if there were several n-searching consumers, some who found P_i to be minimal would accept alternative price offers if P_i were raised.[1]

Although most types of durable goods are purchased only occasionally by any given household, and consumers may only rarely go to the trouble to investigate price/quality conditions at different stores, the dealers themselves experience customer flows at much higher rates, and the law of large numbers suggests that realized profits will almost always be good approximations to the actuarial returns that will be associated with any given price/quality combination. Risk (at least that attributable to consumer search) is therefore not a prominent feature of the market environment of sellers, and we expect the feedback process to lead them eventually to adopt behavior that will maximize actuarial profit. If we make the usual simplifying assumption that the profit functions of firms are identical, this creates an awkward dilemma in that all firms might be

---

[1] If there is a continuous price distribution $F(P)$, and if each buyer investigates exactly n dealers and then purchases at the lowest price, each firm i will find expected sales Q_i equal to $kn[1-F(P_i)]^{n-1}$, where k is the number of potential buyers per seller in the market.

found to converge on the same price, and there would no longer be any justification for consumer search behavior. To show that equilibrium under these assumptions can be characterized by a uniform price, we proceed by assuming the contrary: An "equilibrium" price distribution will be characterized by nonnegative profits and by the condition that no firm i earn profits that are so high as to induce entry:

$$P_i Q_i - C(Q_i) \leqslant K \quad \text{for any } i \tag{6.1}$$

Here, Q_i is the expected number of sales, and $C(Q_i)$ is the cost function of any firm. The parameter K represents the smallest profit that will bring about entry, and we allow it to reflect any expectations that a firm might have regarding the effects of its entry on the price distribution. As Stigler (1961) observed, this condition is likely to require declining average costs: In the limiting case of free entry and a large number of competitors, K becomes zero, and because $dQ_i/dP_i < 0$, condition (6.1) can be satisfied only if $(d/dQ)[C(Q)/Q] < 0$.

Condition (6.1) characterizes equilibrium in terms of entry and demands invariant (or bounded) profits across the price distribution. Equilibrium also requires that marginal changes in a firm's price cannot increase that firm's individual profits. We note, however, that just as firm i will lose sales if it raises its price, other firms may experience sales increases as P_i rises, because their prices will then be more "competitive" compared with P_i. Customers who sample both firms i and j will choose to buy from i if $P_i < P_j$, but if P_i rises so that the inequality no longer holds, firm j will enjoy increased sales (even if P_i rises only to $P_i = P_j$, in which case customers may select randomly). Suppose that $K = 0$ and firm i raises its price to P_j exactly; then firm j will experience an increase in profits because of the fact of declining average costs. In the context of homogeneous products, however, firm i is now identical with firm j, and it, too, must enjoy the same profit level. Because the profits of firms i and j were identical before the increase in P_i (because $K = 0$), firm i must have benefited from its price increase, and we conclude that the price dispersion could not have been an equilibrium phenomenon.[2]

The difference between this conclusion and that found in most of the literature on "equilibrium" price distributions is attributable to our use of condition (6.1). The equilibrium we have just described involves both individual profit-maximizing pricing and free entry into the market; if we

---

[2] This argument is quite different from the one given by Butters (1977) or Diamond (1971) to the effect that if search costs, C, are positive, any firm can raise its price by an amount up to C without losing customers, because that argument does not take into account the possibility that even small changes in price can divert customers to competitors that have already been sampled.

drop this second condition, then the possibility for equilibrium price distributions reappears. (Some suggestion that free entry – or large-numbers competition – will tend to compress a price distribution to a point is also found in the work of Wilde and Schwartz, 1979.) Significant price distributions are sustainable only in the presence of significant barriers to entry, or in the presence of incomplete convergence to equilibrium.

It may be the case that many price dispersions are in fact attributable to these two factors. At the same time, it is unlikely that motivation for search behavior will disappear even in a highly competitive price equilibrium. There is no doubt that the rewards to search consist of more than just price differences: Variations in convenience and quality provide potential payoffs to search that seem to be at least as great as those generated by variations in price. Thus, if we allow for the presence of product differentiation, we expect to continue to observe search behavior even under free-entry equilibrium conditions. Formally, we shall construct our model under an assumption that although firms are concerned only with unit costs, prices, and sales and therefore do not see any significant differences between their own and their competitors' products, consumers may respond differently to product characteristics (such as color, style, or perceived quality) and therefore find significant variations in the desirability of the products.

We characterize a household in two ways: It has a set of tastes for the characteristics of the product, and it has an inclination to investigate more than one supplier before making a final purchasing decision. We shall compress the appeal of the product characteristics into a single variable, v, which itself is comparable to price, so that the household can compare two alternative suppliers, i and j, in terms of the net values $v_i - P_i$ and $v_j - P_j$. Naturally, no purchase will be made at all unless these quantities are positive. Finally, we assume that the v's have an upper bound.

We use a cumulative function $V(v)$ to describe the distribution of the v's that is faced by our household, and we assume $V(v)$ to be continuously differentiable. A similar function $W_i(v)$ describes how the product of firm i is distributed in appeal among its potential customers. In the context of differentiated products, it is, of course, possible for firms to charge different prices simply because of differences in their W distributions. A firm with a wide distribution may come to exploit its very-high-v customers with high prices (becoming an "exclusive" shop), whereas firms with narrow W distributions profit from lower prices. However, we are not interested here in these conventional sources of price differences, and we shall therefore assume that each firm faces the same distribution

$W(v)$ and that $W(v)$ is fixed. For similar reasons, we shall make a strong assumption that households are identical in that each faces the same distribution $V(v)$.[3] Because firms as a whole and consumers as a whole are sampling the same population of v's, it follows from these two assumptions that $V(v)$ and $W(v)$ are identical.

Because all firms and consumers face the same v distributions, P and v must be distributed independently. Let $F(P)$ be the price distribution and $\Lambda(\Delta)$ be the distribution of the net values $v - P$, where $\Delta \equiv v - P$. The density function $\psi(\Delta)$ corresponding to $\Lambda(\Delta)$ is given by

$$\psi(\Delta) = \int_0^\infty V'(P+\Delta)F'(P)\,dP \tag{6.2}$$

Consumer search

Optimal search models vary widely in the amount of prior information that is assumed to be available. At one extreme, Kohn and Shavell (1974) assumed the distribution of values to be completely known. In this case, a sequential search procedure is optimal: Defining Δ' to be the best "offer" that the household has encountered so far in its search, the household goes on searching so long as the cost of search is less than the expected benefit to be obtained from one further sample, that is, whenever

$$C < \int_{\Delta'}^\infty (\Delta - \Delta')\psi(\Delta)\,d\Delta \tag{6.3}$$

Even in the context of fully rational behavior, this procedure suffers from the stringency of its assumption that buyers are fully informed as to the distribution of values but have no idea where any particular dealer falls in that distribution. The more usual Bayesian model, such as the one suggested by Rothschild (1974a) assumes that the consumer is ignorant of the distribution $\psi(\Delta)$, so that the search process must be used both to estimate the parameters of the distribution and to obtain favorable outcomes. In any case, such models are subject to all of the objections we detailed in Chapter 4. We must assume that consumers actually do behave as if they were solving general stochastic optimization problems that are susceptible to analytical solution by professional statisticians in

---

[3] These are quite restrictive assumptions. If automobile dealers sell products ranging from "very small" to "very large," the customer who wants a "very small" car is likely to see quite a different distribution of values than is the customer who wants an intermediate one.

only a few special cases, and we must ignore the fact that in any case the amount of search is likely to be too limited to provide estimates of distributions in which one could have any confidence.[4]

In order to limit the complexity of the problem, we shall impose three restrictions. First, we concern ourselves only with relatively expensive, differentiated products. The reason for using goods with high prices is to ensure (a) that price and quality variations are not overwhelmed by search cost and (b) that no price encountered is ever actually lower than search costs, making further search unnecessary in any case. Second, we shall assume that the buying experience is repeated from time to time in several markets and that the distributions found in those markets are similar (although mean price and quality levels may be entirely different), so that we do not have to introduce the complexity of different Δ distributions. Third, any income effects that arise in consequence of a large number of expensive searches do not affect the valuations, v_i, or the search costs.

The individual approaches firm i and is shown a product with appeal v_i and price P_i, giving a net value Δ_i. He suffers a search cost, C, whenever he seeks out a dealer, and we shall use Δ' to represent the most favorable offer that has been encountered so far in the search. When the consumer investigates a new source, three outcomes are possible:

S: The search is successful in the sense that the new Δ is larger than Δ' by an amount greater than C. The household benefits to the extent $\Delta - \Delta' - C$.

F_1: The search is a failure in that despite an improvement in Δ, that improvement does not cover C, and the household loses $C - \Delta + \Delta'$.

F_2: The search is a disaster in that $\Delta < \Delta'$, and the household wastes its search cost, losing C.

---

[4] For example, if the density function $\psi(\Delta)$ is known to be rectangular over $[0,1]$, the expected number of samples taken during sequential search, n_s, varies with search costs according to $n_s = 1/\sqrt{2C}$. A value of C equal to 10 percent of the standard deviation of the distribution would seem to be a modest cost; nevertheless, in this case that would amount to $C = 0.0289$, and this value substituted into the foregoing equation gives $n_s = 4.16$. Because the median number of searches is even smaller than this, this means that for most sequentially searching households, the question on the margin is essentially whether or not to investigate a third, fourth, or fifth supplier. Because, in principle, the form of $\psi(\Delta)$ is unknown, the rational Bayesian must use his three or four data points to determine both the nature of the distribution and its parameters, and the confidence intervals that would have to be applied to the resulting estimates would be so broad as hardly to be worth the effort.

Our main hypothesis is that the feedback mechanism determines search behavior on the basis of experience with these three cases. If case S is frequently encountered, search will be encouraged (in a sense, the household is convinced that shopping around does pay off). On the other hand, cases F_1 and F_2 discourage search and at the same time encourage purchase from the best of the dealers already sampled (so long as $\Delta' > 0$).

Suppose the individual has already investigated t dealers. The relevant choice is whether to go on to seek out a $t+1$ dealer or to stop the search process and buy from the dealer whose price/quality offer is currently the best among the t known alternatives. This is another simple binary-choice problem, and we use ϕ to describe the likelihood that search will continue and $1-\phi$ for the likelihood that search will be terminated.

This binary-choice problem has a natural symmetry around a zero payoff, and so, as was the case for the lottery problem, the aspiration level, $\hat{\theta}$, has a natural definition. We can also repeat the argument used in the last chapter that under such binary-choice situations, a choice that fails has the same feedback effect as the opposite choice with an equal positive payoff. Thus, we can simplify the general feedback function and apply it symmetrically. If a search is successful, the degree of success will reinforce further search, and we apply the feedback model to ϕ. If the search is a failure, the degree of failure will reinforce *stopping,* and we apply the feedback model to $1-\phi$. Because Θ describes the value of a positive return in either of these cases, because $\hat{\Theta}$ is fixed, and because the value of I is implicit in the formulation, it is possible to write the feedback function in the much more convenient form $E(\phi, R)$, where R is the dollar payoff figure, and

$$E(\phi_i, R_i) \equiv L^i[\phi, i, \hat{\Theta}, \Theta(R_i)] \quad \text{for } i = \begin{cases} \text{``search''} \\ \text{``stop searching''} \end{cases} \tag{6.4}$$

By definition, our values for R will always be nonnegative. Using this formulation, the transition rules are as follows:

Case S: Search is successful, so that the likelihood of further search is increased:

$$\phi_{t+1} = \phi_t + E(\phi_t, \Delta_{t+1} - \Delta_t' - C) \tag{6.5}$$

Case F_1: Search is a failure, because search costs are not fully recovered, so that the likelihood of stopping is increased:

$$1 - \phi_{t+1} - (1 - \phi_t) = E(1 - \phi_t, C + \Delta_t' - \Delta_{t+1})$$

This can be rewritten as

$$\phi_{t+1} = \phi_t - E(1 - \phi_t, C + \Delta_t' - \Delta_{t+1}) \tag{6.6}$$

Case F_2: Search is a disaster, also increasing $1-\phi$:

$$\phi_{t+1}=\phi_t-E(1-\phi_t,C) \tag{6.7}$$

The value of ϕ changes at each step of a search sequence. Define ϕ_T to be its value at the point at which the household happens to terminate the search process (an event that occurs with probability $1-\phi_t$). From (6.5) through (6.7), we can show that ϕ_T has the following properties (proofs of all of these properties are given in the Appendix to this chapter):

Property A: $C>0 \Rightarrow \phi_t<1$ for large t. Hence, search costs prevent indefinite search, and the household will eventually terminate. Thus, $C>0$ implies the existence of a $\phi_T<1$.

Property B: $C=0 \Rightarrow \phi_T \geqslant \phi_0$ for any $\phi_0<1$. This implies that if search costs are zero, search probabilities increase (with probability 1) toward a limit of 1 (which would have the household investigate entire markets).

Property C: Suppose the values of Δ have an upper bound Δ_{max}. $C>\Delta_{max} \Rightarrow \phi_T \leqslant \phi_0$ for any $\phi_0>0$.

Using the distribution $\psi(\Delta)$ and equations (6.5) through (6.7), we can determine an expected value for ϕ_{t+1} as a function of any given (ϕ_t, Δ_t') pair:

$$E[\phi_{t+1}\mid \Delta_t']=\phi_t-\int_0^{\Delta_t'} E(1-\phi_t,C)\psi(\Delta)\,d\Delta$$

$$-\int_{\Delta_t'}^{\Delta_t'+C} E(1-\phi_t,C+\Delta_t'-\Delta)\psi(\Delta)\,d\Delta$$

$$+\int_{\Delta_t'+C}^{\infty} E(\phi_t,\Delta-\Delta_t'-C)\psi(\Delta)\,d\Delta \tag{6.8}$$

As an example of equation (6.8), it is interesting to consider the proportional form of the learning function with a linearized approximation to the function $\alpha(\Theta-\hat{\Theta})$. If we write $E(\phi_t,R)=\delta R(1-\phi_t)$, where the constant δ is small enough given the range of values of R to guarantee that $\delta R<1$, then equation (6.8) reduces to

$$E[\phi_{t+1}\mid \Delta_t']=\phi_t-\delta\phi_t\left[C-\int_{\Delta_t'}^{\infty}(\Delta-\Delta_t')\psi(\Delta)\,d\Delta\right]$$

$$-\delta(2\phi_t-1)\int_{\Delta_t'+C}^{\infty}(\Delta-\Delta_t'+C)\psi(\Delta)\,d\Delta \tag{6.9}$$

The expression in brackets on the right-hand side corresponds to condition (6.3); that is, the sign of this expression reflects the optimal stopping rule of sequential search models. The integral in the third term is always nonnegative, and thus the sign of the third term of (6.9) depends on whether ϕ_t is larger or smaller than $\frac{1}{2}$. According to (6.9), then, the expected transition from ϕ_t to ϕ_{t+1} given Δ_t' depends on an optimal stopping rule subject to a central tendency toward $\phi_t = \frac{1}{2}$.[5]

Equations (6.5) through (6.7) characterize a Markov process that begins with an initial state, ϕ_0, and produces a distribution of possible values for Δ_1' depending on the value encountered from the first dealer. If the household goes on searching, each of these possible values for Δ_1' produces a joint distribution of possible values for ϕ_2 and Δ_2' depending on the value encountered from the second dealer. Corresponding to each pair (ϕ_2, Δ_2') there is a joint distribution of ϕ_3 and Δ_3' if a third dealer is sampled, and so on. Except in the case in which the household buys at the first available supplier, the household is virtually certain to complete its market adventure with a terminal value, ϕ_T, different from the one with which it began. We shall define a density function $h(\phi_T, \phi_0)$ to describe the set of possible ϕ_T's at the end of a typical searching experience, *given that search beyond the first dealer does take place*. (If there is no further search, then $\phi_T = \phi_0$ again.)

So long as $\psi(\Delta)$ is continuously differentiable and $C > 0$, it is clear from our characterization of the learning process that the following hold:

Property D: $h(0, \phi_0) = 0$ for any $\phi_0 > 0$ [from condition (2.6) and the fact that $R_i \geqslant 0$ always].

Property E: $h(\phi_T, \phi_0)$ is continuously differentiable in both variables over the intervals $0 > \phi_0 \geqslant 1$ and $0 \geqslant \phi_T \geqslant 1$.

Property F: $h(1, \phi_0) = 0$ for any $C > 0$ [from condition (2.6)].

Property G: $h(\phi_T, \phi_0) > 0$ for all ϕ_T that fall in an interval $0 < \phi_T \leqslant \phi_0 + a < 1$ for some $a > 0$. (Some successes are always possible; hence, $a > 0$, and a converges to 0 only at $\phi_0 = 1$. Strings of failures of any magnitude between 0 and C, and of any length, are always possible; hence, we can obtain any positive $\phi_T < \phi_0$.)

Although we were able to show that in the linear case our model is

---

[5] This central tendency is common to psychological learning models. It comes about because any learning model that satisfies $0 \leqslant \phi \leqslant 1$ and that incorporates a positive monotonic relation between payoff and ϕ must have a point of inflection in that relation. If an action is already habitual (ϕ is near to its upper bound of 1), further reinforcements can do little to encourage it still more, whereas negative experiences can do a great deal to inhibit it (as we approach the inflection point, ϕ becomes more sensitive to payoff). Conversely, negative experiences do little toward inhibiting actions that are already unlikely, but positive reinforcements may have a large impact on future behavior.

related to an ordinary sequential stopping rule, the Markov process nevertheless differs from most search models in that it indicates that a positive (although perhaps very small) amount of search is consistent with relatively large values of C. A sequential search rule, for example, would permit no search at all if $\psi(\Delta)$ were a rectangular distribution over $[0,1]$ and $C>0.5$. In contrast, the feedback process is compatible with positive search at much higher cost levels. Suppose we define $\xi(\phi_0) \equiv \int_0^1 \phi_T h(\phi_T, \phi_0) \, d\phi_T$ (a function describing the expected value of the terminal ϕ given ϕ_0). In the Appendix it is proved that the following hold:

Property H: For any $C<\Delta_{max}$, there exists a positive number ϵ such that $\xi(\phi_0)>\epsilon$ for any $0<\phi_0 \leqslant 1$.

Property I:

$$\lim_{\phi_T \to 0} \frac{d}{d\phi_T} h(\phi_T, \phi) = 0 \quad \text{and} \quad \lim_{\phi_T \to 1} \frac{d}{d\phi_T} h(\phi_T, \phi) = 0$$

In our discussions of choice under risk, we have noted that although individuals will generally exhibit different choice likelihoods because of their differences in experience, the population as a whole is likely to be characterized by a stationary distribution of choice likelihoods so long as the distribution of alternative states of nature is stationary. In the case of the model under discussion here, there is some ambiguity as to whether we are interested in search likelihoods during search sequences or only in terminal search likelihoods. The first choice treats each sampling of a potential seller as a single "experience," whereas the second treats each market adventure (a search sequence that may or may not terminate with purchase of the desired commodity) as a single experience. Because we are more inclined to the view that the relevant unit of experience is the entire endeavor – going out to look for and buy some particular durable good – we shall use the second interpretation and consider a population-wide distribution of values for ϕ_T. Because we are assuming that the value of ϕ_T with which a household terminated the last process is the value of ϕ_0 with which it begins the next, our equilibrium distribution is characterized by the property that if ϕ_0 is distributed according to $\gamma(\phi_0)$, then the values of ϕ_T are distributed the same way.

We can put this more formally by supposing that the values of ϕ_0 are distributed throughout the population according to some continuous density function $\gamma'(\phi_0)$. If each household proceeds to enter a market, search, and terminate search, then the economy will be characterized by a new density function $\gamma''(\phi_T)$, where

$$\gamma''(\phi_T) = (1 - \phi_T)\gamma'(\phi_T) + \int_0^1 \phi_0 h(\phi_T, \phi_0) \gamma'(\phi_0) \, d\phi_0 \qquad (6.10)$$

In the Appendix to this chapter it is proved that the following holds:

Property J: For every $C>0$, there exists a unique distribution $\gamma(\phi)$ that satisfies (6.10), with $\{\gamma''(\phi)=\gamma(\phi)$ if $\gamma'(\phi)=\gamma(\phi)\}$ for all ϕ and with $\gamma(0)=\gamma(1)=0$.

Despite the existence of $\gamma(\phi)$, it is not the case that the distribution of ϕ_0 throughout a population will always converge (after sufficient market adventures) to $\gamma(\phi)$, because very high feedback effects could destabilize the convergence. Indeed, it is difficult even to find a satisfactory criterion for the stability of the distribution $\gamma(\phi)$. Conceptually it is simplest to look at the behavior of the means of these distributions. Let us define $\overline{\phi_0}$, $\overline{\phi_T}$, and $\bar{\phi}$ as the means of $\gamma'(\phi_0)$, $\gamma''(\phi_T)$, and $\gamma(\phi)$, respectively. Because $\bar{\phi}$ is unique, we can define stability by the condition

$$\frac{d\overline{\phi_T}}{d\overline{\phi_0}}<1 \quad \text{at} \quad \gamma'(\cdot)=\gamma(\cdot) \tag{6.11}$$

In general, this condition is not met for every possible perturbation in $\gamma(\phi)$. Nevertheless, we can prove that for "low" feedback rates, the process is stable in the sense given by (6.11). Suppose that we introduce a rate variable into the feedback function:

$$E'(\phi_{i,t},R_i)=uE(\phi_{i,t},R_i) \quad (0<u\leqslant 1) \tag{6.12}$$

The new function $E'(\cdot)$ has all the properties of $E(\cdot)$, and the value for u can be used to suggest a "rate" of feedback. We can now prove the following (see Appendix):

Property K: For every perturbation in $\gamma(\phi)$ that is s standard deviations away from $\bar{\phi}$ there exists a rate $u_0>0$ such that (6.11) holds for all $u\leqslant u_0$.

Finally, we can use (6.11) to show that increases in search cost will have the expected effect of inhibiting equilibrium search activity:

Property L: For stable distributions, high search costs reduce search activity: $d\bar{\phi}/dC<0$.

An alternative approach to the analysis of this equilibrium is to use the fixed-point approximation to $\bar{\phi}$. Because $\xi(\phi_0)>\epsilon$ for $\phi_0<1$ and $\xi(\phi_0)<1$ (from property F), we have $\epsilon\leqslant\xi(\phi_0)\leqslant 1$ for all $\epsilon\leqslant\phi_0\leqslant 1$. Because the Markov process is continuous, the Brouwer fixed-point theorem guarantees the existence of a ϕ^* such that $\xi(\phi^*)=\phi^*$, with $\epsilon<\phi^*<1$, and ϕ^* can serve as an approximation for $\bar{\phi}$.

Unfortunately, analytic solutions for ϕ^* are inaccessible almost as often as are solutions for $\gamma(\phi)$ itself. To solve for ϕ^* we must find the mean of the distribution $h(\phi_T,\phi)$, and this is a complicated sum that depends on the joint distribution of Δ' and ϕ as the individual passes through a search sequence. In fact, we have been able to obtain a solution

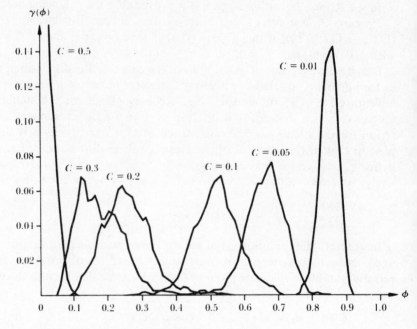

Figure 6.1. Simulated distributions of $\gamma(\phi)$.

for ϕ^* in only one case. Suppose that we consider the distribution $\gamma(\phi)$ as u [the feedback "rate" defined by (6.12)] becomes very small. It turns out that in this case $\gamma(\phi)$ converges to a "spike" around $\bar{\phi}$, and the difference $\bar{\phi} - \phi^*$ converges to zero. In the limit, $\gamma(\phi) = 0$ for $\phi \neq \bar{\phi}$ and $\phi^* = \bar{\phi}$. Equation (6.13) provides the solution equation for $\lim_{u \to 0} \phi^*$ for the case of $\psi(\Delta)$ rectangular over $0 \leqslant \Delta \leqslant 1$:

$$\frac{\phi C}{1-\phi} - Z(\phi) + \frac{2\phi - 1}{\phi} (1-C)^2 Z[\phi(1-C)] = 0 \qquad (6.13)$$

where

$$Z(x) = \frac{2-x}{2x} - \frac{1-x}{x^2} \ln \frac{1}{1-x}$$

Simulations

However difficult the analytic derivation of $\gamma(\phi)$ may be, it is always true that simulation of the feedback mechanism is available, often quite cheaply. Even with as complicated a model as that treated in this chapter,

Table 6.1. *Estimates of* q_n *obtained from simulation*

	$C=0.01$	$C=0.05$	$C=0.10$	$C=0.20$	$C=0.30$	$C=0.50$
$n=1$	0.146	0.340	0.480	0.693	0.841	0.954
$n=2$	0.117	0.217	0.244	0.211	0.130	0.043
$n=3$	0.104	0.145	0.127	0.065	0.023	0.002
$n=4$	0.092	0.098	0.067	0.021	0.004	0.000
$n=5$	0.075	0.060	0.038	0.007	0.002	0.000
$n=6$	0.066	0.044	0.021	0.002	0.000	0.000
$n=7$	0.056	0.031	0.010	0.001	0.000	0.000
$n=8$	0.045	0.021	0.005	0.000	0.000	0.000
$n=9$	0.044	0.015	0.004	0.000	0.000	0.000
$n=10$	0.036	0.010	0.002	0.000	0.000	0.000

a computer can produce stable distributions involving thousands of "households" very quickly (in our experiments, half a second proved to be sufficient to produce stationary distributions for markets of 10,000 consumers). Many simulations of this sort have been run using various distributions $\psi(\Delta)$ and alternative functional forms for $E(\cdot)$. Figure 6.1 describes a typical set of six simulations in which the variable under consideration is search cost. In these, $\psi(\Delta)$ is a simple rectangular distribution, and the feedback function is linear, with $E(\phi_t, R) = 0.2(1 - \phi_t)R$. Examples are given for $C=0.01$, $C=0.05$, $C=0.1$, $C=0.2$, $C=0.3$, and $C=0.5$. Figure 6.1 reflects the property that higher search costs reduce the quantity of search and in addition describes the effect of search costs on the dispersion of the ϕ distribution. Relatively high and relatively low values of C decrease the width of the distribution and also skew it toward the extreme values of $\phi=0$ and $\phi=1$.

Corresponding to $\gamma(\phi)$ is a vector of searching frequencies, Q, each of whose elements, q_n, describes the expected proportion of the population that will search exactly n times. Table 6.1 describes the simulation estimates of q_n for each of the six cases used to construct Figure 6.1.

The mean of $\gamma(\phi)$ is $\bar{\phi}$, and we shall call $\bar{n}$ the corresponding expected number of searches: $\bar{n} \equiv \Sigma n q_n$. Values of $\bar{\phi}$ and $\bar{n}$ obtained from the simulation experiments are reported in rows 2 and 3 of Table 6.2. If the searching likelihood were fixed at $\bar{\phi}$, rather than varying throughout each market adventure, then q_n would be exactly equal to $(\bar{\phi})^{n-1}(1-\bar{\phi})$. That this is in fact a very good approximation for q_n can be seen from Table 6.3, which lists values for q_n and $(\bar{\phi})^{n-1}(1-\bar{\phi})$ for purposes of comparison. In Table 6.3, only three cases are listed, but the other cases reveal

Table 6.2. *Comparison of search propensities from feedback and optimal search models*

	$C=0.01$	$C=0.05$	$C=0.10$	$C=0.20$	$C=0.30$	$C=0.50$
$\bar{\phi}$	0.85	0.67	0.52	0.31	0.16	0.05
$\bar{n}$	7.0	3.0	2.1	1.5	1.2	1.1
ϕ^*	0.85	0.67	0.53	0.33	0.20	0.05
s^2	40.1	6.2	2.4	0.68	0.25	0.06
n_s	7.1	3.2	2.2	1.6	1.3	1.0
σ_s^2	42.9	6.8	2.8	0.92	0.38	0.0
$\bar{v}$	0.72	0.52	0.41	0.27	0.17	−0.02
v_s	0.86	0.68	0.55	0.37	0.23	0.0

Table 6.3. *Comparison of values of* q_n *with values of* $(\bar{\phi})^{n-1}(1-\bar{\phi})$

	$C=0.01$		$C=0.10$		$C=0.30$	
	q_n	$(\bar{\phi})^{n-1}(1-\bar{\phi})$	q_n	$(\bar{\phi})^{n-1}(1-\bar{\phi})$	q_n	$(\bar{\phi})^{n-1}(1-\bar{\phi})$
$n=1$	0.146	0.146	0.480	0.480	0.841	0.841
$n=2$	0.117	0.125	0.244	0.250	0.130	0.132
$n=3$	0.104	0.107	0.127	0.129	0.023	0.021
$n=4$	0.092	0.091	0.067	0.067	0.004	0.003
$n=5$	0.075	0.078	0.038	0.034	0.002	0.001
$n=6$	0.066	0.066	0.021	0.018	0.000	0.000
$n=7$	0.056	0.057	0.010	0.009	0.000	0.000
$n=8$	0.045	0.048	0.005	0.005	0.000	0.000
$n=9$	0.044	0.041	0.004	0.002	0.000	0.000
$n=10$	0.036	0.035	0.002	0.001	0.000	0.000

equally close similarity between the two series. Using $(\bar{\phi})^{n-1}(1-\bar{\phi})$ as an approximation for q_n, and the fact that $\sum_{n=1}^{\infty} na^n = a/(1-a)^2$ for $0 \leqslant a < 1$, we find

$$\bar{n} \sim \sum_{n=1}^{\infty} n(\bar{\phi})^{n-1}(1-\bar{\phi}) = \frac{1}{1-\bar{\phi}} \qquad (6.14)$$

The data provided in Table 6.2 are easily manipulated to demonstrate that the reciprocal of $1-\bar{\phi}$ is an excellent estimate of the realized values for $\bar{n}$.

The fixed-point approximation ϕ^* given in Table 6.2 was obtained from (6.13). These values seem to be quite satisfactorily close to $\bar{\phi}$ in these examples, in spite of the fact that the feedback rate used for the simulation is significantly greater than the limiting zero value that was necessary for the derivation of ϕ^*.

Simulations using different feedback functions and different value distributions have produced similar results, although one can hardly claim to have investigated more than a small fraction of all the possible simple analytic functions. Variations in the feedback function, for example, appear to have a considerable effect on the dispersion of $\gamma(\phi)$, but relatively little influence over its mean: In one case, increasing the feedback coefficient by a factor of 4 altered the simulated values of $\bar{\phi}$ by less than 15 percent of the values in Table 6.2 (and for most values of C, much less). Our impression that $\bar{\phi}$ is relatively stable is reinforced by the closeness of the fixed-point estimate ϕ^*. This latter figure is precisely correct for the limiting zero-coefficient case, and the fact that it is so close for the case of a feedback coefficient of 0.2 indicates that $\bar{\phi}$ is not very sensitive to feedback rates.

The particular examples used for Figure 6.1 are interesting because the rectangular distribution used for $\psi(\Delta)$ permits comparisons with optimal search models. Suppose that this distribution is fully known to households. Optimal sequential search will then produce an expected number of searches, n_s, and a variance in n, σ_s^2, given by

$$n_s = \frac{1}{\sqrt{2C}}$$

$$\sigma_s^2 = n_s^2 - n_s \tag{6.15}$$

Values for n_s and σ_s^2 are listed in rows 5 and 6 of Table 6.2, where they can be compared with $\bar{n}$ and s^2 (the variance of n) from the simulated distributions. The similarities among these numbers are striking, and this comparison might well encourage one in the view that markets indeed operate as if they were composed of households that behave according to principles of optimization. The feedback model presumes that consumers have neither the capacity nor the sophistication necessary to employ optimal search rules; yet it produces a very similar relation between search propensity and search costs. In some cases it produces values of $\bar{n}$ that are indistinguishable from their "optimal" counterparts.

It would be quite a different matter, however, to assert that the market is composed of households that individually behave as if they were maximizers. Although the total amount of search behavior in our model is similar to what would be generated by optimal sequential search, our households actually are doing nothing of the kind. They do not have the information on $\psi(\Delta)$ that would be prerequisite to optimal search behavior, nor do they use any analytic rules to govern their search decisions. Naturally, they do not do as well as fully informed optimizing households can do. The last two rows of Table 6.2 list expected values for realized net payoffs (final Δ' minus total search costs expended) for our adaptive households, given as $\bar{v}$, and for optimal sequential search, given as v_s.[6]

The dynamic responses to particular sequences of quotes are quite different in the two kinds of models. For example, the sequentially searching household that happens to encounter a long string of low-value quotes will continue to search indefinitely, whereas the adaptive household may stop at any point and, in accordance with property A, is certain to stop eventually (this may account for the fact that s^2 in Table 6.2 is generally less than σ_s^2). As another example, suppose a household encounters first a low Δ and then a high one; this will encourage further search, whereas a reversal in the order of the quotes will discourage further search. Under optimal search procedures, in contrast, the decision to investigate a third dealer will be unaffected by the ordering of the first two. In short, it is a distinguishing feature of feedback models that the individual is not a microcosm of the market and that the predominant features of a theory for one are not necessarily the predominant features of a theory for the other.

Dealer behavior

As we suggested in an earlier section, customer flows may be large enough for any seller's risk to be substantially reduced by the law of large numbers. If this is the case, then dealers will eventually come to charge (actuarial) profit-maximizing prices for their products. In this section we shall first consider what those prices might be and then focus on the question of convergence.

Suppose that all consumers investigate exactly n dealers before making a decision. An n-searching consumer who visits firm i encounters a net value Δ_i that depends on that firm's price and on the consumer's taste for its particular product. If $\Delta_i > 0$ and if Δ_i is maximal among the n firms sampled, then he buys from firm i. This occurs with a probability

$$[\Lambda(\Delta_i)]^{n-1} = \left[\int_0^\infty V(P+\Delta_i) F'(P) \, dP \right]^{n-1} \tag{6.16}$$

The P_i for seller i is given, but the v is distributed according to $V(v)$. If there are K customers per seller in the market, then the expected sales of firm i are given by

---

[6] Expected net payoff from optimal sequential search is given by $v_s = 1 - \sqrt{2C}$ if the distribution $\psi(\Delta)$ is uniform.

$$Q_i = kn \int_{P_i}^{\infty} \left[\int_0^{\infty} V(P + v - P_i) F'(P) \, dP \right]^{n-1} V'(v) \, dv \qquad (6.17)$$

where k is the number of potential buyers per seller in the market, and the lower limit to the integration reflects the fact that the consumer will buy only if v exceeds P_i.

It is clear from (6.17) that regardless of the nature of the distribution, F, firm i faces a downward-sloping demand curve for any finite value of n. As P_i rises, the cumulative distribution V falls for every value of v, reflecting the loss of potential customers to competitors. Moreover, the demand curve itself has nonzero elasticity that is (imperfectly) reflected in this model by the range of the integration.

We argued in Chapter 4 that adaptive firms operating under certainty would converge on a so-called Cournot-Nash market equilibrium. For the reasons outlined earlier in this chapter, this equilibrium must be characterized by a single price, and in order to derive this price, we proceed by supposing that all firms other than firm i charge a common price P^*, finding an optimal price for the remaining firm i, and solving for the P^* that leads to $P_i = P^*$. When all other firms charge P^*, the distribution $F(P)$ collapses to a point, and (6.17) becomes

$$Q_i = kn \int_{P_i}^{\infty} [V(P^* + v - P_i)]^{n-1} V'(v) \, dv \qquad (6.18)$$

In a case of constant marginal costs, the net profit of firm i will be

$$(P_i - C_u) Q_i - nkC_0 - FC \qquad (6.19)$$

where C_u is unit production cost, C_0 is the cost of space and personnel necessary to display or demonstrate the product both to those who buy and to those who do not, and FC is fixed cost. If we find the first-order conditions for the maximization of (6.19)[7] and impose our condition that each firm find its profits maximized at the same value of $P_i = P^*$, we find (after some manipulation) that P^* is the solution to (6.20):

$$1 - [V(P)]^n - n(P - C_u)[V(P)]^{n-1} V'(P)$$

$$- n(n-1)(P - C_u) \int_P^{\infty} [V(v)]^{n-2} [V'(v)]^2 \, dv = 0 \qquad (6.20)$$

It is a curious fact that this differentiated-product equilibrium may reflect a positive association between search activity and equilibrium market price. Suppose, for example, that the distribution $V(v)$ is given

---

[7] Because the derivative of (6.19) is positive for $P_i = 0$ whenever $P^* \geqslant 0$ and is negative for sufficiently large P_i, a nonnegative optimal P_i is always available.

by $(v-a)^k$, where $0 \leqslant a \leqslant v \leqslant a+1$ and $k>0$. Then, if $C_u = 0$ and $nk \neq 1$, equation (6.19) can be solved to give[8]

$$1 = \frac{n(n-1)k^2}{kn-1} P \quad \text{if } a \geqslant \frac{kn-1}{n(n-1)k^2} \tag{6.21}$$

$$1 = \frac{n(n-1)k^2}{kn-1} P + (P-a)^{nk}$$

$$+ P(P-a)^{nk-1} \frac{nk(k-1)}{nk-1} \quad \text{if } a < \frac{kn-1}{n(n-1)k^2} \tag{6.22}$$

Suppose that (6.21) applies (this implies pricing in a range where all consumers eventually buy from some dealer), and define P' as the solution to (6.21) with $n+1$ substituted for n. Using (6.21),

$$P' - P = \frac{2 - k(n+1)}{n(n^2-1)k^2} \tag{6.23}$$

If we meet the conditions $n > 1$ and $2 > k(n+1)$, then equation (6.23) implies that P rises as n is increased to $n+1$. (Because $n \geqslant 2$, we note that this result is possible only if $k < 2/3$.)[9]

If all households were assumed to search exactly n times, then equation (6.20) would be used directly to determine the market price. Because search propensity is the product of a feedback process, however, we expect to find that even households with identical search costs can be expected to display a variety of different search behaviors. If, in fact, the inclination to investigate different sources of supply is distributed across the population according to a vector of probabilities, q_n, and the firm is unable to distinguish the search propensities of various customers, then equation (6.20) should be replaced by (6.23), where the qualitative properties of equation (6.20) will be retained:

---

[8] Equation (6.21) applies whenever $P \leqslant a$; (6.22) applies whenever $P > a$. Because $a > 0$, (6.22) can be solved only for $P > 0$. Descartes's rule of signs guarantees that this positive value of P is unique.

[9] The possibility that increased search might have a perverse impact on equilibrium price corresponds to a general property of models of monopolistic competition that has already been observed by Archibald (1961). Interdependence among the demand functions that face individual firms with differentiated products makes it possible for entry of new firms into a market to shift the demand curves of existing firms. If the nature of the interdependence happens to lead to a general decrease in demand elasticities after entry, a new market equilibrium may come about at higher prices than before. In our model, an increase in n, from the point of view of firm i, is equivalent to an increase in the number of its competitors, and the distribution $V(v)$ produces the perverse elasticity consequence.

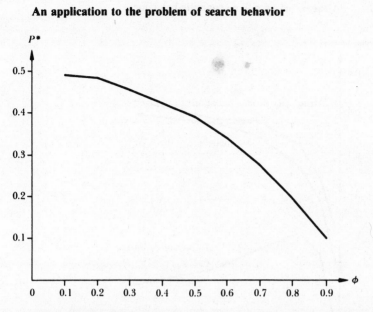

Figure 6.2. Estimated equilibrium market price as a function of average search likelihood.

$$1 - \sum_{n=1}^{\infty} \left\{ [V(P)]^n + n(P - C_u)[V(P)]^{n-1} V'(P) \right.$$

$$\left. + n(n-1)(P - C_u) \int_P^{\infty} [V(v)]^{n-2} [V'(v)]^2 \, dv \right\} q_n = 0 \qquad (6.24)$$

In fact, the problem is made more complicated by the fact that the distribution of searching propensities is determined in part by $\gamma(\Delta)$. In using (6.23) as the profit function for firm i, we are ignoring the fact that changes in P_i will change $\gamma(\Delta)$, and this will lead to some alteration in q_n. Unfortunately, we have no analytic representation of this interdependence, and we must be satisfied with (6.24) as our best approximation of a solution equation for P^*.

If we use the expression $(\bar{\phi})^{n-1}(1 - \bar{\phi})$ as an approximation for q_n, then it is possible to obtain explicit solutions to (6.24), at least in the case of simple distributions. For example, if $V(v)$ is uniform over $0 \leqslant v \leqslant 1$, then $V(v) = v$ and $V'(v) = 1$, and equation (6.24) can be solved to yield (C_u is made equal to 0)

$$P^* \sim \frac{2 - \bar{\phi} - [5\bar{\phi}^2 - 8\bar{\phi} + 4]^{1/2}}{2\bar{\phi}} \qquad (6.25)$$

The graph of this estimate for P^* as a function of $\bar{\phi}$ is shown in Figure 6.2. For the particular value distribution used to derive (6.25), it is clear

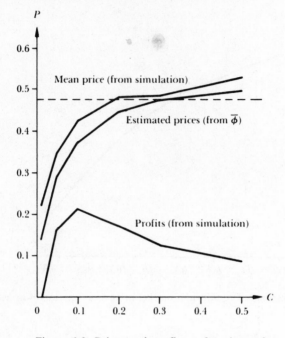

Figure 6.3. Prices and profits as functions of consumer search costs.

that increases in search likelihoods always decrease equilibrium price, and because increases in search cost always decrease search likelihood, we have the expected result that increases in consumer search costs will lead to increases in equilibrium market price. Using the values of $\bar{\phi}$ obtained from the consumer search simulations, we can use (6.25) to obtain the relationship between search cost and estimated market price. This relationship is graphed as the middle solid line in Figure 6.3.

Finally, we note that the solution to (6.24), as well as the approximation (6.25) and the relationships shown in the figures, are independent of the number of firms that are in the market. The number of competitors faced by firm i is not a function of how many potential sellers happen to exist in the market, but a function of how many other sellers have been visited by those customers who happen also to come in firm i's door. Thus, the state of competitiveness of a market is fundamentally a question of customer search behavior rather than of absolute numbers. This fact is reflected in Figure 6.3. High search costs put firms in a nearly monopolistic position, because customers rarely visit more than one potential dealer, and thus market price approaches the monopoly value $P^* = \frac{1}{2}$. Low search costs place firms in more competitive positions, and

P^* is found to be correspondingly lower, although even with very low search cost, $\bar{n}$ proves to be relatively small, and P^* is still significantly above the competitive level (of zero if $C_u = 0$).

The existence of price dispersions

We noted at the start of this chapter that in practice price dispersions exist that seem to be far too broad to be supported by markets containing rationally searching consumers. Certainly, such a thing as a $50.00 price difference between two local camera retailers could not exist for long in a market in which consumers used optimal searching techniques. Feedback processes require time for convergence, and thus price disequilibrium may exist for a period of time, but even here, if dealers do face actuarial income flows, equilibrium should arrive eventually, and with it, a single price.

It is possible, however, that in the case of relatively expensive durables, or specialty products that have limited market volume, dealers do not make sufficiently many sales for the law of large numbers to apply. If this is the case, the feedback process will tend to create price dispersions rather than eliminate them. For example, if consumer search follows the pattern we have described, then $1 - \bar{\phi}$ is an estimate of the fraction of the population that will not proceed beyond the first dealer encountered. For this segment of the market, a dealer is a monopolist and will do best at a correspondingly high price. Other customers will search more, and in a few cases the dealer will be in what is equivalent to a highly competitive market. Over time, such a firm will receive a series of contradictory market signals: High prices sometimes will bring high profits and sometimes will drive customers away. The dispersion in these market signals will slow the learning of the firm even if it should happen to be the case that the analytic forms of the feedback and utility functions imply that equilibrium behavior will maximize actuarial profits at a single price. In contrast to the usual competitive-market model in which product homogeneity forces identical prices on all firms at every instant of time, disequilibrium in this differentiated market is characterized by a variety of different prices, some too high and some too low, and this does not necessarily lead even to general shortages or surpluses at the market level. The main forces tending toward equilibrium are lost, and the disequilibrium will tend to reproduce itself.

Examples of this sort of problem are readily developed using simulation techniques similar to those that have been used several times already. Suppose that we consider a market composed of twenty firms (the actual number of firms is unimportant, for, as we have already noted, it is the search behavior of consumers that determines the competitiveness of the market). At the beginning of each time period, each firm chooses a price, P_i, from the vector of twenty possibilities $0.0, 0.05, 0.10, \ldots, 0.90, 0.95$. For purposes of the simulation, we set $C_u = 0$, considering P_i to be measured as an increment over production cost (and, correspondingly, v must be measured from C_u as an origin). If $V(v)$ is rectangular over $0 \leqslant v \leqslant 1$, then monopoly price in our model will be $\frac{1}{2}$, and the competitive price will be zero. During each period, consumers enter the market, search, and buy in accordance with the models already developed. At the end of the period, firm i has accumulated total sales S_i, and this generates a profit $\Pi_i = P_i S_i - FC$. This profit level then modifies the probability with which any price will be chosen for the next period, following the usual feedback rules. (Note that because this model is characterized by declining average costs, fully competitive behavior will always lead to losses.)

In the case of the simulations actually run, $V(v)$ was rectangular over $0 \leqslant v \leqslant 1$, and the feedback models were linear counterparts of equation (3.1), with $\Theta(\Pi)$ linear in profits, and $\hat{\Theta}$ fixed at $\hat{\Theta} = 0$.

Figure 6.4 describes a typical example in which consumer search costs equaled 0.1 and other parameters were identical with those used in the preceding simulations. Firms' utility functions were $\Theta_i = 0.02\Pi_i$, and fixed costs were all identical at $FC = 2.0$. Initially, all prices were made equally likely (so that expected price was 0.475).

If each of the firms were to experience actuarial cash flows, then this linearized feedback model would imply convergence to a single price equilibrium: Consumer search behavior would correspond to that obtained from our earlier simulation for $C = 0.01$, the likelihood of unprofitable prices would fall to zero (because any price with an expected loss would always lead to an actual loss), and the linearized feedback process would bring about a unique price, as described in Chapter 4. In this case, however, the model was constructed with only 200 consumers entering the market each time period, so that an "average" firm would sell to only a few customers per period, and this is clearly far from an equilibrium distribution. The irregularity of the distribution provides further evidence that the small number of customers per firm leads to ambiguous price/profit experiences. In this particular case, each firm averaged about 7.06 sales per period, but actual sales varied from 0 to 15, depending on the prices charged and which firms were lucky enough to be visited by a large number of consumers. Even with this dispersion in pricing behavior, however, household searching was indistinguishable from that shown for $C = 0.01$ in Figure 6.1. The mean search probability over the last 100 time periods was 0.524, compared with 0.516 in the simple search model.

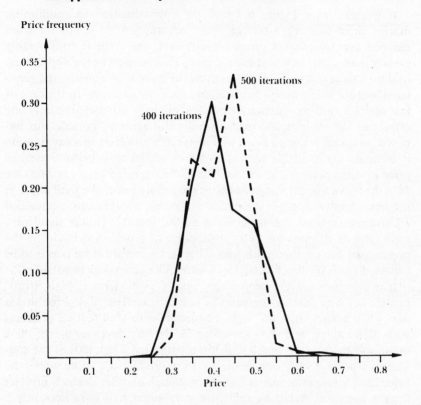

Figure 6.4. Simulated price-probability distributions.

The uniform price-likelihood vector used as an initial condition for the simulation described in Figure 6.4 is quite arbitrary, and price or profit averages taken over the entire period might be overly influenced by this initial state. It is more reasonable, perhaps, to begin with this initial vector, operate the feedback model over several time periods, and then use the product of this simulation as the initial condition for the simulation from which data are to be gathered. In practice, the model was run as described for 400 time periods (using the same parameters as before), and then a 100-period simulation was operated using as initial pricing likelihoods the average output of the 400-period model. Figure 6.4 displays the 400-period and the 500-period distributions for the case of $C=0.01$. The final distribution is not noticeably different from those shown in Figure 6.4. Similar distributions are obtained from this two-stage simulation for other values of search cost. Average profit levels and average market price can be obtained readily over the 100 periods, and these are shown in Figure 6.3.

It is clear from Figure 6.3 that the approximation to equilibrium market price that was obtained from equation (6.25) is not far from realized average market price. Nevertheless, the error is considerably greater than what we would expect, given the closeness of the approximation used to generate (6.25). Moreover, the error is systematic, the simulated average price always being higher than the estimate. In the case of low search cost, this systematic deviation might be attributed to lingering effects of the initial uniform probability distribution, because this imposed an initial expected price well above P^*; however, this explanation is certainly not available for cases of high search cost, because average price in these cases is higher than the initial expected price. In one case ($C = 0.5$), average price is even above monopoly price! We shall argue in the next chapter that the systematic difference between our estimate of P^* and the realized average price is not attributable to any significant errors in our estimate but is a consequence of feedback behavior in the presence of market disequilibrium. That is, an upward price bias is to be expected from feedback processes under quite general circumstances.

It is also interesting to notice that once C is moderately high, firms' profits fall with further increases in search cost. The reason for this is that when search costs are high, consumers often fail to find products with high values, and they therefore fail to buy anything at all. At a monopoly price of 0.5 and a uniform distribution $V(v)$, half of the consumers who visit only one dealer find the product not to be worth the price, and a potential sale is lost, even though another dealer's product (had it been discovered by the consumer) might well have been worth enough to justify purchase. Thus, high search costs have ambiguous consequences on profits: By restricting the competitiveness of the market, they enable firms to approach monopolistic pricing, but by restricting access to information regarding product quality, they inhibit the opportunity for mutually beneficial buyer-seller transactions. When search costs are low, the price effect appears to predominate, but when search costs are high, loss of quality information has the larger impact on profits. (Had the simulation permitted some sort of quality advertising, then this second factor might have been reduced in importance, leaving the price effect to predominate.)

Final notes

Throughout this discussion, search costs have been represented by a constant, and this is an oversimplification in at least two respects. First, it would certainly be more plausible to treat C as an increasing function of n. Indeed, to many consumers, first encounters with automobiles, cameras, or house sellers may be so interesting and informative as to justify the search costs by themselves. Further investigations, however, can be sheer tedium, and to many of us, many searches would become so exasperating that total search costs would exceed their market cost components by substantial margins. Second, should a search process be terminated at a dealer whose offer is not the best, some cost must be incurred in retrieving the optimal bid. Were this fact taken into account, consumers in our model presumably would show less inclination to continue searching whenever a "best" bid has been encountered. For the sake of simplicity, neither of these two modifications has been introduced into the model, and there does not seem to be any reason to expect substantial changes in our general results if they were.

A more awkward problem arises as a consequence of the introduction of product differentiation into the theory. Following the existing literature on search behavior, we have placed most of our emphasis on pricing, treating dealer characteristics as given. In a more general model, however, one might follow the lead of Lancaster (1966), Rosen (1974), and others and describe the optimal choice of product characteristics. The feedback process would then apply to product type as well as to price. Presumably, the model would operate essentially as before, except that convergence to equilibrium from some disequilibrium state would take even longer than in the simple model because of the need for a multidimensional learning process.

This additional variable was not introduced into the model because it is evident that the optimal distribution of prices and product characteristics depends heavily on the circumstances under which differentiation takes place: the effect of differentiation on preferences, on the distribution of consumer tastes, and even on the number of firms in the market. In only a few of the models of optimal product differentiation that are possible, moreover, will it prove to be the case that (a) all firms face identical market conditions and (b) all consumers see the same distribution of product values. Because these conditions are essential to the derivation of simple optimal search rules that could be compared with the results of our model, the question of optimal product differentiation was put aside. Of course, simulation could handle these more general models quite readily, but there would have been no means for direct comparisons with the more conventional search rules.

Finally, we introduced the subject of this chapter with the observation that the object of the feedback process has in this case many of the aspects of a decision style rather than a simple (consumption or production) choice. Even so, we have concentrated on a relatively simple dimension of the search problem, and it is quite possible that the objects of feedback processes in practice are much more sophisticated rules of behavior. Consumer search could be governed by learned rules of thumb that may or may not use arguments that are related to optimal search models, and firms might learn to apply specific mark-up formulas, or to tie price-changing decisions to recent market experiences. The variety of possible models is very large, and obviously many of them would enable firms and consumers to do better for themselves than they do using the naive behavior described in this chapter. Nevertheless, the essential principle that we have demonstrated for our simple examples will apply in any case, and that is that in a stochastic environment the behavior patterns that are acquired by any individual will inevitably incorporate some measure of error. Some consumers will search more than others simply because they happen to have had favorable experiences. Some firms may charge more than others because they have been lucky enough to have been visited recently by low-searching consumers. These "errors" then go on to enrich the stochastic environment in which the learning of others takes place. This point, of course, applies to optimal Bayesian search procedures (Rothschild, 1974b) as well as to the process described here. However, if it is a "rule" that is to be acquired rather than the behavior itself, these errors may include the acquisition of rules that have no "rational" basis: The consumer may come to search whenever $\Delta_t > \Delta_{t-1}$ and to stop otherwise, or he may go on searching whenever the last salesman encountered wore glasses. Many firms will learn to keep prices high at Christmas time, but some may be found to maintain high prices whenever the moon is full. In short, one might modify our model by making rules the objects of the feedback process, but it would be inconsistent with the spirit of this book to assume that consumers will apply only "good" rules.

Appendix

Property A: $C>0 \Rightarrow \phi_t < 1$ for large t.

Proof: Suppose we have a $\phi_t = 1$; then from (2.13) we have from (2.6) that

Case S: $\phi_{t+1} = 1$

Case F_1: $\phi_{t+1} = 1 - L(0, C + \Delta'_t - \Delta_{t+1}) < 1$

Case F_2: $\phi_{t+1} = 1 - L(0, C) < 1$

We would fail to encounter a $\phi_{t+1} < 1$ only if the household encountered an infinite sequence of successes, which is a sequence of Δ'_t's for which $\Delta_{t+1} \geqslant \Delta_t + C$ for all t. If the values of Δ are all bounded, this is impossible.

Property B: $C = 0 \Rightarrow \phi_T \geqslant \phi_0$ for any $\phi_0 < 1$.

Proof: Suppose we have a $\phi_t < 1$. Then, from (2.13),

Case S: $\quad \phi_{t+1} = \phi_t + L(\phi_t, \Delta_{t+1} - \Delta'_t - C) > \phi_t$

Case F_1: $\quad$ does not exist

Case F_2: $\quad \phi_{t+1} = \phi_t - L(\phi_t, 0) = \phi_t \quad$ by (2.7)

Therefore, because $L(\cdot)$ approaches 0 only at $\phi_t = 1$, $\phi_{t+1} \geqslant \phi_t$ always, and because in repeated trials successful searches will arise, search probabilities will rise monotonically toward 1.

Property C: Suppose the values of Δ have an upper bound Δ_{max}. $C > \Delta_{max} \Rightarrow \phi_T \leqslant \phi_0$ for any $\phi_0 > 0$.

Proof: Suppose $\phi_t > 0$.

Case S: $\quad$ never arises

Case F_1: $\quad \phi_{t+1} = \phi_t - L(1 - \phi_t, C + \Delta'_t - \Delta_{t+1}) < \phi_t$

Case F_2: $\quad \phi_{t+1} = \phi_t - L(1 - \phi_t, C) < \phi_t$

Thus, for very large search costs, search probability is monotonically decreasing toward 0.

Property H: For any $C < \Delta_{max}$, there exists a positive number ϵ such that $\xi(\phi_0) > \epsilon$ for any $0 < \phi_0 \leqslant 1$.

Proof: At the tth stage of the search process, Δ'_t is distributed according to some density function $\psi(\Delta'_t)$, and

$$E[\phi_{t+1}] = \int_0^1 E[\phi_{t+1} \mid \Delta'_t] \psi(\Delta'_t) \, d\Delta'_t$$

From equations (6.8) and (2.6) we have

$$\frac{dE[\phi_{t+1}]}{d\phi_t} > 0$$

and

$$\lim_{\phi_t \to 0} E[\phi_{t+1}] = 0 - 0 + \int_0^1 \int_{\Delta'_t + C}^{\infty} L(0, \Delta - \Delta'_t - C) \gamma(\Delta) \psi(\Delta'_t) \, d\Delta \, d\Delta'_t$$

By (2.8), the condition $C < \Delta_{max}$ guarantees that the integral expression is strictly positive, and therefore $E[P_{t+1}]$ has some minimal value $\epsilon_t > 0$. Because at every stage the search process is terminated with a probability $(1 - P_t)$, the value of $\bar{P}_T(P_0)$ is composed of a series of values of $E[P_{t+1}]$ weighted by the convergent series $1 - P_1, P_1(1 - P_2), P_1 P_2(1 - P_3), \ldots$, and therefore there is some value $\epsilon > 0$ with $\bar{P}_T(P_0) > \epsilon$ for any $0 < P_0 \leqslant 1$.

Proposition I: For every $C > 0$, there exists a unique distribution $g^*(\phi)$ that satisfies (2.16), with $g(\phi) = g'(\phi) = g^*(\phi)$ for all ϕ and with $g^*(0) = g^*(1) = 0$.

Proof: Define $\dot{H}(\phi_T, \phi) \equiv (1/\phi_T) h(\phi_T, \phi)$. By Property I, $H(\phi_T, \phi)$ is bounded by $\lim_{\phi_T \to 0} H(\phi_T, \phi) = 0$, and hence from Properties E, F, and G, $H(\phi_T, \phi)$ has a maximal value, M, for some pair (ϕ_T, ϕ) in the interior of $[0,1]^2$. Naturally, $H(\cdot)$ shares Properties E, F, and G with $h(\cdot)$.

Define $\bar{\phi} \equiv \int_0^1 \phi g(\phi) \, d\phi$ and a function

$$f(\phi_T) \equiv \bar{\phi} \int_0^1 \phi H(\phi_T, \phi) g(\phi) \, d\phi$$

Because $g(\phi) \geqslant 0$, we have $f(\phi_T) \leqslant \bar{\phi}^2 M$, and because $H(\phi_T, \phi) \geqslant h(\phi_T, \phi)$ for all $\phi_T \in (0,1]$, we have

$$f(\phi_T) \geqslant \bar{\phi} \int_0^1 \phi h(\phi_T, \phi) g(\phi) \, d\phi$$

Define $k \equiv \int_0^1 f(\phi_T) \, d\phi_T$, where we now have

$$\bar{\phi} \leqslant k \leqslant M \bar{\phi}^2 \tag{6.26}$$

Let $G(\phi_T) = f(\phi_T)/k$, and write the identity

$$G(\phi_T) = (1 - \phi_T) G(\phi_T) + \frac{1}{k} \phi_T f(\phi_T)$$

Multiplying the ϕ_T into $f(\phi_T)$, we obtain

$$G(\phi_T) = (1 - \phi_T) G(\phi_T) + \frac{1}{k} \bar{\phi} \int_0^1 \phi h(\phi_T, \phi) g(\phi) \, d\phi \tag{6.27}$$

Integrating over ϕ_T and rearranging terms,

$$\bar{\phi} \equiv \int_0^1 \phi_T g(\phi_T) \, d\phi_T = \frac{\bar{\phi}^2}{k} \tag{6.28}$$

We note, using (6.26), that $\bar{\phi}_T \geqslant 1/M$. If $\bar{\phi} \geqslant 1/M$, then $k \geqslant 1/M^2$ always, $\bar{\phi} \leqslant 1$ because $\int_0^1 g(\phi) \, d\phi = 1$, and hence $0 \leqslant G(\phi_T) \leqslant M^3$ for all ϕ_T in $[0,1]$.

Define l as a set of continuous functions $g(\cdot)$, with $g(0) = g(1) = 0$, $g(\phi) \geqslant 0$, $\int_0^1 \phi g(\phi) \, d\phi \geqslant 1/M$, and $\int_0^1 g(\phi) \, d\phi = 1$. If l is a closed, bounded, convex subset of L^1, and applying the bound on $G(\phi)$, we can use the Ascoli theorem to show that the function $G(\phi_T)$ defines a compact mapping from l to l (Munkres, 1975). Hence, by Schauder's fixed-point theorem (Smart, 1974), there exists a fixed point $g^*(\phi)$. From (6.28), the value of k at

$g^*(\phi)$ is $\bar{\phi}$, and substituting this into (6.27) we see that $g^*(\phi)$ is a fixed point for equation (2.16) as well.

Now suppose there are two fixed points $g_1(\phi)$ and $g_2(\phi)$. Define

$$\delta(\phi) \equiv \min[g_1(\phi), g_2(\phi)]$$

$$B_i(\phi) \equiv g_i(\phi) - \delta(\phi) \quad (i = 1, 2) \tag{6.29}$$

At a fixed point, equation (2.16) becomes

$$g_i(\phi_T) = \int_0^1 \phi H(\phi_T, \phi) g_i(\phi) \, d\phi$$

and using (6.29) we obtain

$$B_i(\phi_T) = \int_0^1 \phi H(\phi_T, \phi) B_i(\phi) \, d\phi + \int_0^1 \phi H(\phi_T, \phi) \delta(\phi) \, d\phi - \delta(\phi_T)$$

For every ϕ_T in $[0, 1]$, there is an i that gives $B_i(\phi_T) = 0$. By Property G, $\int_0^1 \phi H(\phi_T, \phi) B_i(\phi) \, d\phi \geq 0$, with the strict inequality holding for some of those values of ϕ_T for which $B_i(\phi_T) = 0$ (i.e., those values of ϕ_T that are no more than a units above a ϕ with $B_i(\phi) > 0$). Therefore, $\int_0^1 \phi H(\phi_T, \phi) \delta(\phi) \, d\phi - \delta(\phi_T) \leq 0$ for all ϕ_T, with the strict inequality holding for some ϕ_T. Multiplying by ϕ_T and integrating, we obtain

$$\int_0^1 \phi \delta(\phi) \, d\phi - \int_0^1 \phi_T \delta(\phi_T) \, d\phi_T < 0$$

and because this is impossible, we must have $B_i(\phi) = 0$ for all ϕ, which means the fixed point is unique.

Proposition II: For every perturbation in $g^*(\phi)$ that is s standard deviations away from ψ^*, there exists a learning rate $u_0 > 0$ such that equation (2.17) holds for all $u \leq u_0$.

Proof: Using (2.16), we have

$$\psi_T = \psi_0 + \int_0^1 \phi_0 g(\phi_0) [\xi(\phi_0) - \phi_0] \, d\phi_0$$

The expression $\phi_0 [\xi(\phi_0) - \phi_0]$ is a generally declining function of ϕ_0, because $\xi(\phi_0) > \epsilon$ and $\xi(1) < 1$, and so long as this function has a negative slope, distortions in $g(\phi_0)$ that put greater weight on larger values of ϕ_0 (thereby increasing ψ_0) will necessarily increase ψ_T by less, thus satisfying (2.17). Unfortunately, exceptions to the negative slope are found in the neighborhood of $\phi_0 = 0$. However, we have already noted that the function $\xi(\phi)$

has a fixed point at $\phi = \phi^*$, and so long as ϕ^* is unique, the negative slope is guaranteed in the neighborhood of ϕ^*, and (2.17) holds. Now, as the rate of learning $u \to 0$, $h(\phi_T, \phi^*)$ approaches a "spike" around ϕ^*, $g^*(\phi) \to h(\phi_T, \phi^*)$, $\psi^* \to \phi^*$, and, by the uniqueness of ψ^*, ϕ^* is unique. For any distortion that is, say, s standard deviations away from ϕ^*, we can find a u_0 small enough to put that distortion in the vicinity of ϕ^*, where (2.17) must hold.

Proposition III: For stable distributions, high search costs reduce search activity: $d\psi^*/dC < 0$.

 Proof: Consider any indefinite sequences of quotes $\Delta_1, \Delta_2, \Delta_3, \ldots$. Corresponding to this is a sequence of search probabilities $\phi_0, \phi_1, \phi_2, \ldots$. The expected terminal value of P from this sequence is $\phi^e = \sum_{t=1}^{\infty} \phi_t^2 \prod_{i=1}^{t-1} (1 - \phi_i)$, which is the sum of the stopping probabilities times the associated values of ϕ_t at the time of stopping. From the learning function, we have $\partial \phi_t / \partial C = \partial \phi_{t-1} / \partial C + \partial L(\phi_t, R)/\partial C$, and because every $\partial L(\phi_t, R)/\partial C < 0$, we must have $\partial \phi_t / \partial C < \sum_{i=1}^{t-1} \partial \phi_i / \partial C \leq 0$ for all $t \geq 2$. This condition is readily shown to be sufficient for $\partial \phi^e / \partial C < 0$, and because this applies to all values of ϕ_0 and to all sequences of quotes, it follows that $d\psi_T/dC < 0$ as well. If we begin with an equilibrium distribution $g_1^*(\phi)$, with ψ_1^*, then increasing C will lead to a $\psi_T < \psi_1^*$, and (2.17) implies that the new equilibrium distribution $g_2^*(\phi)$ must have $\psi_2^* < \psi_1^*$.

CHAPTER 7

Inflationary disequilibrium

For our third application of the general feedback theory, we develop a model of asymmetric price behavior in an economy. It is often alleged that prices and wages are influenced by "ratchet" mechanisms whereby certain prices can be readily induced to rise but display considerable resistance to downward pressures. The reluctance of trade unions to accept downward revisions in wage rates is often cited as an example of this phenomenon. Recently, a number of economists (Vining and Elwertowski, 1976; Parks, 1978) have noticed the existence of a positive association between the mean rate of inflation (or, in Parks's version, a proposed measure of the rate of unexpected inflation) and the variance of individual price changes around this mean. The most common argument is that high rates of inflation are responsible for instability in relative prices, and Parks, in particular, has outlined a number of theories to that effect. The data, however, are equally consistent with a reversal in the direction of causality, in which disequilibrium in individual markets is considered to be responsible for inflation, through the proposed ratchet mechanism.

It is difficult to find any convincing theoretical underpinning in rational behavior for this ratchet, however. Even in the frequently cited case of the labor union, it is not clear why the asymmetric price behavior would be in the self-interest of workers. (Why not simply seek as high a wage as possible in any period?) This being the case, it is well worthwhile to exploit the fact that feedback processes are well defined for disequilibrium and look for some source of asymmetry within this mechanism. Such an approach is of special interest because it suggests the possibility of a microeconomic view of inflation that could be compared with existing aggregative models of the process.

By "disequilibrium" we refer to a short-run state wherein the sellers in a market are not behaving identically, but are selling similar goods at different prices or are imposing different supply restrictions on their products. We argued in the last chapter that such a state may be normal for a market in which a feedback process determines behavior, but even if the market is usually characterized by a single price equilibrium, a short-run disequilibrium may arise because of some exogenous factor price change, a factor supply restriction, or a sudden change in the composition of the

131

market. These events in themselves need not produce disequilibrium (all suppliers might conceivably respond to a factor supply restriction by imposing identical rules of rationing on their customers), but differences in inventory reorder dates, differences in exposure to a changed market (farmland may vary in distance from a proposed highway), and differences among managers' responses to external shocks will ordinarily produce temporary variations among even highly competitive sellers.

From the consumer standpoint, all of these variations amount simply to different firms imposing different prices, ranging from "discounts" to "exorbitant" prices together with delivery delays.[1] For our purposes, it is convenient to compress all of the dimensions of cost into a single price variable P_i that we shall describe as the "price" charged by firm i.

Consumers may well be unaware of the circumstances that have produced the disequilibrium, and even when they do recognize that a disequilibrium exists, they do not have ready access to the detailed market information that would be required before they could exploit the situation deliberately. This is not a setting, for example, in which one could reasonably estimate a market price distribution and apply optimal search procedures. However, we can apply a feedback model, because even when consumers do not consciously "search," they do "remember," and each experience with a supplier, and its price, will influence the choice of supplier when subsequent occasions for consumption of the good arise. For the sake of contrast to the durables market that was treated in the last chapter, we shall use as an archetype the supermarket shopper who always buys something from a visited supplier, although how much is bought depends naturally on the price charged at that location. This assumes, in effect, that even in the short run, market forces are sufficient to prevent prices from rising so high that consumers would be willing to incur the cost of abandoning the seller and seeking out a competitor before buying anything at all.

A model of supermarket selection

We shall apply our model to a household by using the elements of the vector Φ_t to describe the likelihood that the household will purchase from firms $1, \ldots, n$ during period t. We define the units of t so that only one firm is visited per period. Suppose that the household visits firm i and finds a lower price than was encountered at some previous supplier j. We naturally expect this experience to lead to an increased tendency to buy

[1] "Infinite" prices – that is, permanent unavailability of the product – will be assumed not to arise, as it would be more appropriate to catalogue such events under "catastrophe" rather than "disequilibrium."

from i and a decrease in the likelihood of future visits to j. Whether or not we wish a model in which the propensity to visit j can fall toward zero as an asymptote depends on how we visualize our selection mechanism. Sophisticated search procedures may, under some circumstances, produce a significantly higher asymptote: If the shopper is consciously searching for a low price under unstable conditions, the location j may continue to be visited regularly as part of a conscious information-gathering effort.

Formally, we use the difference $P_j - P_i$ as the net payoff and set $I = i$ in equation (2.1), concluding that $\phi_{i,t+1} > \phi_{i,t}$ and $\phi_{j,t+1} < \phi_{j,t}$ in accordance with condition (2.2). If the price at firm i were higher than P_j, then the argument would be reversed: It is the trip to firm j that is reinforced, and we set $I = j$ and payoff equal to $P_i - P_j$, concluding that $\phi_{i,t+1} < \phi_{i,t}$ and $\phi_{j,t+1} > \phi_{j,t}$. If $P_i = P_j$ (as might occur if the same firm were encountered twice), then there is no effect on the values in Φ_t, and the current likelihood vector will be preserved.

Our procedure of applying the model to whichever firm has the lower price has the incidental consequence of guaranteeing that Θ is nonnegative, and we need not concern ourselves with the definition of $\hat{\Theta}$, or with the questions whether or not, under more general circumstances, $L(\cdot)$ is symmetric around $\Theta = \hat{\Theta}$ and whether or not "punishments" have as well-known behavioral consequences as positive payoffs.

In principle, comparisons between firms' prices may extend over many time periods. Ideally, perhaps, we might assume that each new price is compared with all previously encountered prices, with the strength of the learned adjustment declining with increases in the time lag between the two samples. The mathematics of such a model would be extraordinarily cumbersome, however, and we shall therefore confine this chapter to just a piece of the process, restricting the model to comparisons across adjacent time periods. Because similar models can be constructed to compare any pair of time periods, and because such models would have qualitative implications identical to those of the model we shall use, there seems to be very little lost in making such a simplification. A consequence of this assumption is that when a price P_i is encountered, a comparison is made between that and the preceding price P_j, but we do not attempt to specify comparisons with the prices of any other firms k. Because there is no particular reason why the comparison between P_i and P_j should influence the willingness to buy from third firms whose prices are not (by this assumption) being considered, we shall apply the feedback to $\phi_{i,t+1}$ and $\phi_{j,t+1}$, but we shall leave $\phi_{k,t+1} = \phi_{k,t}$ for all $k \neq i, j$. Because it no longer matters which price was sampled first, this procedure permits us to suppress the index i in the feedback function if we indicate what comparison is being made by replacing Θ by the indexed Θ_{ij}. It follows that $L^i(\Phi_t, \Theta_{ij}) = -L^j(\Phi_t, \Theta_{ij})$.

Following similar reasoning, there is no cause for expecting the value of $\phi_{k,t}$ for some third firm, k, to affect the outcome of a comparison between the prices of firms i and j, and thus the only relevant terms in the argument Φ_t would seem to be $\phi_{i,t}$ and $\phi_{j,t}$. From condition (2.6), however, we know that whenever $P_i < P_j$, we must have $-L^j(\Phi_t, \Theta_{ij}) < \phi_{j,t}$, and the importance of this bound suggests that it might be natural to assume further that whenever $P_i < P_j$, the function $L^i(\cdot)$ depends only on the element $\phi_{j,t}$ in the vector Φ_t. (In fact, the "proportional" model is a special case of this formulation.) The implications of our model do not seem to be affected in any significant way if we use this assumption, but the notation is simplified so dramatically as to make its adoption very compelling; for this reason, we shall replace $L^i(\phi_t, \Theta_{ij})$ with the form $L(\phi_{j,t}, \Theta_{ij})$ whenever $P_i < P_j$.

Define $B(i)$ and $W(i)$ as subsets containing all firms whose prices are respectively lower ("better") and higher ("worse") than that of firm i:

$$B(i) \equiv \{j \mid P_j < P_i\}$$
$$W(i) \equiv \{j \mid P_j > P_i\} \tag{7.1}$$

For a particular household, the value of Φ_t depends on its shopping history. Suppose that we know this history up to period $t - 2$, so that the vector Φ_{t-1} is known. Define $\Phi_t^i \equiv \phi_{1,t}^i, \ldots, \phi_{n,t}^i$ as the conditional value of Φ_t given that i was visited during $t - 1$. Now the value of $\phi_{i,t+1}$ depends on whether firm i was sampled during t or $t - 1$, and on the difference between its price and that of the other firm that was encountered over those same two periods. The likelihood that any firm j was encountered is given by the elements of the vectors Φ_t and Φ_{t-1}, and we can use these likelihoods, together with the feedback model, to determine an expected value for $\Phi_{i,t+1}$:

$$E[\phi_{i,t+1}] = E[\phi_{i,t}] + \sum_{j \in W(i)} \{\phi_{j,t-1}\phi_{i,t}^j L(\phi_{j,t}^j, \Theta_{ij}) + \phi_{i,t-1}\phi_{j,t}^i L(\phi_{j,t}^i, \Theta_{ij})\}$$

$$- \sum_{j \in B(i)} \{\phi_{j,t-1}\phi_{i,t}^j L(\phi_{i,t}^j, \Theta_{ij}) + \phi_{i,t-1}\phi_{j,t}^i L(\phi_{i,t}^i, \Theta_{ij})\} \tag{7.2}$$

where $E[\phi_{i,t}] = \Sigma\phi_{j,t-1}\phi_{i,t}^j$ and firms' prices are assumed to be held constant.

Equation (7.2) refers to learned adjustments that come about from actual encounters with sellers. Naturally, the household may also be exposed to price information through other sources: word of mouth, newspaper advertisements, catalogues, or posted displays of price lists.

This sort of communication is to be discussed in the next chapter, but in any case it does not seem likely to have any significant effect on the character of the model; once we move to the market level, the information flows are presumably similar to Φ_t, because the sources of information concerning a firm's price are all closely related to the volume of that firm's sales. Therefore, although it might generalize the model somewhat to introduce two probability vectors (one for direct household encounters, and the other for other information flows), we shall be content to carry on with equation (7.2) as it stands.

The process described by equation (7.2) can be extended over several periods. Corresponding to every sequence of choices j, k made during $t-1$ and t, there is a value Φ_{t+1}^{jk} that can then be used to determine an expected value for $\phi_{i,t+2}$. Weighting these expected values by the likelihoods of j during $t-1$ and the conditional likelihoods of k during t, we can obtain a value of $E[\phi_{i,t+2}]$. In similar fashion, we can obtain values of $E[\phi_{i,t+h}]$ over any number h of time periods. Using the conditions (2.1) through (2.8) of the learning function, we can ascribe the following properties to each of these estimates:

A. $E[\phi_{i,t+h}]$ is a continuous function of the elements of Φ_{t-1} and the price vector and is continuously differentiable in the elements of Φ_{t-1}. This follows from the fact that $L(\cdot)$ is continuously differentiable and from the fact that taking weighted averages is a continuous operation. The derivative of $E[\phi_{i,t+h}]$ with respect to price elements is not continuous at the points $P_i = P_j$, however, because even though $L^i(\Phi_t, I, 0) = 0$, different functions apply when $P_i > P_j$ and when $P_j > P_i$.

B. $\{P_i = P_j$ for all $i, j\} \Rightarrow E[\phi_{i,t+h}] = \phi_{i,t}$ for all h.

C. Define M to be the set of all firms whose prices are minimal. Then, for all $i \in M$, $\sum_{i \in M} \phi_{i,t} < 1$ implies $E[\phi_{i,t+h}] > \phi_{i,t}$. That is, if there are any firms making sales at prices higher than the minimum, then the sales of firms in M can be expected to grow. For firms in M, the set $B(i)$ is empty, and $\phi_{i,t+1} > \phi_{i,t}$ whenever a firm with a higher price is encountered. So long as $\phi_{j,t} > 0$ for some higher-priced firm j, the expected value of ϕ_i will rise over time.

D. For the highest-priced firms, sales can be expected to fall. That is, $E[\phi_{i,t+h}] < \phi_{i,t}$. This is because the set $W(i)$ is empty for the highest-priced firms. However, it is possible for firms whose prices are above the prices of many of their competitors to enjoy at least temporarily growing values of ϕ. For example, if prices, Φ_{t-1}, and Φ_t were uniformly distributed, equation (2.3) would give $E[\phi_{i,t+1}] > \phi_{i,t}$ for every firm whose price is below the mean. The reason for this is that for Φ_t uniform, most of the price comparisons in which these firms are involved are favorable, and the consumer learns to go to them more often. As time passes, the highest-priced firms lose and the lowest-priced firms gain in household visits, and as a consequence, the intermediate-priced firms are subjected to unfavorable comparisons more and more frequently, until they, too, begin to suffer consumer losses. Eventually, of course, if the prices do not change, only the lowest-priced firms will retain the household as a customer. That is, $\lim_{h \to \infty} E[\phi_{i,t+h}] = 0$ for all i not in M. This, of course, is the counterpart of the general convergence theorem proved in Chapter 2.

Market demand

If there are N consumers in the market who are following the adjustment process just described, then we can aggregate their behaviors to obtain a market demand. For example, if initially all consumers have the same values of Φ_t, then we can use $E[\phi_{i,t+h}]$ directly to estimate the market share of firm i at time $t+h$.

Because different households normally have different shopping histories, their vectors Φ_t will not be the same, and the aggregation of N versions of equation (7.2) cannot be performed directly. We shall use an approximation to this aggregation, therefore, by using expected values at the market level in place of the individual $\phi_{i,t}$'s in equation (7.2). The same approximation can be used for the conditional elements $\phi_{i,t}^j$, as this will introduce no more than a second-order error into the model. Thus, if we define $S_{i,t}$ to be the "market share" of firm i at time t (the fraction of the population that can be expected to visit firm i at time t), our approximation to an aggregation of equation (7.2) across the population N becomes

$$S_{i,t+1} = S_{i,t} + \sum_{j \in W(i)} \{S_{j,t-1} S_{i,t} + S_{j,t} S_{i,t-1}\} L(S_{j,t}, \Theta_{ij})$$
$$- \sum_{j \in B(i)} \{S_{j,t-1} S_{i,t} + S_{j,t} S_{i,t-1}\} L(S_{i,t}, \Theta_{ij}) \qquad (7.3)$$

As it stands, this model is strongly reminiscent of Phelps and Winter's image (1970) of demand conditions in a market characterized by "noninstantaneous customer response to price changes." Although equation (7.3) is not precisely equivalent to it, the feedback theory may be interpreted as formal support for the market-adjustment equation that Phelps and Winter accepted without derivation. However, the primary objective of that study was the application of optimal control to a firm's pricing problem in such a market, and as an application of traditional optimization techniques in a partial-disequilibrium setting, the Phelps-Winter model encounters severe difficulties with the formulation of plausible expectations functions. Indeed, their analysis requires that each firm disregard entirely the possibility that its competitors follow decision rules similar to its own. We shall follow quite a different course here and assume that the pricing behavior of firms obeys the same kind of learning process that we used to obtain the shopping behavior of consumers.

Firms' profit functions

We could apply the feedback mechanism formally by associating a probability with each of a finite set of prices that might be chosen by a firm, and then use ex post profit level as a reinforcer that would induce a transition from one probability vector to another. The mathematics of such a model would be formidable, however, and it proves to be sufficient for our purposes just to describe the schedule of payoffs – that is, the functional dependence of profit on price – and then appeal to the proposition that adaptive firms will incline toward charging prices that are associated with the largest profits.

The variable P was defined to include consumer costs that go beyond simple product price, but we shall assume that sales restrictions that impose such costs on consumers also reduce the cost to the firm of providing the product (by reducing inventory costs or by avoiding the need to pay temporarily "exorbitant" factor prices), so that for any given level of sales, profit varies directly with P. Conventional demand elasticities need not be restricted, beyond the assumption of a concave household expenditure function $R(P)$, so that expected revenue during t to firm i from that household will be $\phi_{i,t} R(P_i)$. This means that in our terminology, "market share" refers to the fraction of households that visit firm i, but not to the fraction of total market revenue that is received by that firm.

Suppose that T is the length of the accounting period over which a firm evaluates its profits. There is no particular reason for T to match the length of a typical consumer cycle. If $T<1$, then equation (7.3) applies to only a fraction $1/T$ of consumers, and profits will be earned only from this fraction. If $T>1$, then total sales are obtained from a series of learning cycles, and profits earned over T are the sum of (changing) profits over the period.

The longer the accounting period, the greater the dependence of market share on the firm's current price. That is, if we have $T \leqslant 1$, then the number of customers who approach firm i is determined entirely by previously established buying habits, and the price charged by the firm influences sales in this period through the mechanism of the demand function alone. Such a firm might well come to behave as a monopolist, as in the case described by Diamond (1971). For greater values of T, customers learn to avoid high-priced firms, and sales within the accounting period are determined by consumer adjustments as well as demand elasticity. This dependence of the apparent revenue flow on the length of the accounting period is not so unconventional as it may at first appear. T in our ex post learning model operates like a discount rate in a full-information planning model. Short accounting periods have effects similar to high discount rates, and long accounting periods will lead to learned behavior similar to that which would arise if the discount rate were very low.

We noted in the last section (property A) that $E[\phi_{i,t+h}]$ is not continuously differentiable in the elements of the price vector. The same restriction therefore applies to $S_{i,t+h}$. We could smooth $S_{i,t+h}$ if we were to introduce a smooth distribution of firms along the price continuum [so that a change in P_i would continuously transfer firms from one of the sets $B(i)$ and $W(i)$ to the other], but this would require the assumption of atomistic firms, and we mean this theory to apply to imperfectly competitive markets as well. Instead, we shall introduce a continuous distribution function that is to be regarded as an approximation to the array of prices that are charged by the competitors of firm i. This procedure is necessary because we wish to investigate the slope of the profit function of firm i, and otherwise that slope is not always defined. Thus, let $f(s,x)$ be a joint density function that describes the distribution of market shares, s, and prices, x, that can be observed during period $t-1$ among the competitors to firm i. We shall assume that $f(\cdot)$ is continuous, and, by definition,

$$\int_0^1 \int_0^\infty f(s,x)\,dx\,ds = 1 - S_{i,t-1} \tag{7.4}$$

Define $f'(s,x)$ as a similar density function that applies during time t.

Suppose that firm i charged a price P_i' during period $t-1$ and is now charging P_i during time t. We can now use a continuous version of equation (7.3) to describe the expected market share for firm i during period $t+1$:

$$S_{i,t+1} = A + S_{i,t} \int_0^1 \left(\int_{P_i}^\infty L(s,x-P_i)f(s,x)\,dx \right.$$
$$\left. - \int_0^{P_i} L(S_{i,t},P_i-x)f(s,x)\,dx \right) ds \tag{7.5}$$

where

$$A \equiv S_{i,t} + S_{i,t-1} \int_0^1 \left(\int_{P_i'}^{\infty} L(s, x - P_i') f'(s, x) \, dx \right.$$

$$\left. - \int_0^{P_i'} L(S_{i,t}, P_i' - x) f'(s, x) \, dx \right) ds$$

The terms described by A in equation (7.5) are matters of history and are outside the control of firm i during period t. They are functions of the firm's previous price P', the market share with which it entered the period, and the price/market-share distribution of other firms during t.

Because $\partial L(\phi, \Theta)/\partial \Theta > 0$ from condition (2.1), and $L(\phi, 0) = 0$, it is easy to see that $\partial S_{i,t+1}/\partial P < 0$; that is, increases in price will lead to reductions in the expected market share of firm i in period $t+1$. We expect a similar result if firm i chooses a price P_i and maintains it for several periods. In this case, however, the problem is made more complicated by the fact that in calculating $S_{i,t+2}, S_{i,t+3}$, and so on, we must take account of the effect of P_i in determining market shares of firms other than i. Because of the mathematical complexity of this problem, proofs that for any h, $S_{i,t+h}$ decreases with increases in P_i generally require the use of special cases or simplifying approximations whenever $h > 1$.[2] In order to avoid these difficulties, we shall confine the model that follows to the case in which $T = 2$. This permits us to retain the general form of equation (7.5) without losing the essential character of our model in which the firm is confronted with a very short run monopoly position together with a longer-run sensitivity of market share to price.

Define $S_T(P)$ to be the sum of the expected market shares of the firm over the two periods: $S_T(P) \equiv S_{i,t} + S_{i,t+1}$. The expected revenue to be received by the firm over T is then proportional to $R(P)S_T(P)$. Because the introduction of production cost does not seem to alter our model in any significant way, it is convenient for us to disregard costs and use $R(P)S_T(P)$ as the firm's profit function. (Of course, if marginal cost is constant, it may be introduced notationally by defining P to be the excess of price over marginal cost.) We shall make the conventional assumptions that $R(P)$ has a maximum at some unique price, that $R(0) \leqslant 0$, and that the second derivative, $R''(P)$, exists and is negative throughout.

[2] One possible procedure, for example, is to assert that the normalized density functions, $f(s, x)$ divided by $1 - S_{i,t}$, are unaffected by changes in P so long as the prices charged by all the competitors of firm i are unchanged. This assumes, in effect, that the aggregate market shares of firms other than i are a function of P, but that the distribution of this aggregate among individual firms is not. Substituting this into equation (2.6) eliminates the interaction between P and the distribution functions leading to unambiguous reductions in $S_{i,t+h}$ when P is increased.

Because $S_T(P) > 0$, and $\partial S_T(P)/\partial P < 0$, it follows that the product $R(P)S_T(P)$ also has a maximum (or several maxima), and this maximum (or these maxima) must arise at some price less than the monopoly price [the P that maximizes $R(P)$].

Because of the stochastic nature of household buying behavior, realized revenue during T may not correspond to the product $R(P)S_T(P)$, and a firm that learns to price from its own profit history might not choose a maximizing value of P even if the function $R(P)S_T(P)$ were stationary over time. For example, we have already described cases in which the concavity of the learning function will induce apparently risk-averse pricing. In order to avoid this complication, we shall assume that each firm faces a very large number of customers, so that is is almost always sufficient to replace the distribution of values of ϕ_i with the certainty equivalent S_i in determining realized revenue.

Equilibrium

Our basic proposition is that firms learn to price from their market experiences, so that prices that are associated with large payoffs are encouraged, whereas prices that produce lower payoffs are used less and less frequently. If the payoff function $R(P)S_T(P)$ is stationary, the firm will eventually learn to charge only profit-maximizing prices. In this context, the appropriate equilibrium concept is the single-price Nash-type equilibrium in which n firms (with identical cost functions) share the market equally and in which, given a common price P^* being charged by its competitors, a firm with a share of $1/n$ of the market finds that its own profit function is maximized at P^* as well. So long as a unique price P^* is optimal, the learning by firms will preserve the stationary value of $R(P)S_T(P)$, and the market will stay in equilibrium.

It is shown in the Appendix that if it exists, this unique price P^* is given by

$$2R'(P^*) - \frac{n-1}{n} L_2\left(\frac{1}{n}, 0\right) R(P^*) = 0 \tag{7.6}$$

Equation (7.6) reflects the expected property that if $n = 1$, the equilibrium price is the (unique) monopoly price that maximizes $R(P)$. For larger values of n, $R'(P^*)$ must exceed the monopoly value, because by condition (2.2), $L_2(\cdot)$ is positive, and from the concavity of $R(\cdot)$, we conclude that for larger values of n, equilibrium price is below monopoly price.

The equilibrium price does not decrease monotonically with increases in n; in fact, as n becomes very large, the equilibrium price actually returns toward the monopoly price again. We observed earlier that whenever $P_i < P_j$, condition (2.6) requires that $L^i(\Phi_t, \Theta) < \phi_{j,t}$. In equilibrium, $\phi_{j,t} = 1/n$, and therefore as n grows indefinitely large, it follows that $L^i(\Phi_t, \Theta)$ approaches 0. Applied to our simplified form of the learning equation, this requires $\lim_{n \to \infty} L(1/n, \Theta) = 0$ for any value of $\Theta \geqslant 0$. Because $L(\cdot)$ is continuously differentiable, this requires in turn that $\lim_{n \to \infty} L_2(1/n, \Theta) = 0$ for any $\Theta \geqslant 0$. Equation (7.6) then converges toward $R'(P) = 0$ when n is large, and we are back to monopoly pricing. This result is not a contradiction to the standard proposition that large numbers of firms contribute to competitive pricing ($P^* = 0$), because it arises in a context of poor buyer information. In effect, n is an index of the number of different firms that a household can be expected to visit over its lifetime. As n grows large, the likelihood that any buyer will visit the same seller twice approaches zero, and consequently the loss of market share that will follow from monopoly pricing becomes negligible. The empirical counterpart to this case is a "tourist trap" (or, more precisely, the set of all tourist traps together. Because tourists rarely visit the same shop twice, high prices are no deterrent to future sales, and thus geographic areas with large transient populations are likely to experience prices at monopoly levels even when there are many potential sellers in the same area.

The equilibrium we have defined requires not only that the stationary point described by (7.6) provide a maximum for the product $R(P)S_T(P)$ but also that this maximum be unique. If there are several maximal values for P, then a firm might learn to ignore distinctions between them, and although moving from one price to another might not affect current profits, it would alter future market shares. The function $S_T(P)$ would no longer be stationary, and we would have no equilibrium.

Much more interesting is the possibility that a single price equilibrium does not even exist: The stationary point described by P^* may not maximize individual firms' profit functions. In fact, examples in which the second-order conditions are violated at P^* are very easy to find (the general derivation is provided in the Appendix). Suppose that the revenue function is derived from a linear demand curve: $R(P) = aP - bP^2$, and the learning function takes the form $L(\phi, \Theta) = \Theta\phi/(\Theta + K)$, where K is some positive constant. Obtaining the necessary derivatives, and substituting them into (7.6), we can solve for P^*:

$$P^* = \frac{a}{2b} + \frac{2}{E} - \left[\left(\frac{a}{2b} \right)^2 + \left(\frac{2}{E} \right)^2 \right]^{1/2} \tag{7.7}$$

where $E = (n-1)/n^2 K$.

Using the derivation provided in the Appendix, the second derivative has the sign of

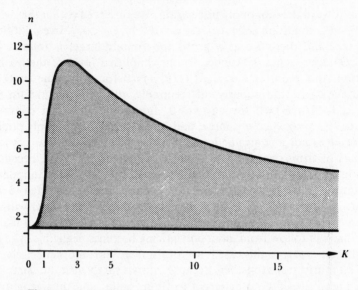

Figure 7.1. Combinations of n and a learning parameter K that preclude stationary equilibria.

$$-4b - \frac{2(nE-1)}{n}(a - 2bP^*) \qquad (7.8)$$

The shaded area in Figure 7.1 describes the combinations of n and K that produce a positive second derivative for the class of cases $a=1$ and $b=0.01$. For example, if $n=3$ and $K=2$, equation (7.6) gives $P^*=14.86$, but (7.8) has a value of $+0.27$. A negative second derivative arises for large values of n, because for large n the price approaches monopoly levels and the concavity of the revenue function dominates the sign. Large values of K also lead to a negative sign, because a large K signifies a low consumer learning rate, and this low learning rate has the effect of insulating a firm from its competitors. Price again tends toward monopoly levels, and again the concavity of the revenue function will determine the sign of (7.8).

The main implication of these results is that under many circumstances it is impossible for a firm's market-share function $S_T(P)$ to be stationary. At different points in time, different prices are profit-maximizing, and because of the lags inherent in the feedback process, no firm can be expected to learn to charge a fixed price.

It might be possible to define a kind of "long-run" price distribution. If we restrict the set of alternative prices to a finite number $P_1, \ldots, P_m$ and define a vector $Q_{i,t}$ to be the vector of probabilities with which firm i

chooses to charge each of these prices during an accounting period T that begins at t, then we can use realized profits over T as the reinforcers in a learning model to determine $Q_{i,t+1}$. Actual prices charged during this period also determine market-share equations $S_{i,t+2}$ for each firm in the market, and the process is repeated. If we were to consider an indefinite sequence of such iterations and then calculate mean values for each element in Q_i, we could use the fact that the learning model is a compact operator to show that these mean values are found in a unique price distribution.

This long-run distribution, however, would be of little practical interest, because there is no reason to expect the elements of $Q_{i,t}$, or even the mean values of these elements over all firms during t, to correspond to it. For small values of n, the iterations we have described will take the entire market through stochastic cycles, and there is no way to know where in such a cycle a market might be found at any specified time. Moreover, attempts to "smooth" the process by increasing the number of firms would be inappropriate here, because, as we have noted, large values of n change the equilibrium properties of the model, and the distribution will collapse into a single-price Nash equilibrium.

Disequilibrium

The main argument of this chapter is that disequilibrium can be inflationary. Specifically, if we replace an equilibrium at P^* with a price distribution around P^*, we shall not discover equilibrating forces that drive prices back to P^* in the short run. Instead, we shall encounter generally upward price pressures that will lead to mean prices higher than P^*. Formally, this comes about because of the concavity of the feedback process. The slope of the profit function faced by a firm depends in part on the responsiveness of market share to changes in price, and this in turn depends on the responsiveness of $L(S_{i,t}, P_i - x)$ to changes in P_i; that is, it depends on $L_2(S_{i,t}, P_i - x)$. However, increases in the dispersion of prices around P^* generally increase the values of $P_i - x$, and by the concavity of $L(\cdot)$, this *reduces* $L_2(S_{i,t}, P_i - x)$. Thus, the opportunity cost of price increases in terms of loss of market share is reduced, and any firm charging the old equilibrium price P^* will find higher profits to be associated with higher prices (a formal proof of all of this is provided in the Appendix).

The argument is easily expressed in heuristic terms: The price charged by a firm is held below monopoly levels by conventional competitive forces. Increases in price dispersions weaken those competitive forces by isolating firms from one another in the market. Small price adjustments that look important when firms are charging similar prices look unimportant when prices are far apart. Of course, firms with low prices may be selling much more product than others, but for any firm, the marginal sales loss from increasing price is reduced in the presence of large price differences among firms. Thus, increases in price dispersion lead to decreases in competitive pressures, and prices naturally tend more toward monopoly levels.

In order to implement the feedback model, we must argue that managers no longer "know" or even "think" that they know what the new optimal price is. Instead, the pricing behavior of each manager is described by some probability density function [which in turn contributes to the function $f(s, x)$ that is faced by his competitors]. One might imagine that each manager consciously experiments with different prices, using perhaps some Bayesian decision rule, although a more strict learning interpretation would hold that pricing decisions are random (or are determined by unknowable internal psychological variables) and are governed only by the established density function. The learning process is slowed by the fact that individual pricing histories add "noise" to the profit function [through changes in the term A in equation (7.5)]; nevertheless, until market shares are substantially altered, higher profits will be associated with prices above P^*, and managers will learn to charge higher prices on average.

Beyond this initial upward pressure on prices, it is difficult to provide a formal description of the dynamic course of events, because with different firms displaying different pricing histories, market shares will change, and the profit functions of firms begin to differ. If firms with lower market shares have profit functions that are maximized at prices that are lower than the prices that maximize the profit functions of firms with larger market shares, then cyclic patterns will develop. On the other hand, if large market shares are associated with relatively low profit-maximizing prices, then the initial price increase may begin to be offset as customers move to lower-priced firms, further increasing their market share, and rendering higher-priced firms insignificant in the average. We note, however, that as a firm's market share becomes very large ($S_{i,t}$ approaches 1), optimal price approaches the monopoly price [because $f(s, x)$ approaches 0 for all (s, x) as $S_{i,t}$ approaches 1, and the profit function is then maximized at $R'(P) = 0$]. It is impossible, therefore, for the market to converge to a state in which one firm with a minimal price dominates the market, because such a firm will learn of the profitability of monopoly-level prices, and its price will rise. Thus, some cyclic pricing behavior will always occur.

We can provide a qualitative impression of the dynamic course of events if we suppose for the moment that as a consequence of this cyclic pricing pattern, firms maintain market shares that are near to $1/n$, and if we suppose that there exists a single price P_g that maximizes the profit function over a range of market shares in the neighborhood of $1/n$. Because firms will then be identical, we can argue that each will learn from the same reinforcement (reward) structure, and hence the prices charged by each will obey the same distribution. Let us use a density function $g(P)$ to describe the likelihood with which any firm will charge a price P. Because with all firms identical we have $f(1/n, x) = [(n-1)/n]g(P)$, we know from our previous argument that P_g is an increasing function of the spread of $g(P)$ and that at the point of the initial disturbance, $P_g > P^*$. As firms learn to associate higher profits with higher prices, naturally the value of $g(P)$ will increase for higher values of P and decrease for lower values of P. This rightward shift in $g(P)$ will increase P_g still more because it reduces the frequency of low prices and hence reduces the frequency with which a high-priced firm loses market share through unfavorable comparisons with its competitors. Thus, $g(P)$ will shift further rightward as firms learn that still higher prices are profitable.

This inflation cannot go on indefinitely, however, because of the concavity of the revenue function: The price P_g can never rise as high as the monopoly level. Eventually, the rightward shift of $g(P)$ will have to slow down. As $g(P)$ begins to stabilize, firms will face more stationary profit functions, and they will become more adept at pricing at P_g. This, in turn, will reduce the spread of $g(P)$, and our argument will operate in reverse: P_g declines. Finally, the system moves back toward the original equilibrium as firms learn P_g, $g(P)$ contracts, and P_g falls. Clearly, however, this restoration toward equilibrium must be extremely slow compared with the original inflation, because as P_g falls, firms' previous learning becomes obsolete. Prices that formerly were profitable are now too high, and the contraction in $g(P)$ is impeded. The problem is that $g(P)$ must contract around P^*, not around its mean, and this process requires that firms continually learn and then unlearn the use of all the prices above P^*.

We expect the same general description to apply in cases that lack a single-price Nash equilibrium. We note that such markets will be characterized in general by prices that exceed the value of P^* that satisfies (7.6). The reason for this is that so long as market shares are approximately equal, all profit functions will be maximized at prices that exceed $\bar{x}$ unless $\bar{x}$ itself is above P^*. The market could not sustain for long a price distribution with mean below P^*, because all firms would come to learn that higher prices are more profitable, and $\bar{x}$ would rise.

If there is no single-price Nash equilibrium, then there may be no stable price distribution that can be used as a benchmark for evaluating the consequences of disequilibrating shocks. Nevertheless, it is still the case that if we replace the distribution $f(s,x)$ with some mean-preserving $f^*(s,x)$, the profit function for firm i will be maximized at a higher price than before. Thus, our proposition still holds that if the market is subjected to a disequilibrating disturbance, prices will be inclined to rise above the levels that would have been observed otherwise. The dynamic course of events will then be similar to what we have described for the simple case, except that the market will not return to the earlier cyclic pattern.

Discussion

The belief that inflation is partially attributable to exogenous disturbances to an economy is hardly a new one. So-called structural models already attribute inflationary pressures to the disequilibria that may arise from different growth rates in different sectors of the economy; see Frisch (1977) for references. These models suffer to some extent from their neglect of market interdependence (the possibility that disequilibrium in one sector will shift demand in another) and from their reliance on asymmetric models of market behavior: Excess demand is said to raise prices and wages, whereas excess supply is said to encounter "downward rigidity" of one sort or another.

Although the argument of this chapter also concludes that disequilibrium has inflationary consequences, there is no appeal to asymmetric behavioral paradigms to achieve this result. The argument is instead that in markets with more than one firm, prices are driven by competitive forces below monopoly levels. When any such market is disturbed, the introduction of random elements into each firm's pricing behavior will have the short-run effect of increasing the isolation of each firm from its competitors. Once this happens, monopolistic (or more nearly monopolistic) pricing becomes more attractive, and prices will be found to be higher than they would otherwise have been.

Our model also differs from structural models in that it applies to single markets, thereby avoiding the market-independence problem. Our general argument can be plausibly extended to more than one market, however: An exogenous shock to market A is likely, through consumer substitutions and budget constraints, to alter the price that will clear market B. This second market will therefore be thrown out of equilibrium, and the model that we have developed then applies to both markets. So long as the disequilibrium in market A does not lower the demand in B so far as to offset the upward price pressure in B, the result will be a general inflation.

Because demand curves are downward-sloping, this process of increasing price will naturally lead to declining sales, and there is therefore no inconsistency if higher-than-usual unemployment accompanies the inflation. The origins of the inflation do not arise in the labor market, however, and policies that increase unemployment cannot be expected to restrain the inflation (beyond simply depressing the economy). In fact, from a policy standpoint, the theory here argues that traditional policy tools may be wholly inappropriate for dealing with price increases. The origins of this inflation are microeconomic in nature, having to do with dislocations among markets, and no aggregated monetary or fiscal devices can have any direct effect on these dislocations. Indeed, by introducing new shocks into the system, policies introduced to control inflation may only worsen the problem. Even price controls, which by definition would be effective in temporarily halting price increases, would, through their own power to dislocate an economy, serve as causal factors in subsequent price increases once they were relaxed.

To the extent that traditional policy tools are of any relevance, the theory given here would argue for an accommodating monetary expansion. We have noted that the restoration of equilibrium will require a slow deflation as firms' pricing behaviors converge to P^*. Because P^* is below the mean of the disequilibrium price distribution, this convergence is made difficult by the destabilizing effect of having a distribution converge not to its mean but to some point below it. Restoration of equilibrium (albeit at higher prices) may be facilitated by an expansionary monetary policy that maintains the mean of $g(P)$ and that slowly raises P^* until, at equilibrium, P^* and the mean of $g(P)$ are equal. Even this policy, however, becomes defensible only after $g(P)$ has begun to contract and prices have begun to fall. Accommodating monetary expansion during the inflation itself would only accelerate the inflation by raising P^* and would provide no stabilizing influence.

Finally, we recognize that in deriving our results we have been forced to impose a large number of simplifying assumptions on the underlying reinforcement model, and one might have some legitimate concern that our conclusions depend in some essential way on these restrictions. It appears, however, that the essential mechanism for our results rests on the concavity assumption. It is this assumption that implies that the marginal influence of price over shopping behavior is reduced when prices are widely dispersed, compared with when they are close together. This assumption, in turn, represents only a modest strengthening of the monotonicity assumption in the context of a bounded dependent variable. Because these are quite normal properties of learning models in general, there is reason to be confident that our main conclusions will prove to be robust under quite a variety of different formulations.

Appendix

Using the definition of $S_T(P)$ and equation (7.5), we have

$$\frac{\partial R(P)S_T(P)}{\partial P} = R'(P)S_T(P) - R(P)S_{i,t}Z(P) \tag{7.9}$$

where

$$Z(P) \equiv \int_0^1 \left[\int_P^\infty L_2(s, x-P)f(s,x)\,dx + \int_0^P L_2(S_{i,t}, P-x)f(s,x)\,dx\right] ds \tag{7.10}$$

In order to obtain a Nash equilibrium, we set $S_{i,t} = 1/n$ and define a function $f_k(s,x)$ that satisfies (7.4) and whose properties are that $f_1(s,x) = f(s,x)$ and $\lim_{k\to\infty} f_k(s,x) = 0$ for all $s \neq 1/n$ and $P \neq P^*$. We shall use $Z_k(P)$ to represent the value of equation (7.10), with $f_k(\cdot)$ replacing $f(\cdot)$.

Now, if $P > P^*$,

$$\lim_{k\to\infty} Z_k(P) = \lim_{k\to\infty} \int_0^1 \int_0^P L_2(1/n, P-x)f_k(s,x)\,dx\,ds$$

and using (7.4) we obtain

$$\lim_{k\to\infty} Z_k(P) = L_2(1/n, P-P^*)(1-1/n) \tag{7.11}$$

Similarly, if $P < P^*$,

$$\lim_{k\to\infty} Z_k(P) = L_2(1/n, P^*-P)(1-1/n) \tag{7.12}$$

Expressions (7.11) and (7.12) converge to the same value as P approaches P^*, and $S_T(P^*)$ takes the value $2/n$. Substituting into (7.9), we find the stationary equilibrium at $s = 1/n$ and $\partial R(P)S_T(P)/\partial P = 0$ at $P = P^*$ to be described by

$$2R'(P^*) - \frac{n-1}{n}L_2(1/n, 0)R(P^*) = 0 \tag{7.6}$$

The second derivative of the profit function is given by

$$\frac{\partial^2 R(P) S_T(P)}{\partial P^2} = R''(P) S_T(P) - 2R'(P) S_{i,t} Z(P) S_{i,t} Y(P) \tag{7.13}$$

where $Z(P)$ is defined as before, and

$$Y(P) \equiv \int_0^1 \left[-\int_P^\infty L_{22}(s, x-P) f(s,x) \, dx - L_2(s,0) f(s,x) \right.$$

$$\left. + \int_0^P L_{22}(S_{i,t}, P-x) f(s,x) \, dx + L_2(S_{i,t},0) f(s,x) \right] ds$$

If we define $f_k(s,x)$ as before and follow the same procedure as was used to obtain (7.11) and (7.12), we can show that if $P > P^*$ and $S_{i,t} = 1/n$,

$$\lim_{k \to \infty} Y_k = L_{22}(1/n, P - P^*)(1 - 1/n) \tag{7.14}$$

Similarly, if $P < P^*$ and $\phi_{i,t} = 1/n$;

$$\lim_{k \to \infty} Y_k = -L_{22}(1/n, P^* - P)(1 - 1/n) \tag{7.15}$$

In this case there is a discontinuity at the point $P = P^*$ because $L_{22}(1/n, 0) \neq 0$, and there is a sign reversal between equations (7.14) and (7.15). The reason that this arises in this model is that the nature of the dependence of market share on price rests on whether one is charging more than one's competitors (and therefore losing market share) or charging below one's competitors (and therefore gaining market share). With this in mind, the sign of the right-hand side of equation (7.13) at the stationary point described by (7.6) is the sign of

$$2R''(P^*) - \frac{n-1}{n} [2R'(P^*) L_2(1/n, 0) - \delta(P) R(P^*) L_{22}(1/n, 0)] \tag{7.16}$$

where

$$\delta(P) \equiv \begin{cases} +1 & \text{for } P < P^* \\ -1 & \text{for } P > P^* \end{cases}$$

We know that $R''(P^*) < 0$, $R'(P^*) > 0$ (because P^* must be below the monopoly price), $R(P^*) > 0$, $L_2(1/n, 0) > 0$ [by condition (2.1)], and $L_{22}(1/n, 0) < 0$ (by concavity). Therefore, in the case of price decreases $(P < P^*)$, expression (7.16) is unambiguously negative, and the second-order conditions are satisfied in the downward direction. However, in the case of price increases $(P > P^*)$, the third term in (7.16) is positive. If this term is large enough to make expression (7.16) positive, the second-order conditions are violated in the upward direction, and we must conclude that there does not exist any single-price Nash equilibrium in this market.

Now define a price distribution $f^*(s,x)$ with the following properties:

(a) $\displaystyle\int_0^1\int_0^\infty f(s,x)\,dx\,ds = 1 - S_{i,t-1}$

(b) $\displaystyle\int_0^1\int_0^\infty xf^*(s,x)\,dx\,ds = \int_0^1\int_0^\infty xf(s,x)\,dx\,ds$

(c) $\displaystyle\frac{\int_0^1 f^*(s,x)\,d\phi}{\int_0^1 f(s,x)\,ds}$

is monotonically increasing in the differences $x-\bar{x}$ for $x>\bar{x}$ and $\bar{x}-x$ for $\bar{x}<x$, where $\bar{x}$ is the mean price charged by the competitors of firm i weighted by their market shares. $\bar{x}$ is given by

$$\bar{x} = \frac{1}{1-S_{i,t}}\int_0^1\int_0^\infty xf(s,x)\,dx\,ds$$

Thus, $f^*(s,x)$ is a neutral disturbance to the market in that it increases the spread of competitors' prices (from the point of view of firm i) while preserving the mean.

If we evaluate $Z(P)$ as given by equation (7.10) at the mean $P=\bar{x}$ using the two alternative price distributions, it is clear from the concavity of $L(\cdot)$ that $Z^*(\bar{x}) < Z(\bar{x})$, where $Z^*(\bar{x})$ represents the value of the function with $f^*(s,x)$ replacing $f(s,x)$. The reason is that the probability weights on values of x close to $\bar{x}$ [for which $L_2(\cdot)$ is large] are reduced, whereas the weights for values of x farther from $\bar{x}$ [for which $L_2(\cdot)$ is small] are increased, and therefore the value of the entire integral must fall.

Now suppose that the market is initially in a single price equilibrium, with each firm selling to a $1/n$ share of the market at a price P^*, and that the market is then subjected to some exogenous disturbance. Different managers respond in different ways to this shock, depending on experience, market position, and other chance elements, but the disturbance is neutral in that the prices they now charge are distributed around a mean $x=P^*$. Necessarily, the value of $Z^*(P)$ is smaller than the old equilibrium $Z(P)$, and referring to equation (7.9) it is unambiguous that the slope of the profit function is now positive at the point $P=P^*$, so that each firm will find maximum profits at some price $P>P^*$.

CHAPTER 8

Advertising and imitation

It is a striking fact that every modern free-enterprise economy includes the institution of advertising. Its influence is inescapable, and it is certainly difficult to imagine any description of contemporary economic life that does not dwell at some length on its role in the determination of market processes. The fact that there is no systematic analysis of advertising to be found in the conventional economic theory of consumption would be astonishing were it not that the evident capacity of advertising to alter choice behavior is so plainly inconsistent with the optimization paradigm on which the theory is founded. Indeed, the conventional belief that advertising can induce fully informed consumers to buy what they otherwise would not buy has been a continuing source of embarrassment to economists who adhere to traditional utility-maximization models.

In defense of the traditional theory, there do exist many forms of advertising that are at least potentially consistent with optimization. If we were to confine ourselves to its information content, stressing as examples retail advertisements that describe current prices, the existence of special sales, or product availability, we could address the phenomenon by means of standard Bayesian decision techniques. As work by Boyer (1974) implies, there can be little doubt that a substantial portion of (printed) retail advertising does perform such a function, and to this extent there is no incompatibility with the rest of economic theory. On the other hand, this explanation cannot reasonably be applied to advertising that primarily serves to differentiate such technically homogeneous products as beer, aspirin, cigarettes, soap, or various paper products, and Boyer's data support this conclusion.

One might deal with some other cases of advertising, and still remain within the boundaries of traditional theory, if one were to argue that advertising itself is sometimes a part of the product. Some economists actually treat advertising as if it were a "good" for which consumers would be willing to pay. Frech and Rochlin (1979), for example, describe advertising as a public good that is presented to the market in the form of a "tie-in" sale: The product cannot be purchased without at the same time contributing to the cost of the associated advertising. Examples in which advertising may take on the properties of consumption goods can be found. Cigarette advertising, for example, seems designed to project highly complimentary images on smokers of particular brands. One series of advertisements employs actors presented in extremely masculine roles in rugged western settings (and it is not surprising that smokers of that brand are overwhelmingly men); another stresses youth and leisure in attractive and athletic circumstances. It is possible that consumers of these products associate themselves with the idealized qualities that are presented in the advertisements and that the purchase of a given brand of cigarette amounts in fact to the purchase of a complimentary self-image. If this is true, then the advertising is a consumption good. Sexually suggestive ads for soaps and other products might be addressed in similar terms. At the same time, this is not a very satisfactory approach to the problem, because it falls into the methodological trap that has been referenced often in this book. When a proposed explanation of an empirical phenomenon requires that we assume novel properties for a utility function that cannot be observed directly, the utility-maximization model itself is reduced to a tautology, and we find ourselves stating in effect that people react to advertising because people react to advertising.

The images that are projected in consumer-oriented advertising seem to be designed to exploit a phenomenon that is much broader in scope than is advertising itself, and that is the tendency for consumers to imitate one another. This tendency toward imitation is well documented, and it even provides the foundation for a few economic models. Leibenstein's analysis (1950) of "bandwagon" and "Veblen" effects focused on this process, and more recently Conlisk (1980) demonstrated that, for some consumers, imitation may actually be a superior behavioral mode compared with optimization, because it avoids the costs that are inherent in making independent decisions. That is, imitation may actually be rational!

In practice, of course, imitation may be no more than a selective form of experimentation: If a friend announces that some new restaurant serves delicious food, one may be inclined to go there oneself, not in blind imitation of the friend but as an information-gathering experiment that has been suggested by the friend's experience. It is not plausible, however, that all imitative behavior can be accounted for with such rationalistic devices. They certainly cannot account for the extraordinary susceptibility of teenagers to popular fashions of behavior. The effectiveness of "peer pressure" in inducing young people to acquire faddish and even dangerously unhealthful behaviors and the apparent power of television sports heroes to induce consumers to alter their beer-drinking habits provide persuasive evidence that imitative behavior goes well beyond rational experimentation and efficient information handling and that it includes a variety of passive responses that might in some cases be harmful to the individual.

We are not especially concerned here with the question why people should engage in passive imitation. Perhaps it is no more than the outgrowth of some biologically determined set of instincts that are themselves our inheritance from a genetically distant past. It is much more important for our purposes that we construct a plausible model of how imitative behavior operates than it is to speculate on its ultimate causes. Our basic hypothesis here will be that the experiences of others, and our observations of them, act as surrogate experiences of our own. In the case of advertising, we imagine ourselves in the role of the sports hero, the youthful owner of a new automobile in some romantic setting, or the housewife rescued by a super cleanser, and we react with the sense of success and pleasure that these little stories provide. Imitation of friends and acquaintances follows a similar pattern. If we observe others who engage in some behavior and then display satisfaction with its outcome, our own behavior responds as though we ourselves had undergone the experience. This interpretation suggests that imitation might be analyzed by means of the same feedback formulation we have been using for ordinary experiences. Because it is likely that these surrogate experiences will have much less influence over our own choice probabilities than will firsthand encounters with the behavior and its consequences, we cannot use the model as it stands, but must make some distinction between the two types of experiences. Nevertheless, the formulation can follow the same general rules.

We continue to use Φ_t to describe an initial vector of choice probabilities for an individual at time t. We add the new condition that external demonstration effects will modify Φ_t to some new value Φ_t', where these new probabilities describe the actual likelihoods with which choices are made. When some alternative is chosen, and its consequences realized, Φ_t' is then modified to a new vector Φ_{t+1} according to the same feedback model [equation (2.1)] we have used throughout.

Our interpretation of demonstration as surrogate experience indicates that the transition from Φ_t to Φ_t' is governed by a series of functions similar to equation (2.1):

$$\phi_{j,t}' - \phi_{j,t} = M^j(\Phi_t, W) \tag{8.1}$$

The elements of the vector $W = \{w_1, \ldots, w_n\}$ in equation (8.1) represent the magnitudes of the demonstration effects themselves. In the case of advertising, each element, w_j, might reflect the dollar expenditure on advertising in favor of the corresponding choice A_j. In the case of fads or demonstration effects, an element w_j might reflect the number of other consumers who have chosen A_j, or it might combine the number of such consumers with an index of their expressed enthusiasm over the consequences of that choice. Ordinarily, $\phi'_{j,t}$ will be monotonically increasing in w_j, although exceptions to this rule surely exist. If those who are "hip" despise the habits of the "middle class," then increases in the number of persons who choose A_j may actually decrease the selection likelihood for this alternative on the part of certain members of the avant-garde. In general, however, we shall preserve the positive monotonic characterization. If the elements of W are all zero, then $\Phi'_t = \Phi_t$:

$$\frac{\partial \phi'_{j,t}}{\partial w_j} > 0 \tag{8.2}$$

$$\{w_j = 0 \quad \text{all } j\} \Rightarrow \phi'_{j,t} = \phi_{j,t} \quad \text{for all } j \tag{8.3}$$

Increases in the elements of W have the obvious primary effect of increasing the selection probabilities of the corresponding alternatives. There is an equally important but less obvious secondary effect of such increases, however. Any external influence that increases the selection likelihood of some choice A_j will increase the likelihood that an individual will gather actual (as contrasted to surrogate) experience with that choice, and this will act to reduce the ultimate impact of any demonstration regarding A_j. If the payoff to A_j is large, then imitation will only tend to accelerate an already existing dynamic trend in selection probabilities toward that alternative. If the experience with A_j is unfortunate, then the demonstration will be offset to some extent and may have no long-run impact at all.

Advertising

We noted that there is a scarcity of economic analysis concerning the mechanism of advertising. Most of the existing literature on the subject begins with a premise that advertising does influence demand and then focuses on optimal advertising levels (Dorfman and Steiner, 1954) or on possible relationships between advertising and market structure (Comanor and Wilson, 1979). Almost all of this literature displays a tendency to ignore the utility payoffs that accompany goods that are advertised, and, in particular, no attention is paid to the fact that an immediate consequence of advertising must be an increase in consumers' familiarity with product payoffs. Some go so far as to suggest that consumer preferences are either irrelevant or (what is the same thing) wholly manipulable. Galbraith (1960) suggested that "wants can be synthesized by advertising," and he later elaborated this belief into a discussion of the mechanisms of "demand management" (1971). Approaches such as this treat advertising as an independent psychic force that exerts direct control over consumer behavior and that can be discussed quite separately from the values of the goods and services themselves. From the perspective afforded by the feedback model, however, this is an oversimplification that approaches self-contradiction: If advertising is effective at all, its most notable consequence must be an expansion of firsthand experience with the associated products, and it makes no sense at all to ignore the role of that experience in the determination of future choice behavior.

The only exceptions to the general observation that discussions of advertising neglect product payoff values seem to arise in the aforementioned works that treat advertising as a good in itself, and in discussions of advertising in the context of imperfect information. Works by Nelson (1974) and Schmalensee (1978) do focus on payoff values, and the Schmalensee article is of particular interest in that it exploits a Markov information-gathering mechanism that has much in common with the feedback model treated here.

In order to treat both primary and secondary demonstration effects simultaneously, we must turn to mathematically simplified versions of our model. For the transition from Φ'_t to Φ_{t+1} we shall use the proportional model, which, from (2.13), provides the following:

For $i \in S$:

$$E[\phi_{i,t+1}] = \phi'_{i,t} + \phi'_{i,t}[\alpha_i - \bar{\alpha}'_s] + \phi'_{i,t} \sum_{j \in F} \frac{\phi'^2_{j,t}\beta_j}{1 - \phi'_{j,t}} \qquad (8.4)$$

For $i \in F$:

$$E[\phi_{i,t+1}] = \phi'_{i,t} - \phi'_{i,t}\bar{\alpha}'_s + \phi'_{i,t} \sum_{\substack{j \in F \\ j \neq i}} \frac{\phi'^2_{j,t}\beta_j}{1 = \phi'_{j,t}} - \phi'^2_{i,t}\beta_i \qquad (8.5)$$

where

$$\bar{\alpha}'_s \equiv \sum_{j \in S} \phi'_{j,t}\alpha_j$$

The definitions here correspond to those given in Chapter 2. If the individual has an aspiration payoff target $\hat{\Theta}$, then the set S contains all potentially "successful" actions – those that will produce a return at least as large as $\hat{\Theta}$. The set F contains "failures" – choices whose payoffs fall below $\hat{\Theta}$. For convenience, we have also accepted the independence assumption that permits us to use the strict equalities in equations (8.4) and (8.5).

Suppose that we confine ourselves to a case in which there is only one alternative A_k whose selection is encouraged through advertising. It is possible that (through the mechanism of stimulus generalization) this advertising directly increases the selection likelihoods of some other alternatives as well – this might be the case if advertising for one particular brand of cigarette were to encourage the smoking of other brands also. However, advertising has generally been regarded by economists as a mechanism for providing product differentiation; indeed, it is very much in the interest of advertisers to provide images that do not generalize readily, because only then do advertisers capture the entire benefits of their efforts. For this reason we shall presume that advertising or demonstrations specifically directed at the choice A_k always reduce the selection likelihoods for all of its alternatives, so that $\phi'_{j,t} < \phi_{j,t}$ for all $j \neq k$.

In Chapter 2 we considered two alternative views of the feedback process: one in which the aspiration level, $\hat{\Theta}$, was fixed, and another in which aspirations rose over time. For either model, we concluded that the selection likelihoods of inferior alternatives (those in the set F) would eventually converge toward zero, and, further, both the changing-aspiration model and the fixed-aspiration model with proportional feedback would ultimately lead to the selection of a single optimal choice. Similar arguments apply to any unadvertised choice whose payoff is smaller than that of the advertised choice A_k. That is, it is easy to see that $\phi_i \rightarrow 0$ for any $i \in F$ where $\Theta_i < \Theta_k$. However, these arguments no longer extend to advertised alternatives. Even though the payoff to A_k may be below aspirations, the discouragement that would ordinarily follow from experience with that choice may be offset by the actions of the advertising. Put more formally, we may have $k \in F$, meaning that the payoff to A_k is below aspirations and is considered to be a "failure," but we cannot show that ϕ'_k necessarily converges toward zero. We can certainly demonstrate that $E[\phi_{k,t+1}] < \phi_{k,t}$ for such a case, but it does not follow that $E[\phi'_{k,t+1}] < \phi'_{k,t}$, because the advertising will increase the value of any $\phi'_{k,t+1}$ over $\phi_{k,t}$. Once we have acknowledged this possibility, we no longer have the means to demonstrate that the selection likelihoods of other alternatives will converge toward zero either. The persistent selection of the inferior alternative A_k has the effect of making other choices look good by comparison, even though they may be quite inferior to the optimal choice. Suppose, for example, that there exists some choice A_j, where $j \in F$, but $\Theta_j > \Theta_k$. That is, the choice A_j will ordinarily be regarded as a "failure," but it is nevertheless better that the advertised choice A_k. It is clear from (8.5) that we cannot guarantee that we shall get $E[\phi_{j,t+1}] < \phi'_{j,t}$, and without specifying more precisely the nature of the mechanism that transforms $\phi_{j,t+1}$ into the (smaller) $\phi'_{j,t+1}$, we cannot be assured that (the expectation of) the selection likelihood of this alternative will decline over time. The same arguments apply a fortiori to choices that are regarded as successes (and are therefore in the set S). This is particularly true if aspiration levels arise out of payoff experience, because frequent selection of the advertised alternative A_k will act to keep aspiration levels small.

We can summarize these qualitative conclusions with three general observations. First, we can no longer show that the feedback mechanism will ultimately lead to an equilibrium dominated by a single optimal choice. Instead, many alternatives will continue to be chosen with positive probability, even if they are not themselves advertised. Second, the most inferior choice (in terms of payoff) that enjoys a positive selection probability in this equilibrium must be an advertised choice. [This is in direct contradiction to the conclusions drawn by P. Nelson (1974), who managed to convince himself that large advertising budgets are actually indicators of high quality.] Our third conclusion, a corollary of the first, is that advertising has the effect of sheltering certain unadvertised alternatives whose payoffs exceed that of the advertised good, but that would, under other circumstances, eventually have disappeared from view. In cognitive terms, we say that experience with imitation maintains a lower payoff experience than would otherwise arise, and this permits other choices to continue to deliver (relative) satisfaction and hence to receive continuing reinforcement that would not exist if the optimal choice were made regularly.

It is evident that the case of imitation does not admit a unique "equilibrium" set of selections, but produces a distribution similar to that arising under uncertainty. Each alternative that survives with a positive selection likelihood alters the choice probabilities in its own way whenever it is chosen, and thus the probability vector itself cycles continually among its possible values. Our best approach to the analysis of this situation is to use the fixed-point approximation to an "equilibrium" that was used in previous chapters. This approximation has proved to be easiest to apply when the proportional form of the feedback function is used, and therefore we shall use equations (8.4) and (8.5) as they stand. For similar reasons, we use a linear version of the transition function $M(\cdot)$. If only one alternative, A_k, is to be encouraged through imitation, then we can use the unscripted variable w to represent our quantitative measure of this effect and write

$$\phi'_{k,t} = \phi_{k,t}(1 - w) + w$$

$$\phi'_{j,t} = \phi_{j,t}(1 - w) \tag{8.6}$$

Different models with various configurations of payoff values and aspiration levels do not produce significant differences in our main conclusions, and so we shall use the simplest model here. We let $\hat{\Theta}=0$ and consider the payoff to the advertised product, Θ_k, to be positive. In such a model, the selection likelihoods of all choices with negative payoffs ("failures") will converge toward zero, and we shall be left with positive selection probabilities for only those alternatives in the set S. Because $\phi_j' \to 0$ for all $j \in F$, we need consider equation (8.4) alone in the form

$$E[\phi_{i,t+1}] = \phi_{i,t}' + \phi_{i,t}'[\alpha_i - \bar{\alpha}_S'] \tag{8.7}$$

The term $\bar{\alpha}_S'$ in (8.7) is defined as in (8.4) and (8.6). Applying equation (8.6) to the expectation, we obtain

$$E[\phi_{i,t+1}'] = (1-w)E[\phi_{i,t+1}] \quad (i \neq k)$$

$$E[\phi_{k,t+1}'] = (1-w)E[\phi_{k,t+1}] + w \tag{8.8}$$

At a fixed point, $E[\phi_{i,t+1}'] = \phi_{i,t}'$ for all i, and we shall call such values ϕ_i^*. There is a corresponding expected value of α at the fixed point that we shall call α^*, where $\alpha^* = \sum_{i \in S} \phi_i^* \alpha_i$. Combining (8.7) and (8.8) at the fixed-point solution, and using this notation, we obtain

$$w\phi_i^* = (1-w)(\alpha_i - \alpha^*)\phi_i^* \quad \text{for all } i \neq k \tag{8.9}$$

$$w\phi_k^* = (1-w)(\alpha_k - \alpha^*)\phi_k^* + w \tag{8.10}$$

Not all alternatives in S have positive selection likelihoods at our equilibrium point, for we note that equation (8.9) can be solved by a value $\phi_i^* = 0$. For those alternatives that do have positive selection likelihoods, we have

$$(\alpha_i - \alpha^*) = \frac{w}{1-w} \tag{8.11}$$

Equation (8.11) implies that $\alpha_i - \alpha^*$ is positive for all i with ϕ_i^* positive. That is, at our equilibrium, we may have positive selection probabilities for alternatives that are not the best, but this will occur only for choices whose payoffs are nevertheless large enough to produce values of α that exceed the expected value of α^* from the equilibrium probability vector as a whole. This is a specific example of the "sheltering" phenomenon that was introduced earlier. In the absence of imitation, α^* will achieve its maximal value, and hence, in equilibrium, no inferior alternatives can maintain positive selection probabilities. The positive selection likelihood of the imitative choice maintains α^* below this maximal value and makes these inferior alternatives possible. It is difficult to evaluate the stringency of the restriction that only those alternatives that offer relatively large payoffs will be sheltered in this way. We note first that the average α^* includes the values of α that correspond to those alternatives that are sheltered as well as α_k itself, and thus α^* may be considerably below what one might expect from consideration of the optimal choice alone. Moreover, we recall that α is itself a concave function of payoff, and in the vicinity of the optimal payoff choice it is possible that relatively wide variations in Θ will produce small variations in α, so that quite a wide variety of different choices might benefit from this sheltering effect.

The mechanism of imitation does not always guarantee that the choice A_k will enjoy positive selection probability in equilibrium, for w may be too small to overcome the influence of the payoff differences that apply. In the case of our proportional model, however, it is impossible for ϕ_k' to fall below w, because this stimulus operates directly on ϕ_k, and this variable is always nonnegative. It follows that our equilibrium value of ϕ_k^* is always greater than w, and thus we can use (8.10) to obtain

$$\phi_k^* = \frac{w}{w - (1 - w)(\alpha_k - \alpha^*)} \tag{8.12}$$

We may refer to our previous conclusion that the advertised alternative, A_k, will be the lowest-payoff choice that still enjoys a positive equilibrium selection probability. This implies $\alpha_k < \alpha^*$, which in turn guarantees $0 < \phi_k^* < 1$, and it is clear from (8.12) that ϕ_k^* increases from $\phi_k^* = 0$ at $w = 0$ to $\phi_k^* = 1$ at $w = 1$. Differentiation of (8.12) yields

$$\frac{d\phi_k^*}{dw} = -\frac{(\alpha_k - \alpha^*) + w(1 - w)(d\alpha^*/dw)}{[w - (1 - w)(\alpha_k - \alpha^*)]^2} \tag{8.13}$$

It is interesting to evaluate the slope given by (8.13) at the endpoints $w = 0$ and $w = 1$:

$$\frac{d\phi_k^*}{dw} = \frac{1}{\alpha^* - \alpha_k} \quad \text{at} \quad w = 0 \tag{8.14}$$

$$\frac{d\phi_k^*}{dw} = (\alpha^* - \alpha_k) \quad \text{at} \quad w = 1 \tag{8.15}$$

We have not solved for the value of this slope at intermediate values of w, and so it cannot be specified for all values of w. Nevertheless, it is clear from the endpoint conditions (8.14) and (8.15) that ϕ_k^* is a generally concave function of w. Because both α_k and α^* must be positive but strictly less than 1, the slope must be strictly greater than 1 at the endpoint $w = 0$. At $w = 1$, we have $\phi_k^* = 1$, and this implies $\alpha^* = \alpha_k$ at this point. Therefore, $d\phi_k^*/dw = 0$ at the limit $w = 1$.

The property of (8.14) that we wish to stress is the fact that the sensitivity of ϕ_k^* to imitation is primarily a matter of payoff values. This is a manifestation of our earlier contention that the effectiveness of advertising cannot be divorced from payoff utility, because advertising itself brings about experience with payoffs. Quantitatively, we note that imitation has the most impact in those cases in which it makes the least difference in outcome value. If α_k is very little different from α^* (which means that Θ_k is very little different from the maximal payoff value), then imitation may strongly bias selection probabilities toward A_k. If Θ_k is enough below the maximal payoff opportunity for α_k and α^* to be widely separated, the effectiveness of advertising is correspondingly reduced. The inverse form of (8.14) implies that quite sharp differences may exist in the responsiveness of choice behavior to advertising when we vary the degree of similarity of payoffs. When α^* is very close to α_k, small increases in w have the potential for increasing the value of the slope $d\phi_k^*/dw$ at $w=0$ by several orders of magnitude.

This result is of considerable interest to any analysis of advertising. It suggests that advertising is not the irresistible psychic force that some have feared, driving consumers into consumption habits that are grossly inferior to those that would have developed in its absence. Instead, it will be found most often in markets consisting of such similar products that it makes very little difference which directions purchasing habits take. Empirical evidence provided by Nelson (1974) strongly supports this conclusion. He found the highest advertising/sales ratios to occur among such technically homogeneous products as perfume, pharmaceuticals, soaps, beers, and cigarettes, whereas more differentiated products such as automobiles and clothing receive far less advertising expenditure. Pharmaceuticals, which are required by law to be technically identical, receive ten times the advertising effort relative to sales value as do automobiles, even though the latter are themselves not remarkably heterogeneous. Our model suggests further that advertising will have much more impact on brand selection than on the generic composition of consumption bundles. Advertising for cigarettes, automobiles, soaps, or beers will influence the distribution of purchases among suppliers but will have much less impact on the total consumption of these commodities, because qualitatively different consumption choices will entail more significant payoff differences. In all of these cases, advertising works best where it makes the least difference.

A further insight to be gained from a feedback model of advertising is that we can then rationalize the rather peculiar informational properties of most commercial messages. Advertising, particularly that on television, does not by any means convey information efficiently. The general absence of hard facts in television commercials is notorious, and from an information standpoint, their repetition at intervals of 15 to 20 minutes is inexplicable. The view of advertising as a form of information dissemination has never coped successfully with these observations. Perceived as surrogate experiences, however, commercial emphases on satisfaction rather than facts are entirely understandable. Instead of informing, the purpose of an advertisement in our model is the simulation of satisfaction, and this goal is met admirably. Moreover, although we have treated a single advertising–purchase cycle in our model, we could as well have included several injections of advertising in the transition from Φ_t to Φ_t', and each step in such a series would be described in a form such as equation (8.1). Advertising in our model will have cumulative effects, and this means that repetitious advertising will be effective.

Fads

Advertising constitutes a rather contrived source for imitation in that the relevant choices and their consequent payoffs have only been represented in some form, and these representations may not be entirely factual. A more literal example of imitation arises if one individual is encouraged to make some choice because of the frequency with which that choice is made by others. Suppose that different consumers (of clothing, vacation resorts, music, etc.) are significantly different in personal tastes, so that the optimal choice of one would be definitely inferior from the point of view of another. This condition will introduce a substantial amount of variety into consumption habits across the economy. Now introduce a new commodity that is not optimal for everyone (although it may be for some), but whose consumption is extremely noticeable (such as ostentatiously brand-labeled clothing, special-purpose athletic gear used as everyday apparel, and the like). Such distinctive commodities encourage imitation in ways that the ordinary and less novel sets of heterogeneous consumption goods do not. If the acquisition of such a good is identified as a choice of A_k, then we might use a variable Ψ_t to represent the fraction of a population of one's acquaintances who make the choice A_k during a period t, and let the magnitude of our imitation effect vary positively with Ψ_t. The question is whether or not the consumption of this good can develop into a fad in which everyone (or nearly everyone) is induced by imitation to abandon their optimal choices in favor of A_k.

For the sake of a simple model, we shall continue to use the proportional example given in (8.6) through (8.8) and make w a linear function of Ψ_t: $w = K\Psi_t$. The coefficient K is some positive constant smaller than one. Using (8.7) and (8.8), we can determine the expected value of $E[\phi_{k,t+1}']$ for some imitating individual choice maker:

$$E[\phi'_{k,t+1}] = \phi'_{k,t} + K\Psi_t(1 - \phi'_{k,t}) - \phi'_{k,t}(1 - K\Psi_t)(\bar{\alpha}'_s - \alpha_k) \tag{8.16}$$

The mechanism of imitation induces a positive choice probability for an alternative whenever there is some significant fraction of other consumers who make that choice. This fact is reflected in equation (8.16) by the fact that whatever the value of $\phi'_{k,t}$, a positive value of K will bring about the condition $E[\phi'_{k,t+1}] > 0$. This condition in turn implies that some imitators will actually choose A_k during period $t+1$, thus themselves becoming examples for future imitation. If enough individuals are imitators, then we observe a fad – a condition in which there are enough imitators to provide a kind of self-sustaining chain reaction in which more and more people turn to the choice A_k period after period.

Not everyone is susceptible to imitation. If it is the case that only some fraction γ of the population can be influenced in this manner, then the fraction Ψ of the population that chooses A_k cannot exceed γ. For a preliminary simple model, we shall suppose that those people who are potential imitators are homogeneous to the extent that each has the same inclination to imitate the behavior of others, and each receives the same payoff value from the selection of A_k. The preferences of the rest of the population are of no concern, because they are not affected by imitation in any case. We begin in a state in which each imitator has the same (small) likelihood of choosing A_k. Nonimitators do not choose A_k, except for a few for whom A_k is the optimal alternative – these may provide the stimulus for the subsequent imitation, but the mathematics are simplified if we assume the number of persons of this type to be negligibly small. The expected fraction of the population for which A_k is the choice during t is then γ times $\phi'_{k,t}$, where the probability ϕ' refers to imitators. Similarly, the expected value of Ψ_{t+1} is $\gamma E[\phi'_{k,t+1}]$. If the population is large enough for us to be willing to replace Ψ_{t+1} with its expectation, then we can substitute Ψ_t/γ and Ψ_{t+1}/γ for $\phi'_{k,t}$ and $E[\phi'_{k,t+1}]$ in equation (8.16). It is convenient to rewrite this equation so as to provide the proportionate change in the value of Ψ from period t to $t+1$. Using R to represent this ratio, we obtain

$$R = \frac{\Psi_{t+1}}{\Psi_t} = 1 + K\gamma - K\Psi_t - (1 - K\Psi_t)(\bar{\alpha}'_s - \alpha_k) \tag{8.17}$$

If imitation is to produce a self-perpetuating choice mechanism, then we must have $R > 1$ for small values of Ψ_t. At such small values, $\bar{\alpha}'_s$ is very near to the value of α at the optimal choice, because inferior alternatives are only rarely taken. If we call this value α_m, then at the point $\Psi = 0$, equation (8.17) becomes

$$R = 1 + K\gamma - (\alpha_m - \alpha_k) \tag{8.18}$$

A self-perpetuating fad can arise only if $K > \alpha_m - \alpha_k$. If this condition is satisfied, then we shall have $\Psi_{t+1} > \Psi_t$ at small values of Ψ_t, and the frequency with which A_k is chosen will increase.

Our fixed-point approximation to equilibrium in this model is characterized by the condition $R = 1$, where the selection frequency for A_k during t is equal to its expectation in $t + 1$. The equilibrium fraction of the population that chooses A_k is called Ψ^*, and this value is obtained by solving (8.17) for Ψ^* at the value $R = 1$:

$$\Psi^* = \frac{K\gamma - (\alpha'_s - \alpha_k)}{K[1 - (\alpha'_s - \alpha_k)]} \tag{8.19}$$

In the special case of only two alternatives, we can write $\alpha'_s = \alpha_k \phi + (1 - \phi)\alpha_m$. At the fixed-point equilibrium, $\Psi^* = \gamma\phi$. Substituting these two conditions into (8.19), we can solve for Ψ^* explicitly:

$$\Psi^* = \gamma \tag{8.20}$$

The implication of (8.20) is that in equilibrium, all imitators choose A_k, and all others do not. Our equilibrium in this case is not some distribution of choice likelihoods, but a single point at which $\phi_k^* = 1$ for all imitators and $\phi_k^* = 0$ for all nonimitators. The reason for this deterministic outcome can be found in equation (8.17). If the initial condition $K > \alpha_m - \alpha_k$ is satisfied for some individual, then the choice A_k becomes more likely, and the probability that the optimal alternative A_m will be selected is correspondingly reduced. This, however, lowers the expected payoff level, which reduces the perceived loss that is associated with A_k. The more frequently the alternative A_k is chosen, the more closely total payoff experience will come to match the payoff to A_k, and the smaller will be the expected discouragement attached to A_k. The condition $R > 1$ at the point $\phi_k' = 0$ thus guarantees $R > 1$ at all higher values of ϕ_k' up to $\phi_k' = 1$. Finally, although the unique solution given by equation (8.20) was obtained for the special case of a two-alternative model with identical preferences among imitators, it is clear from (8.17) that this extreme outcome is a potential equilibrium solution for the model whatever the circumstances might be.

It might appear that if we were to drop the assumption that imitators all value A_k similarly, the equilibrium would be found away from the endpoint $\phi_k^* = 1$. Such is not the case, however, at least in this linearized model. From equation (8.16) it is clear that if anyone chooses A_k, then no imitator will select A_k with probability less than $K\Psi_k$. The sequence of choices and payoffs that accompany any proposed equilibrium state other than $\phi_k^* = 1$ will encounter occasions when ϕ_k is large. This circumstance in turn will make the difference $\bar{\alpha}'_s - \alpha_k$ small, and ϕ_k will be accelerated toward the endpoint $\phi_k^* = 1$. Thus, fixed-point solutions of a set of conditions such as (8.16) (one such equation for each imitator) may contain values of ϕ_k^* less than 1, but these will all be unstable, and the system will converge on $\phi_k^* = 1$ for all imitators.

This model is entirely consistent with the characteristics of fads as we see them in practice. Further, its properties may be of some aid in understanding the rapidity with which fads seem to spread. It is clear that the rate of increase of the selection likelihood ϕ_k is most inhibited in the vicinity of $\Psi = 0$, partly because there are few people to imitate, but primarily because the payoff expectations of potential imitators are greatest at this point, providing the maximum disincentives for the inferior A_k. As we move away from $\Psi_k = 0$, this disincentive falls, and the tendency for Ψ_k to grow accelerates. The spreading popularity of the fad slows only when the population of potential imitators is nearly consumed.

A second implication of this model is that a commodity whose consumption has been stimulated by a process of imitation is more likely to fall from favor through a mechanism of displacement (through another fad) than through any kind of gradual decline. It is certainly true that if novelty or unorthodoxy provide the rewards to consumption of a good, its course as a fad may be self-destructive – the very frequency of its choice degrading the payoffs from its use. Nevertheless, in the vicinity of the equilibrium, payoff experiences (or payoff "expectations") have become consistent with the given choice, so that reduced payoffs that would have been too small to initiate the fad (at $\Psi_k = 0$) are nevertheless consistent with the equilibrium at $\Psi = \gamma$. Thus, payoffs may have to fall a considerable distance before consumption of this good will decline on its own. A new fad, however, will operate quickly and effectively to displace the old, and consumption of the old good can decline as precipitously as it grew before.

Our condition for the initiation of a fad amounts to a condition that the payoff loss engendered by imitation not be large. We require that K exceed the difference $\alpha_m - \alpha_k$, and because not everyone is an imitator ($\gamma < 1$), and we do not expect K to be especially large (except in the case of teenage consumers), this amounts to a requirement that A_m and A_k produce payoffs that are similar in magnitude. This appeals to the general impression that fads arise in consumption situations in which imitation entails very small value losses. The goods in question may be close substitutes for commodities that would have been acquired in any case, or they are inexpensive items that have no major impact on one's overall welfare. It is evidently appropriate that (again excepting teenagers) fads are often seen to be little more than insignificant humorous details of human behavior.

Advertising and fads share a common feature in our model, and that is that imitation does affect choice behavior, but it is most effective when it has inconsequential results. Many critics of optimization models of behavior point to the widespread incidence of advertising and the popularity of faddish consumption behavior as evidence of the unrealism of the maximization assumption, and it is true that these phenomena stand as significant qualitative challenges to orthodox maximization. There does not seem to be any reasonably straightforward (and nontautological) means for dealing with these phenomena within the conventional framework. The model of choice behavior guided by experience that has been outlined here does certainly provide a more effective approach to the problem. At the same time, our own analysis suggests that as a quantitative source of bias away from optimal outcomes, imitation is not very important. The reason is the one given earlier in this chapter: If behavior is guided by experience, imitation can never play more than an accessory role in the choice mechanism. Far from displacing rival influences over choice making, every instance of imitation brings about an expansion of experience, and it is this accumulated experience that ultimately governs behavior.

CHAPTER 9

An application to migration

The comparative-statics theory of optimal labor-force location is straight-forward. Workers are presumed to compare geographic employment locations with respect to wage rates, risks of unemployment, and quality of life, and markets are in equilibrium when workers in general see alternative employment locations as approximately equivalent once all these variables are taken into account. Thus, equilibrium wage rates (for given skill levels) might be lower in areas characterized by attractive climatic conditions or stimulating cultural environment and higher in areas with high unemployment or high levels of industrial pollution.

A particularly important application of this theory has arisen in the field of development economics. Attention in this case is confined to the relationship between wage rates and unemployment. In most studies (e.g., Harris and Todaro, 1970; Todaro, 1974; Stiglitz, 1974) it is presumed that rural workers in less developed countries are fully employed and that the urban labor supply is determined not by prevailing urban wage rates alone but by a composite of urban wages and the (typically high) urban unemployment rate. Individual workers are assumed to compare the income that they can earn from (guaranteed) employment in rural agriculture at a low wage to what could be received in the city, where the expected urban income is computed from the higher urban wage and various assumptions regarding the probability of finding employment there.

The question of greatest concern to economists working in this field is not the comparative-statics equilibrium distribution of the work force but the dynamic process of rural–urban migration as a continuing phenomenon. Todaro, for example, presented as his main hypothesis the relation

$$\frac{\dot{S}(t)}{S(t)} = F\left(\frac{V_u(t) - V_r(t)}{V_r(t)} \right) \tag{9.1}$$

where S is the size of the urban labor force and $\dot{S}$ is its time derivative, $V_u(t)$ is the discounted present value of expected urban income, and $V_r(t)$ is the discounted present value of expected rural income. The Harris-Todaro study similarly draws attention to migration as an

166

ongoing phenomenon with the introductory observation that "migration not only continues to exist, but, indeed, appears to be accelerating."

Despite these indications that the central problem of migration is its persistence, possibly reflecting a continuing dynamic adjustment process, these studies all revert to the simple comparative-statics equilibrium model in order to produce their main conclusions. Typically, models are formulated in which the expected urban wage is made equal to the rural wage (i.e., in which migration is zero), and the resulting equilibrium urban unemployment rate is investigated in the light of various tax and minimum-wage policies. Even the original Todaro study concentrated on a state in which migration is zero, except for an "equilibrium" amount that is calculated by dividing the rate of urban job creation by the employment rate and then subtracting the rate of natural urban population growth.

This reluctance to work with the migration phenomenon itself may be attributed to the fact that dynamic models such as that of equation (9.1), plausible as they certainly are, are not derived from any formal theory but are simply stated as initial hypotheses. It is an indisputable fact that a fully rational household must take account of the presence of unemployment in the city and thus must compare rural income to an expected value for urban income, but this fact can be used to derive an equilibrium model for which migration is zero only when the returns from the two alternatives are equal. It cannot be used to explain a stable rate of change when the returns are unequal. Finite rates of migration can exist only if many individuals who could migrate do not do so even if the expected urban wage substantially exceeds the rural wage. Of course, a variety of independent variables come to mind that could be used to account for this sluggishness (and many of these play important roles in econometric studies of migration), but none of them are introduced explicitly into the theory. As it stands, equation (9.1) states, in effect, that migration decisions are based on a rational comparison of income alternatives but that a large fraction of the population irrationally fails to act on this comparison. That the size of this fraction should vary inversely with the difference between V_u and V_r is plausible, but it is nowhere explained by the theory itself. In short, optimization theory, not being defined for disequilibrium, is simply inadequate to the task.

A second weakness in this optimization view of the migration process is that it requires that rural residents be informed regarding both urban wages and the prevailing unemployment rate and then be able to make decisions based on the appropriate expected-value calculations. The quality of wage and unemployment data in less developed countries is notoriously inadequate for such purposes, however, even at central governmental levels, and it is quite implausible that rural residents should have access to reliable data, even assuming that once they had it they would possess the analytical sophistication to use it. One might reasonably suggest that it is this lack of information that produces the sluggishness leading to finite migration rates. A model that would incorporate the possibility of imperfect information would certainly be an improvement over the static models we have described. Such an introduction into the traditional optimizing framework would not entirely resolve the problem, however. The image of a rural agricultural laborer in a less developed country turning to optimal Bayesian decision techniques in choosing whether or not to migrate simply puts too great a strain on one's credulity. The need is for a model that reduces the analytic sophistication presumed of individuals, not one that increases it.

Strictly speaking, all of these models represent oversimplifications in that workers are presumed to respond to the expected value of wages rather than the expected utility of wages. It is quite reasonable to expect risk-averse behavior in anything as important as a locational decision, and risk-averse workers would be inclined to avoid the city if it offered an expected wage that was no higher than the rural wage. The proper model would consider expected values of some concave (preference) function defined over wages. Moreover, by ignoring this detail, workers have been implicitly assumed to be identical in that they all have identical preference functions.

Migration

Our model of experientially determined behavior is well suited for application to the migration process. First, it is already dynamic in its formulation, and it requires no adaptation to suit it to disequilibrium circumstances. Second, it is well defined for situations in which decision makers are poorly informed, having access only to information contained in their immediate experience. As it happens, our variables are similar in spirit to those that are already found in sample surveys of migration (Todaro, 1976). These studies generally treat migration as a stochastic process, using migration probability as the usual dependent variable. Our treatment is similar, but it proves to be much more interesting if we shift the focus slightly, concentrating on the location decision rather than the decision to move.

The location decision is one in which the mechanism of imitation may play an important part. It is possible that an individual rural worker may "try out" a move to an urban area and thus gain firsthand experience with conditions there. The inconvenience and expense that would accompany such an experiment, however, would normally inhibit individual trials, and we can expect to find an increased reliance on communications from acquaintances and relatives who have already made such moves. The relative who has gone to the city and has found a high-paying job there provides an example to those back home, and this surrogate experience increases the likelihood that the example will be imitated by others. If the relative had failed to find employment and had returned home discouraged, the likelihood that others would try migration would be correspondingly reduced.

We have already suggested that the imitation mechanism has the same qualitative effect as firsthand experience, although in the last chapter we differentiated firsthand experience from secondhand experience with two different feedback models. Here we shall simplify the model by incorporating demonstrations in a different way. We suppose that decisions to locate in an urban area are made more by extended family or tribal units than by individuals and that the experience from one member's move to the city influences every member of that unit more or less equally. Thus, the decision variable (the probability of locating in the city) applies not to one individual but to several in parallel. This formulation has the dual advantage of simplifying our analysis considerably and of introducing a bit of verisimilitude, · which often is lacking in individually oriented models. The importance of family-unit or even tribal-unit decision making in less developed countries is well known, and it is useful for us to acknowledge it here. Moreover, it is commonly observed that migration to high-wage areas is often better described as a temporary export of labor that, if successful, leads to income transfers back to the family unit. If this is the case, then it is a family decision that has been reinforced, not just an individual one.

Because our purpose is to focus on the economic factors that may influence migration, we shall concentrate on the economic experience of the worker. A more general model could make similar use of variables reflecting such factors as age, education, family size, and population density in order to derive a more complete view of the migration process. Here, however, we shall characterize the objective situation as follows: There is one major urban center to which migration is possible. If a member of family unit j locates in this city, he (or she) will find "modern-sector" employment that pays a high wage, W_u, with a probability q. If he fails to find such a job, there still may exist various forms of marginal employment that will pay a very low wage, W_0. If he does not live in the city, rural employment guarantees an income of W_r. (We could, with no loss, distinguish a wage for rural employment from a still lower rural unemployment wage. In keeping with the models already cited, however, we presume that all rural workers are equally employed.) In general, we have $W_u > W_r > W_0$. It is not necessary that every member of family unit j should have the same employment likelihood; ordinarily, q should depend on quite a number of variables such as the age of the worker, the length of his stay in the city, and, most important, whether or not he had a modern-sector job in the previous period. In the face of the potential complexity in determining this probability, however, it is common to assume (following Harris-Todaro) that jobs are distributed randomly, and because we are concerned in this chapter only with demonstrating the usefulness of the dynamic adjustment model, we shall preserve this assumption. This makes q equal to the employment rate itself, E/S, where E is the number of modern-sector jobs.

Because there are only two relevant alternatives (location either in the city or in the rural area), we can simplify our notation somewhat. Here we shall use ϕ_t^j to represent the probability that a member of family unit j will be found in the city during period t, and $1 - \phi_t^j$ the probability of location in the rural area. As usual, the value of ϕ_t^j is determined from each individual's own experience and that communicated from others, and there is no presumption that anyone "knows" anything about the statistical or economic characteristics of the market in general.

It continues to be useful for us to employ the simple proportional model to generate examples of the mechanism that we have in mind. Within this general framework there are at least two reasonable alternative specifications of the process. The first, which we shall term model I, treats all wage income as "good." Thus, the aspiration level, $\hat{\theta}$, is made equal to zero. In this model, if a worker lives in the city and has a job, we write

$$\phi_{t+1}^j = \phi_t^j + \alpha_{ju}(1 - \phi_t^j) \tag{9.2}$$

where α_{ju} is the value of the function $\alpha(W)$ at the point W_u. This function has the usual properties in that it is positive and concave and is bounded by 0 and 1. By retaining the j subscript, we are permitting different family units to respond differently to the payoff experience.

By specifying a probability as the dependent variable, we have already departed significantly from the traditional model. We note that even though $\phi_{t+1}^j > \phi_t^j$ in equation (9.2), the worker may nevertheless go back to the rural sector at the end of the period; that is, he goes home with probability $1 - \phi_{t+1}^j$. In both the Todaro and Harris-Todaro models it is assumed that anyone who migrates to the city stays there so long as the expected urban economic opportunities are greater. In fact, however, some out migration, even among the urban employed, is a common phenomenon in less developed countries, and a dynamic model ought to reflect that fact.

The value that is taken by ϕ_{t+1}^j depends on whether or not the worker lives in the city and whether or not he finds a job. If the worker fails to get an urban job, then

$$\phi_{t+1}^j = \phi_t^j + \alpha_{j0}(1 - \phi_t^j) \tag{9.3}$$

where α_{j0} is the value of the function $\alpha(W)$ at the wage W_0.

For a worker located in the rural sector, earning W_r with certainty, a similar formula is applied to the likelihood $1 - \phi_t^j$, which is the probability of staying there, and this reduces to

$$\phi_{t+1}^j = \phi_t^j(1 - \alpha_{jr}) \tag{9.4}$$

where α_{jr} is the value of the function $\alpha(W)$ at the wage W_r.

Combining (9.2) through (9.4) with their associated likelihoods, and simplifying, we can obtain an expected value for ϕ_{t+1}^j:

$$E[\phi_{t+1}^j] = \phi_t^j + \phi_t^j(1 - \phi_t^j)(\bar{\alpha}_j - \alpha_{jr}) \tag{9.5}$$

where $\bar{\alpha}_j \equiv q\alpha_{ju} + (1 - q)\alpha_{j0}$.

If N represents the total population available for urban/rural employment (which we assume to be fixed for our purposes), and N_j the number of workers in unit j, then the expected urban population at time t is given by

$$S(t) = \sum_{j=1}^{K} N_j \phi_t^j \tag{9.6}$$

where K represents the total number of units.

The expected urban population at time $t+1$ is given by

$$S(t+1) = \sum_{j=1}^{K} N_j E[\phi_{t+1}^j] \tag{9.7}$$

Expected migration, $M(t)$, is the difference $S(t+1) - S(t)$, and using equation (9.7), this becomes

$$M(t) = \sum_{j=1}^{K} N_j \phi_t^j(1 - \phi_t^j)(\bar{\alpha}_j - \alpha_{jr}) \tag{9.8}$$

Finally, if we accept the Harris-Todaro assumption that all workers are identical, we give every city dweller the same chance of employment, $q = E/S$, and ignore the subscript j that distinguishes the responsiveness of different families to experience. These assumptions make all α's equal (to some $\bar{\alpha}$), and equation (9.8) becomes

$$M(t) = (\bar{\alpha} - \alpha_r) \sum_{j=1}^{K} N_j \phi_t^j(1 - \phi_t^j) \tag{9.9}$$

Because the summation term is positive whatever the values of the individual probabilities, this implies that $M(t)>0$ whenever $\bar{\alpha}>\alpha_r$. If, over the relevant range, the function $\alpha(W)$ could be treated as approximately linear in W, then this would reduce to the condition that net migration into the city is positive whenever the expected value of the urban wage exceeds the rural wage, and this is the main proposition we wished to reproduce. More realistically, the function $\alpha(W)$ is concave in W, and in this case equation (9.9) produces a result similar to that of optimization subject to risk aversion: Migration into the city persists so long as the expected value of some concave function of the wage is higher in the city than it is in rural areas.

Properties of model I

The migration model given by equation (9.1) was not explicitly derived from any underlying dynamic adjustment theory, and there has naturally been some debate over its most appropriate form. Todaro, for example, used the size of the urban labor force, S, as the base from which to measure the rate of migration. Zarembka (1970) objected to this specification on the grounds that it is the rural population that provides the migrants, so that therefore $N-S$ should be used as the base. In fact, equation (9.9) does not support either of these positions. In order to get a simple picture of the operation of equation (9.9), let us assume that all individuals are identical in the sense that everyone has the same probability of living in the city. This will make $\phi_t^j=S(t)/N$ for all j. Now equation (9.9) becomes

$$M(t)=(\bar{\alpha}-\alpha_r)S(t)\left(1-\frac{S(t)}{N}\right)$$ (9.10)

or

$$\frac{M(t)}{N-S(t)}=\frac{S(t)}{N}(\bar{\alpha}-\alpha_r)$$ (9.11)

This formulation differs from those of Todaro and Zarembka in that the adjustment mechanism applies to the entire population. In this model, $M(t)$ is the net summation of rural–urban and urban–rural migration, whereas Zarembka and Todaro considered only the effects of wage differentials on the rural population, presuming, contrary to fact, that those who move to the city never go back "home."

The migration process described by equation (9.9) will eventually lead to a stable population distribution. Net migration will reach zero if $\bar{\alpha}=\alpha_r$, and the comparative-statics properties of an economy in such an equilibrium can be evaluated as usual. Even in this equilibrium, of course, many individual workers are changing location; it is only the net flow of migrants that is zero.

Migration model II

Model I, as just described, is useful for comparing the feedback model with more traditional theory, but it does not exploit the potential in our model for making substantive distinctions between actions that are successful and those that are not. One would expect that a worker who migrated into the city, and who then failed to find profitable employment, would feel chagrin at this experience, and the family unit that sent him would be disappointed, recognizing that it has suffered because of the loss of a potential rural worker. This aspect of the problem is readily introduced through the use of a positive aspiration level for wages. Because the worker is guaranteed a wage of W_r if he locates out of the city, a wage greater than this would certainly appear to be a "success," and a lower wage would be treated as a "failure." Thus, the rural wage, W_r, is a natural standard against which the urban experience might be measured.

Our model is only slightly altered by this modification. If the worker locates in the city and finds a high-paying job there, then the probability ϕ_t^j is modified to ϕ_{t+1}^j according to

$$\phi_{t+1}^j = \phi_t^j + \alpha_{js}(1 - \phi_t^j) \tag{9.12}$$

where α_{js} is the value of the function $\alpha_j(\cdot)$ at the point $W_u - W_r$.

If the worker locates in the city and fails to earn the high wage, receiving only W_0 instead, then the likelihood of locating in the city the next period is reduced according to

$$\phi_{t+1}^j = \phi_t^j(1 - \beta_j) \tag{9.13}$$

where β_j is a positive, concave function of the difference $W_r - W_0$.

Because the worker in the rural area receives exactly the aspiration wage, there is no change in the probability of location in the city, and in this case $\phi_{t+1}^j = \phi_t^j$.

Following the same procedures that were used to obtain (9.8), we can derive the expected migration rate for model II:

$$M(t) = \sum_{j=1}^K N_j[q\alpha_{js}(1 - \phi_t^j) - (1 - q)\beta_j\phi_t^j] \tag{9.14}$$

If we again assume that family units are similar with respect to their responses to experience, we can ignore the j subscripts and use $\alpha_{js} = \alpha_s$ and $\beta_j = \beta$ for all j and reduce (9.14) to

$$M(t) = q\alpha_s[N - S(t)] - (1 - q)\beta S(t) \tag{9.15}$$

Model I in the last section produced positive migration rates whenever the expected gain from urban location exceeded the rural wage. The counterpart of this condition, using the notation of model II, requires the benefit of urban over rural income times the likelihood of urban employment to exceed the likelihood of unemployment times the associated loss:

$$q\alpha_s - (1 - q)\beta > 0 \tag{9.16}$$

If α and β are approximately linear in their arguments, then condition (9.16) will hold whenever the expected urban wage is higher than the rural wage. If we compare equation (9.15) to this condition, however, it is clear that model II makes migration a function of the absolute size of the urban area as well as the unemployment rate proper. This rather surprising result comes about because our model describes net migration flows rather than simple one-way population movements. A given unemployment rate in the city will produce a certain likelihood that a rural resident will migrate to the city, and a certain likelihood that city residents will move out. The actual numbers of such migrants depend on the population bases to which these likelihoods are applied. If the rural population is extremely large, then even a small probability of movement into the city may lead to a relatively large number of actual migrants, whereas a relatively large exit probability may not generate very many actual departures if the urban population is small. From this perspective, the distribution of population between urban and rural sectors of the economy becomes an important independent determinant of migration, and it is clear that the population-base question is much more complex than has been implied by other authors, or by the simpler model I. In general, the smaller the urban area relative to the entire economy, the greater the imbalance between in-migration and out-migration, and the higher the final urban unemployment rate is likely to be.

Equilibrium

According to traditional theory, net migration comes to an end when the expected urban wage is equal to the rural wage, or, in more sophisticated models, when the expectation of some concave (preference) function of urban wages is equal to the value of the same concave function evaluated at the rural wage. This is the implication of model I as well. Model II is more complicated and must be treated in more detail.

It is clearly inappropriate to treat urban population size and the unemployment rate as independent variables in equilibrium, because higher population inevitably leads to a lower probability of employment at the high wage. If the number of modern-sector high-wage jobs is fixed at E, then the equilibrium urban population size, given by S^*, and the equilibrium employment probability, given by q^*, are related according to $q^*S^* = E$. Applying this condition to equation (9.16), we can solve for q^* when net migration is zero:

$$q^*\alpha_s\left[N - \frac{E}{q^*}\right] - (1-q^*)\beta\frac{E}{q^*} = 0 \qquad (9.17)$$

It is convenient to use the simplifying expressions $\delta \equiv \beta/\alpha_s$ and $R \equiv E/N$ and write the solution for q^* as

$$q^* = \frac{1}{2}R(1-\delta) + \frac{1}{2}[R^2(1-\delta)^2 + 4\delta R]^{1/2} \qquad (9.18)$$

The traditional model will have no net migration when the expression in (9.16) is equal to zero. Using the same notation as (9.18), this implies an employment probability q_T given by

$$q_T = \frac{\delta}{1+\delta} \qquad (9.19)$$

The curves in Figure 9.1 describe the solutions for q^* given by (9.18) for various values of δ and R. For purposes of comparison, the function in (9.19) is also provided, labeled q_T. It is evident from the diagram that in cases in which R is large (i.e., in which the number of modern-sector jobs represents a substantial fraction of total employment) the equilibrium employment rate projected by our feedback model will exceed that predicted from traditional models. It is useful to determine the parameter values at which the two models are identical. Substituting q in (9.19) for q^* in (9.18), we obtain

$$\delta = \frac{2R}{1-2R} \qquad (9.20)$$

Because R is necessarily positive, it is possible for the two models to produce equivalent results only in cases with $R < 0.5$. For values of $R > 0.5$, there is no value of δ that will solve (9.20), and as the curves in Figure 9.1 indicate, the feedback model produces a lower urban unemployment rate whatever the values of the other parameters.

The relative implications of the two models are reversed when the modern sector is relatively small. For many (although not all) values of δ, the feedback model produces an urban unemployment rate that exceeds that suggested by other models. The reason for this has already been given: If the rural population base is very large, even a small probability

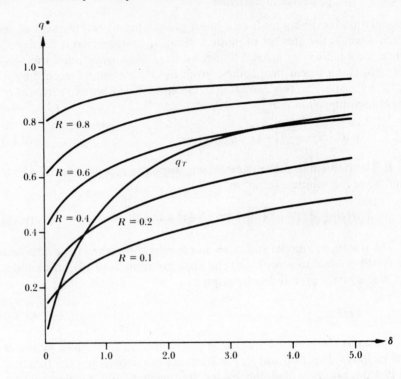

Figure 9.1. Employment rate as a function of $R \equiv E/N$ and $\delta \equiv \beta/\alpha_s$.

of migration may produce a large number of actual migrants, and these will not be offset by departures from a small urban area. Thus, small urban areas are likely to have higher unemployment rates (other parameters being equal) than are larger ones.

City size in equilibrium is given by E/q^* in model II and by E/q in model I. In general, model II suggests that city size is less sensitive to parameter changes than does model I. Figure 9.2 consists of four panels describing the dependence of city size (as a proportion of total work force) on the variable δ. Each panel corresponds to a different value of $R = E/N$ ranging from $R = 0.1$ to $R = 0.8$. For small values of R, S^* is greater than S_T for all reasonable values of δ, whereas for large values of R this condition is reversed, and S^* is smaller than S_T.

It may be useful to consider the unemployment rate as a proportion of the total work force rather than just the urban population. If we call U^* the equilibrium national unemployment rate for model II, then we have $U^* = R(1/q^* - 1)$. Model I will produce an unemployment rate U_T that is similarly defined. Figure 9.3 consists of four panels describing the depen-

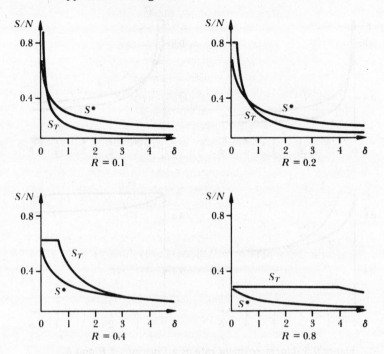

Figure 9.2. City size (S^*/N) as a function of R and δ.

dence of these unemployment rates on δ for various values of R. Again, we find U^* to be less sensitive than U_T. For small values of R we have a higher unemployment rate for model II, whereas this condition is reversed for larger values of R.

In summary, we note that this is another case in which the characterization of behavior in terms of a dynamic adjustment process not only provides a defined adjustment mechanism out of equilibrium but also alters our view of the equilibrium state. Traditional optimization models define equilibrium as a condition with no migration at all. Our dynamic model, by way of contrast, is in equilibrium when net migration is zero, and this is a condition in which in-migration just balances out-migration. It is this difference that has introduced the relevance of the population bases into our models. Conditions in the city induce a certain probability of in-migration from rural areas, and the inflow that results then depends on the size of the population to which this probability applies. Thus, small cities are inclined to grow because there is a small population base for generating out-migration, and there is a relatively large non-resident population from which in-migrants may be drawn. Larger cities

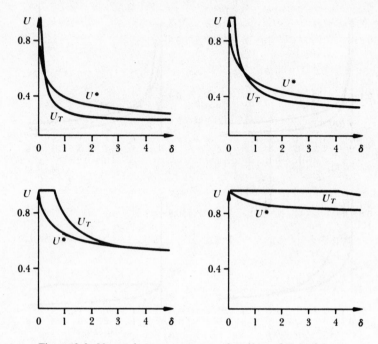

Figure 9.3. Unemployment rate as a function of R and δ.

experience a reversal of this condition, and their growth is thereby stabilized. In comparison with traditional comparative-statics models, our theory produces cities more homogeneous in size and national unemployment rates that are less dependent on the actual number of high-wage jobs.

CHAPTER 10

Conclusions

The various applications of an experience-driven theory of behavior that have been treated in this book have been drawn from a diverse set of fields, but with a single purpose – that of demonstrating the broad usefulness of the theory and its capacity to generate insights that fall outside the scope of the maximization paradigm. At the same time, the sacrifices that the theory has required have been minor: The general outlines and conclusions of comparative-statics equilibrium theory remain in force.

At no point in this book has there been a desire or purpose of renouncing "traditional" economic analysis. The objective has been one of supplementation, adding structure that enables us to address short-run disequilibrium situations as well as long-run equilibrium, and structure that can bring more realism to our treatment of risk and decision making over time. No challenge is intended to the proposition that, given the opportunity to gain experience, consumers and firms come to handle their affairs efficiently and effectively, and certainly no exception is taken to our belief in the capacity of market mechanisms to allocate resources among these same actors according to familiar principles. This book is not intended to stimulate a revolution in our thinking, but to demonstrate that it is possible to write down what seem to be obvious properties of economic adjustment mechanisms and to develop from them empirically useful insights that can be applied to circumstances for which the literal application of maximization theory has always seemed inadequate if not wholly inappropriate.

Equilibrium optimization

Our treatment of optimization as the (usual) equilibrium condition naturally preserves the standard welfare theorems concerning the allocative efficiency of various market mechanisms. At the same time, equilibrium optimization is not invariably satisfied. Moreover, one cannot undergo exposure to literature surrounding the psychology of behavior without losing some confidence in the proposition that self-interest is always effectively pursued by human agents. One may even come to wonder if the concept of self-interest is sufficiently well defined to serve

179

as a cornerstone of economic theory. Problems arise at several levels, and it is worthwhile to review some of them here.

In the examples of lotteries and in the treatment of advertising and demonstration effects, we described situations whose equilibrium properties did not correspond to optimization. In these cases, individual market behavior is not a true reflection of individual self-interest, and thus most conventional welfare theorems fail. In fact, these examples correspond to just those kinds of situations in which economists have always had the least confidence in the suitability of optimization models. At least since the time of Veblen, advertising has been seen to be a source of (potentially) irrational consumer behavior, and examples abound in which consumer behavior under risk seems ineffective at best and wholly irrational at worst (Arrow, 1982). The models developed in this book provide support for the suspicion that fully rational behavior may be a casualty in the presence of advertising or risk, but they also add a useful qualification to these conclusions. Although consumers indeed fail to represent their own self-interest effectively in these models, the deviations from optimality that are obtained are inclined to be relatively small. We find significant changes in equilibrium behavior to be most likely when those changes impose relatively minor losses: Our models suggest that advertising for grossly inferior products will be ineffective in equilibrium, and the model of the demand for lottery tickets implies that lotteries may be attractive only when ticket prices are quite small.

This is not a universal consequence of feedback principles. The search equilibrium and the migration behavior that we have described display deviations from standard comparative-statics optimization, and these do not rely on a condition that differences in payoff magnitudes be small. Even here, however, a related qualification is in order: Large losses in payoff naturally make large payoff gains available to those who employ institutions and behavioral rules that succeed in avoiding them, and thus these situations encourage the acquisition of more effective decision styles. This is one of the reasons why we have made the definition of a choice alternative broad enough to include both simple actions and the use of such sophisticated rules as expected-value maximization or even mathematically complex portfolio selection routines. If the payoff to the use of an elaborate decision rule is high, or is demonstrated by others to be high, it will come to be used frequently (but not by everyone – in a stochastic environment, some will have unsuccessful experiences with such a rule and will reject it). Thus, market equilibrium situations in which experience with simple actions will lead to significant payoff losses will come to be characterized by more sophisticated rules that, whether they are understood by their users or not, provide, on average, higher returns.

One cannot make the generalization that all cases of inefficient equilibrium behavior will be confined to economic problems with trivial payoff differences. Those individuals to whom superior rules have never been demonstrated or whose experience has happened to be unfortunate will still be trapped into inferior behavioral modes (the nontrivial phenomena of cigarette smoking and drunken driving come immediately to mind). Nevertheless, if there is a general tendency for equilibrium violations of optimality to arise more frequently in cases in which these violations do not much matter, that fact will greatly weaken many of the standard objections to the general use of optimization theory under equilibrium conditions.

Myopia

Because they allow no direct influence from future events, feedback mechanisms are inherently myopic in character. Even with experience as our only teacher, however, the future will not be left out entirely; one can still observe the consequences that others have encountered from their own past actions, and hence demonstration effects enable individuals to imitate actions that have proved to be beneficial to others and to avoid actions that have proved to be harmful. Myopia cannot be entirely eliminated by this means: Events that have never occurred before cannot be learned about, and therefore changed environmental circumstances will not be reflected in the payoffs that others have received from past actions. A good empirical example of this problem is provided by the evidence that the numbers of individuals entering various careers respond to changes in economic opportunities, but only after significant lags (Freeman, 1975).

Myopia in our theory is not as extreme as that found in some maximization models. The traditional "cobweb" theory that proposed that farmers choose their output quantities in response only to current prices (thus producing dramatic price changes at crop time) suggested in effect that farmers could go through a series of cycles in product prices without ever learning to avoid their consequences. Our experience-driven theory will not produce such a result. A simple application of the theories given in Chapter 4, in which output quantity is the relevant choice, will produce models that will either converge to a single (optimal) output or at worst produce distributions of individual outputs that in the aggregate will be quite stable. More sophisticated models in which farmers acquire decision rules to guide their responses to market price might generate possible behaviors that would be even better at dealing with the potential instability of agricultural prices. Thus, equilibrium in our experience-driven model may approximate the full-optimization counterpart as expressed in Muth's "rational-expectations" theory (1961).

There is a difference, however, between learning to deal with cyclic events that are a part of one's experience (or others' experiences) and choosing an optimal course of action for dealing with future circumstances that have never occurred before. In such cases, the myopia in our model remains in force, and there is no possibility of a convergence to some counterpart of a dynamic rational-expectations equilibrium. These observations have obvious implications for the description of dynamic equilibrium price paths. For example, consider Hotelling's two-part proposition (1931) that (a) the price (net of extraction costs) of an exhaustible resource should increase at the interest rate subject to the condition (b) that at the date of exhaustion the price has risen to exactly that point at which the quantity demanded of the resource is zero. Part (a) of this proposition is obtained from a simple dynamic arbitrage condition and is therefore readily assimilated by experience. Indeed, this price rule may come to be applied as part of a feedback equilibrium decision system. Part (b), however, makes reference to conditions that are a part of no one's experience, and thus there is no way that it can be made the object of a feedback convergence mechanism. So far as our theory is concerned, we can expect an equlibrium in which prices rise at the appropriate rate, but we cannot expect the equilibrium price level to match some "rational" long-run value. Our model leaves the price level arbitrary (for a time), leaving open the possibility of the sudden and unexpected price breaks (up or down) that are commonly associated with speculative "bubbles" (Cross, 1982).

The myopia in feedback models extends in both directions in that recent experience always has a greater influence over behavior than has the more distant past. These are models in which the actual sequence in which events occur can make a difference (as we observed in the model of search equilibrium), and it is this fact that all historical events are never given equal weight that is responsible for the inefficiency that general experiential models have in dealing with problems involving risk. As examples of this mechanism, we might find that automobile seat belts are more likely to be buckled immediately after one has witnessed an accident, or that asset holdings change character as the experience of the 1930s recedes into the past.

Self-interest

A potentially more far-reaching concern for welfare economics has to do with the definition of "self-interest" itself. This is a problem that has been sidestepped in this book through the use of an orthodox utility function. Once we abandon the characterization of an individual as a fully informed calculator of optimal behavior, however, we implicitly abandon complete knowledge of self-interest, and it is natural to ask if people really "know" what is "good" for them in the first place. So far as the logic of their structure is concerned, our models require only that certain outcomes stimulate repetitions of the behaviors that brought them about and that alternative payoffs differ in their capacities to induce such repetitions. It is useful to recall the standard Darwinian observation that genes that proliferate through evolution are those that support successful reproduction of organisms and not those that make those organisms "happy" or "successful" in any other sense. Our theory provides a close parallel in that there is no essential requirement that payoffs that bring about repetitions in behavior also contribute to the well-being of the individual. From a welfare standpoint, such a requirement would obviously be very desirable. One is tempted to appeal to an evolutionary argument to restore this linkage, noting that behavioral responses that are harmful would not evolve successfully, so that in a Darwinian equilibrium the determinants of behavior (whatever they may be) and self-interest (defined as genetic success) must be coincident. Such an argument presupposes that evolutionary equilibrium has been achieved, however, and we have no assurance that this is in fact the case. Opportunities for drunken driving are very recent in evolutionary history, and supposing that there is a gene or set of genes that make some individuals susceptible to this behavior, not nearly enough time has passed for this genotype to have been eliminated from the pool. Compulsive teenage players of electronic video games are surely not enhancing their long-run chances for success (genetic or otherwise), and yet this behavior is evidently strongly encouraged by the payoffs that are provided. The point is that if we are in a state of transition, only short-run analyses are appropriate, and we have no guarantee that in every case the biological determinants of behavior are consistent with self-interest in the twentieth century, however appropriate they may have been thousands of years ago.

The fact that an experience-driven theory of behavior does not depend on complete cognizance of self-interest is responsible for many of the intellectual divisions between economists and other social scientists. From the perspective of conventional optimization theory, cigarette smokers, drunken drivers, those who build their houses on floodplains or on slippery mud-clay hillsides, and even suicides and alcoholics either are the victims of incomplete information or are meeting the demands of their own self-interests, whatever "outsiders" may believe. The appropriate social policies for dealing with such persons can only be (a) to provide them with information and (b) to leave them alone. These are not the only policies that are compatible with an experience-driven theory of behavior, however, because such a theory leaves open the possibility that some behaviors are motivated by payoffs that are not beneficial to anyone (Cross and Guyer, 1980). Thus, policies that limit alcoholism, reduce cigarette smoking, and prevent suicide acquire support from a feedback analysis, although they cannot be justified through any reference to traditional economic theory. This seems to be a good direction for us to take, if only because it appeals so strongly to common sense to believe that imperfect behavioral adaptation can lead to significant losses in welfare and that there is good reason to try to limit these losses.

Making money

One of the standard arguments in support of the use of optimization as a behavioral paradigm states that a failure to achieve optimization on the part of a significant number of market agents should leave open profit-making opportunities for others who do not suffer from similar behavioral deficiencies or who are in a position to exploit the nonrational behavior in other ways. In competitive situations, the "optimizers" should succeed in displacing the "nonoptimizers" altogether, so that (using a natural selection model) only optimizers will remain. The validity of such displacement arguments clearly depends on the context; it applies much more readily to firms than to consumers, and it is more relevant to competitive markets than it is to situations involving small numbers of firms. Even in the case of competitive markets, however, the selection argument is not airtight. Equilibrium without optimization is supportable indefinitely if no one happens to optimize, or if the capacity to optimize is a special talent that is available to only a few entrepreneurs.

In fact, one can point to quite a number of institutions that do draw their subsistence from nonoptimal equilibrium market behavior of others. (Whether or not these institutions make "profits" in the economic sense, of course, depends on the structure of the relevant industry, not on the question of individual rationality.) We have already provided one such example in our model of state-run lottery games. In that case, profits are clearly available because of the explicit entry barriers that are in place to limit competition, but it is easy to extend the model to include gambling establishments in general. Other types of institutions profit by providing higher-level decision rules of one sort or another that, for a price, enable and encourage behavior that is closer to optimal than are more easily learned lower-order responses. Educational institutions in general are obvious examples; one is particularly impressed by the role of certain technical and professional training programs that seem to stress rote learning and the acquisition of decision rules whose intellectual foundations are at best imperfectly understood by their trainees. A curious example of another sort was provided by the proliferation of "Christmas clubs" in savings institutions during the 1950s and 1960s. These amounted only to savings plans that encouraged routine deposits during the year with the object of having a useful sum of spending money available during the holiday season. These programs had a cost in that they paid reduced interest rates (compared with ordinary passbook savings), and hence participation in them was inferior to a self-imposed regime of regular saving; yet they proved to be extremely popular. From an optimization standpoint, the use of Christmas clubs was not rational, but as providers of decision rules in settings that would otherwise induce imperfect equilibrium behavior, they proved to have a substantial market.

The vulnerability of those engaging in nonoptimal behavior to exploitation by those who optimize is particularly relevant in asset markets. Because these markets incorporate a significant element of risk, we have here a setting in which the myopic experiential mechanism is conducive to nonoptimal equilibrium behavior. It is characteristic for these markets to be composed of a variety of different types of participants; for our purposes, let us consider just two stylized examples – "amateurs" (or amateur speculators) and "professionals." Whereas the amateurs may follow relatively simple (or at least naive) decision rules, the professionals are individuals and firms who have developed more sophisticated decision rules, or whose volumes of holdings are large enough for actuarial cash flows to dominate experience. If the professionals engage in profitable arbitrage, the market will operate as if all participants are optimizers, and we are justified in using the optimization paradigm to describe the equilibrium. This is not the end of the story, however, because the amateurs continue to engage in transactions that tend to push market variables away from this equilibrium and restore arbitrage opportunities for the professionals. We may end up with a free-entry counterpart of the state lottery game: In this equilibrium the amateur speculators lose money systematically to a competitive industry of professionals who do not, on average, make large profits (because of the free-entry condition) but who do succeed in covering opportunity costs.

Experimental economics

These conclusions lead to a few further comments on the use of laboratory experiments to test the predictions of rational market behavior. We must note, for example, that economic necessity (as well as humanity) dictates that when human subjects are used in laboratory experiments, the payoffs must be quite small compared with the payoffs in "real" markets. Otherwise, the cost of obtaining evidence from samples of adequate size would exceed the generosity of any foundation, and the harm that would have to be imposed on those unfortunate subjects who failed to perform "well" would challenge the conscience of almost any experimenter. In the light of our feedback theory, this appears to be a significant restriction: For reasons that we have already cited, we expect equilibrium deviations from rationality to be most pronounced when the inferior choices incur relatively minor payoff losses. This suggestion extends to the possibility that deviations from rationality that are found in small-payoff laboratory experiments may not be generalizable into significant sources of insight into real market behavior. There do exist a few experimental situations in which equilibrium behavior seems to move toward rationality as payoff increases (Atkinson, 1962), and others that do not find any such effect (Grether and Plott, 1979), but even these are confined to very small payoff differences, and the problem of extrapolation from the laboratory to the market remains unresolved.

There is a great deal of ambiguity as to what hypotheses a laboratory market experiment should be testing. There are at least four reasonable alternatives. First, we may be testing the validity of a short-run maximization paradigm. In this case, it will be appropriate to place naive subjects in an unfamiliar situation, describe some rules, and test for the immediate implementation of optimization or, where necessary, the use of Bayesian information-gathering techniques. Second, we may be testing an experience-driven adjustment mechanism similar to that described in this book. In that case, the same experiment might be appropriate, but we would then design the procedure to simplify an evaluation of a dynamic convergence process. Third, we may focus on the proposition that the rules of optimization apply in the (experimental) long run without any regard for the intermediate stages of adjustment. This is the hypothesis that is most commonly treated in practice, although this version has the usual disability of suggesting a theory of equilibrium without providing any corresponding theory of convergence.

Fourth, it is implicit in the models derived in this book that human subjects in laboratory experiments will not react to brand new situations in newly appropriate ways, but will carry with them responses that have already been learned outside of the laboratory. Our fourth hypothesis is therefore that experiments serve to uncover decision styles and rules of thumb that are typical of established real-world environments. Under this interpretation, however, the naive subject (the college sophomore) is not at all appropriate for the purpose, because the necessary background experience is limited and may be confined to a few atypical situations. Such subjects may actually bring with them unrealistic and stylized impressions of how markets work, thus tending to obscure rather than reveal important behavioral regularities.

This fourth hypothesis has an intriguing corollary. We have noted that a number of experiments have revealed violations of the expected-utility hypothesis that are interpretable as violations of the "independence" axiom. M. Machina has suggested to me that under conditions of "temporal" risk (i.e., in which there is a significant lag between action and realized outcome, and in which other decisions must be made during this period), efficient behavior is not identical with that under static risk and expected-utility maximizing behavior under temporal risk will produce apparent violations of the independence axiom that are similar to those revealed by the "Allais paradox" (Allais, 1953) and the experimental work of Kahneman and Tversky (1979). Because "temporal" risk is in fact the rule outside the artificial environment of the laboratory, the possibility arises that what is observed in an experiment is not a self-contained example of how people behave under risk, but an *image* of how people have learned to react to real-world conditions of risk. If experimental subjects are bringing their decision rules with them into the laboratory, it is this latter hypothesis that is being put to test.

This interpretation is given support by a further experimental result. It is found that subjects' selections among risky alternatives are quite insensitive to changes in the wealth level around which the payoffs are centered; see the discussion of Machina (1982). From the standpoint of expected-utility maximization, this should occur only if the utility function is linear, which would be inconsistent with the widespread incidence of risk-averse behavior. If these subjects are simply carrying with them into the laboratory behavior that has been acquired over a long period of time, then this insensitivity to wealth changes is exactly the result one might expect.

Conclusion

There are innumerable avenues of study that can be opened up by an experience-driven theory of behavior, and we have only touched on a few of them here. Some of these are merely intriguing possibilities that have been suggested by hearsay evidence (such as an alleged fact that hospital workers are unusually avid purchasers of life and disability insurance). Others, such as a thorough analysis of savings behavior and the role of durable assets, could assist in the analysis of such major issues as social insurance programs and the welfare of the elderly.

It would be useful as well to deal with undesirable restrictions that, for convenience, we have imposed on our models. Our use of an independence assumption for much of the discussion has made simple models possible, but it has abstracted from the human ability to make inferences (both correct and false) about future events on the basis of selected past circumstances. The "man in the street" often holds strong views concerning "balance" in government budgets, for example, and yet the economic consequences of such "balance" (or lack or it) are still matters of controversy among professional economists, and they cannot be a part of anyone's ordinary experience. Relaxation of our independence assumption may enable some analysis of how payoffs under one situation or state of nature may be generalized into market behavior elsewhere and how such generalization may produce systematic deviation from optimality.

Another interesting line of research would focus on the cardinality of the dependent variable in a feedback model. We noted that the concavity of our feedback mechanism produces behavior that is indistinguishable from risk aversion – a property that is usually attributed to concave utility functions. One might go further, noting that payoffs may be given cardinalist rankings based on the magnitudes of their behavioral effects (in our case, the size of the probability adjustments).

References

Alchian, A. A. 1950. "Uncertainty, Evolution and Economic Theory." *Journal of Political Economy* 58:211-22.

Allais, M. 1953. "Le Comportement de l'Homme Rationnel devant le Risque. Critique des Postulats et Axiomes de l'Ecole Americaine." *Econometrica* 21: 503-46.

Allison, J. 1981. "Economics and Operant Conditioning." In *Predictability, Correlation, and Contiguity*, edited by P. Harzem and M. D. Zeiler, pp. 321-53. New York: Wiley.

Archibald, G. C. 1961-2. "Chamberlin vs. Chicago." *Review of Economic Studies* 29:2-28.

Arrow, K. J. 1962. "The Economic Implications of Learning by Doing." *Review of Economic Studies* 29:155-73.

1982. "Risk Perception in Psychology and Economics." *Economic Inquiry* 20: 1-9.

Arrow, K. J., Karlin, S., and Suppes, P. (editors). 1960. *Mathematical Methods in the Social Sciences*. Stanford University Press.

Atkinson, R. C. 1962. "Choice Behavior and Monetary Payoff: Strong and Weak Conditioning." In *Mathematical Methods in Small Group Processes*, edited by J. Criswell, H. Solomon, and P. Suppes, pp. 23-34. Stanford University Press.

Atkinson, R. C., Bower, G. H., and Crothers, E. J. 1965. *An Introduction to Mathematical Learning Theory*. New York: Wiley.

Ayllon, T., and Azrin, N. 1966. *The Token Economy*. New York: Appleton-Century-Crofts.

Bailey, M. J., Olson, M., and Wonnacott, P. 1980. "Marginal Utility of Income Does Not Increase: Lending, and Friedman-Savage Gambles." *American Economic Review* 70:372-9.

Battalio, R. C., Kagel, J. H., and Green, L. 1979. "Labor Supply Behavior of Animal Workers: Towards an Experimental Analysis." In *Research in Experimental Economics*, edited by V. Smith, pp. 231-54. Greenwich, Conn.: Jai Press.

Battalio, R. C., Kagel, J. H., Rachlin, H., and Green, L. 1981. "Commodity-Choice Behavior with Pigeons as Subjects." *Journal of Political Economy* 1: 67-91.

Baumol, W. J., and Quandt, R. E. 1964. "Rules of Thumb and Optimally Imperfect Decisions." *American Economic Review* 54:23-46.

Baumol, W. J., and Stewart, M. 1971. "On the Behavioral Theory of the Firm." In *The Corporate Economy: Growth, Competition and Innovative Potential*, edited by R. Marris and A. Wood. Cambridge: Harvard University Press.

Bernouilli, D. (1738) 1954. "Exposition of a New Theory of the Measurement of Risk." *Econometrica* 22:23-36 (translation).

Bishop, R. L. 1962. "The Stability of the Cournot Oligopoly Solution: Further Comment." *Review of Economic Studies* 29:332-6.

Boyer, K. 1974. "Informative and Goodwill Advertising." *Review of Economics and Statistics* 56:541-8.

Bruner, J. S., Goodnow, J. J., and Austin, G. A. 1957. *A Study of Thinking*. New York: Wiley.

Bush, R. B., and Estes, W. K. (editors). 1959. *Studies in Mathematical Learning Theory*. Stanford University Press.

Bush, R. R., and Mosteller, F. 1955. *Stochastic Models for Learning*. New York: Wiley.

Butters, G. 1977. "Equilibrium Distributions of Sales and Advertising Prices." *Review of Economic Studies* 44:465-92.

Clarkson, G. P. E. 1963. "A Model of Trust Investment Behavior." In *A Behavioral Theory of the Firm*, edited by R. M. Cyert and J. G. March, pp. 253-67. Englewood Cliffs, N.J.: Prentice-Hall.

Comanor, W. S., and Wilson, T. A. 1979. "Advertising and Competition: A Survey." *Journal of Economic Literature* 17:453-76.

Commission on Review of the National Policy toward Gambling. 1976. *Gambling in America*. U.S. Government Printing Office.

Conlisk, J. 1980. "Costly Optimizers Versus Cheap Imitators." *Journal of Economic Behavior and Organization* 1:275-93.

Coombs, C. H., Dawes, R. M., and Tversky, A. 1970. *Mathematical Psychology*. Englewood Cliffs, N.J.: Prentice-Hall.

Cross, J. G. 1973. "A Stochastic Learning Model of Economic Behavior." *Quarterly Journal of Economics* 87:239-66.

1982. "On Baubles and Bubbles." Unpublished manuscript, University of Michigan.

Cross, J. G., and Guyer, M. 1980. *Social Traps*. Ann Arbor: University of Michigan Press.

Cyert, R. M., and DeGroot, M. H. 1970. "Bayesian Analysis and Duopoly Theory." *Journal of Political Economy* 78:1168-84.

1971. "Interfirm Learning and the Kinked Demand Curve." *Journal of Economic Theory* 3:272-87.

1973. "An Analysis of Cooperation and Learning in a Duopoly Context." *American Economic Review* 63:24-37.

1974. "Rational Expectations and Bayesian Analysis." *Journal of Political Economy* 82:521-36.

Cyert, R. M., and March, J. G. (editors). 1963. *A Behavioral Theory of the Firm*. Englewood Cliffs, N.J.: Prentice-Hall.

Darby, M. R., 1972. "The Allocation of Transitory Income Among Consumers' Assets." *American Economic Review* 62:928-41.

Darwin, C. 1859. *The Origin of the Species by Means of Natural Selection.* New York: D. Appleton & Co. (1929).

Dawkins, R. 1976. *The Selfish Gene.* Oxford University Press.

Day, R. H. 1971. "Rational Choice and Economic Behavior." *Theory and Decision* 1:229–51.

Day, R. H., and Groves, T. (editors). 1975. *Adaptive Economic Models.* New York: Academic Press.

Day, R. H., Morley, S., and Smith, K. R. 1974. "Myopic Optimizing and Rules of Thumb in a Micro-Model of Industrial Growth." *American Economic Review* 64:11–23.

Diamond, P. A. 1971. "A Model of Price Adjustment." *Journal of Economic Theory* 3:156–8.

Doob, J. L. 1953. *Stochastic Processes.* New York: Wiley.

Dorfman, R., and Steiner, P. O. 1954. "Optimal Advertising and Optimal Quality." *American Economic Review* 54:808–25.

Duesenberry, J. S. 1952. *Income, Saving, and the Theory of Consumer Behavior.* Cambridge: Harvard University Press.

Earley, J. S. 1956. "Marginal Policies of 'Excellently Managed' Companies." *American Economic Review* 46:44–70.

Edwards, W. 1961. "Probability Learning in 1000 Trials." *Journal of Experimental Psychology* 62:385–94.

Ehrlich, I. 1973. "Participation in Illegitimate Activities: A Theoretical and Empirical Investigation." *Journal of Political Economy* 81:521–65.

  1975. "The Deterrent Effect of Capital Punishment: A Question of Life and Death." *American Economic Review* 65:397–417.

Farrell, M. J. 1970. "Some Elementary Selection Processes in Economics." *Review of Economic Studies* 37:305–19.

Feather, N. T. 1961. "The Relationship of Persistence at a Task to Expectation of Success and Achievement Related Motives." *Journal of Abnormal and Social Psychology* 63:552–61.

Fisher, I. 1930. *The Theory of Interest.* New York: Macmillan (Augustus M. Kelley reprint, 1961).

Fisher, F. M. 1961. "The Stability of the Cournot Oligopoly Solution: The Effects of Speeds of Adjustment and Increasing Marginal Costs." *Review of Economic Studies* 28:125–35.

Frech, H. E., and Rochlin, C. B. 1979. "Advertising as a Privately Supplied Public Good." *Economic Inquiry* 17:414–18.

Freeman, R. B. 1975. "Supply and Salary Adjustments to the Changing Science Manpower Market: Physics, 1948–1973." *American Economic Review* 65: 27–39.

Friedman, M. 1953. "The Methodology of Positive Economics." *Essays in Positive Economics.* University of Chicago Press.

  1957. *A Theory of the Consumption Function.* Princeton University Press.

Friedman, M., and Savage, L. J. 1948. "The Utility Analysis of Choices Involving Risk." *Journal of Political Economy* 56:179–304 (reprinted in *Readings in Price Theory.* Homewood, Ill.: Irwin).

192   References

Frisch, H. 1977. "Inflation Theory 1963–75: A Second Generation Survey." *Journal of Economic Literature* 15:1289–317.

Galbraith, J. K. 1960. *The Affluent Society.* Boston: Houghton Mifflin.

1971. *The New Industrial State.* Boston: Houghton Mifflin.

Garber, J., and Seligman, M. E. P. (editors). 1980. *Human Helplessness, Theory and Applications.* New York: Academic Press.

Gorman, W. M. 1967. "Tastes, Habits, and Choice." *International Economic Review* 8:218–22.

Grant, D. A., Hake, H. W., and Hornseth, J. P. 1951. "Acquisition and Extinction of a Verbal Conditioned Response with Differing Percentages of Reinforcement." *Journal of Experimental Psychology* 41:1–5.

Grether, D. M., and Plott, C. H. 1979. "Economic Theory of Choice and the Preference Reversal Phenomenon." *American Economic Review* 69:623–38.

Hahn, F. H. 1962. "The Stability of the Cournot Oligopoly Solution." *Review of Economic Studies* 29:329–31.

Hamilton, W. D. 1964. "The Genetical Evolution of Social Behavior." *Journal of Theoretical Biology* 7:1–16.

1972. "Altruism and Related Phenomena, Mainly in Social Insects." *Annual Review of Ecology and Systematics* 3:193–232.

Harris, J. R., and Todaro, M. P. 1970. "Migration, Unemployment, and Development: A Two-Sector Analysis." *American Economic Review* 60:126–42.

Herrnstein, R. J. 1970. "On the Law of Effect." *Journal of the Experimental Analysis of Behavior* 13:243–66.

Herrnstein, R. J., and Loveland, D. 1975. "Maximizing and Matching on Concurrent Ratio Schedules." *Journal of the Experimental Analysis of Behavior* 24:107–17.

Hilgard, E. R., and Marquis, D. G. 1961. *Conditioning and Learning.* New York: Appleton-Century-Crofts.

Hilgard, E. R., and Bower, G. H. 1968. *Theories of Learning.* New York: Appleton-Century-Crofts.

Himmelweit, S. 1976. "A Behavioral Model of Learning in Production." *Review of Economic Studies* 43:329–46.

Hoenack, S. A., and Weiler, W. C. 1980. "A Structural Model of Murder Behavior." *American Economic Review* 70:327–41.

Hotelling, H. 1931. "The Economics of Exhaustible Resources." *Journal of Political Economy* 39:137–75.

Houthakker, H. S., and Taylor, L. D. 1970. *Consumer Demand in the United States*, 2nd ed. Cambridge: Harvard University Press.

Intriligator, M. D. 1971. *Mathematical Optimization and Economic Theory.* Inglewood Cliffs, N.J.: Prentice-Hall.

Kagel, J. H., and Battalio, R. C. 1980. "Token Economy and Animal Models for the Experimental Analysis of Economic Behavior." In *Evaluation of Econometric Models*, edited by J. Kmenta and J. B. Ramsey, pp. 379–401. New York: Academic Press.

Kagel, J. H., Battalio, R. C., Rachlin, H., Basmann, R. L., Green, L., and Klemm, W. R. 1975. "Experimental Studies of Consumer Demand Behavior Using Laboratory Animals." *Economic Inquiry* 13:22–38.

Kahneman, D., and Tversky, A. 1979. "Prospect Theory: An Analysis of Decision Under Risk." *Econometrica* 47:263–91.

Katona, G. 1970. *The Powerful Consumer Demand in the United States*, 2nd ed. Cambridge: Harvard University Press.

Knight, F. H. 1921. *Risk, Uncertainty and Profit*. Boston: Houghton Mifflin.

Kohn, G., and Shavell, S. 1974. "The Theory of Search." *Journal of Economic Theory* 9:93–123.

Koopmans, T. C. 1957. *Three Essays on the State of Economic Science.* New York: McGraw-Hill.

Kuhn, T. S. 1970. *The Structure of Scientific Revolutions*, 2nd ed. University of Chicago Press.

Lancaster, K. 1966. "A New Approach to Consumer Theory." *Journal of Political Economy* 74:132–56.

Lave, L. B. 1962. "An Empirical Approach to the Prisoner's Dilemma Game." *Quarterly Journal of Economics* 76:424–36.

Leibenstein, H. 1950. "Bandwagon, Snob, and Veblin Effects in the Theory of Consumers' Demand." *Quarterly Journal of Economics* 64:183–207.

Lewin, K., Dembo, T., Festinger, L., and Sears, P. 1944. "Level of Aspiration." In *Personality and the Behavior Disorders, Vol. 1*, edited by J. V. Hunt, pp. 333–78. New York: Ronald Press.

Luce, R. D., and Raiffa, H. 1957. *Games and Decisions.* New York: Wiley.

McCall, J. J. 1970. "Economics of Information and Job Search." *Quarterly Journal of Economics* 84:113–26.

Machina, M. J. 1982. "'Expected Utility' Analysis without the Independence Axiom." *Econometrica* 50:277–323.

Machlup, F. 1946. "Marginal Analysis and Empirical Research." *American Economic Review* 36:519–54.

1967. "Theories of the Firm: Marginalist, Behavioral, and Managerial." *American Economic Review* 57:1–33.

McManus, M., and Quandt, R. E., 1961. "Comments on the Stability of the Cournot Oligopoly Model." *Review of Economic Studies* 28:136–9.

March, J. G., and Simon, H. A. 1968. *Organizations.* New York: Wiley.

Marris, R. 1963. "A Model of the 'Managerial' Enterprise." *Quarterly Journal of Economics* 77:185–209.

Marshak, J., and Radner, R. 1972. *Economic Theory of Teams.* New Haven: Yale University Press.

Mirrlees, J. A., and Stern, N. H. 1972. "Fairly Good Plans." *Journal of Economic Theory* 4:268–88.

Munkres, J. R. 1975. *Topology.* Englewood Cliffs, N.J.: Prentice-Hall.

Muth, J. F. 1961. "Rational Expectations and the Theory of Price Movements." *Econometrica* 29:315–35.

Nelson, P. 1974. "Advertising as Information." *Journal of Political Economy* 82:729–54.

Nelson, R. R., and Winter, S. G. 1973. "Toward an Evolutionary Theory of Economic Capabilities." *American Economic Review* 63:440–49.

1982. *An Evolutionary Theory of Economic Change.* Cambridge: Harvard University Press.

Norman, M. F. 1972. *Markov Processes as Learning Models*. New York: Academic Press.

Olton, D. S. 1979. "Mazes, Maps, and Memory." *American Psychologist* 34: 583–96.

Parks, R. W. 1978. "Inflation and Relative Price Variability." *Journal of Political Economy* 86:79–95.

Penrose, E. T. 1952. "Biological Analogies in the Theory of the Firm." *American Economic Review* 42:804–19.

Phelps, E. S. 1970. "Money-Wage Dynamics and Labor Market Equilibrium." In *Microeconomic Foundations of Employment and Inflation Theory*, edited by E. S. Phelps. New York: Norton.

Phelps, E. S., and Winter, S. G. 1970. "Optimal Price Policy under Atomistic Competition." In *Microeconomic Foundations of Employment and Inflation Theory*, edited by E. S. Phelps, pp. 309–37. New York: Norton.

Pollack, R. A. 1970. "Habit Formation and Dynamic Demand Functions." *Journal of Political Economy* 78:745–63.

Reinganum, J. F. 1979. "A Simple Model of Equilibrium Price Dispersion." *Journal of Political Economy* 87:851–8.

Rosen, S. 1974. "Hedonic Prices and Implicit Markets." *Journal of Political Economy* 82:34–55.

Rothschild, M. 1973. "Models of Market Organization with Imperfect Information: A Survey." *Journal of Political Economy* 81:1283–308.

1974a. "Searching for the Lowest Price When the Distribution of Prices Is Unknown." *Journal of Political Economy* 82:689–712.

1974b. "A Two-Armed Bandit Theory of Market Pricing." *Journal of Economic Theory* 9:185–202.

Rubin, P. H., and Paul, C. W. 1979. "An Evolutionary Model of Taste for Risk." *Economic Inquiry* 42:585–96.

Salop, S., and Stiglitz, J. 1977. "Bargains and Ripoffs: A Model of Monopolistically Competitive Price Dispersion." *Review of Economic Studies* 44: 493–510.

Samuelson, P. A. 1948. *Foundations of Economic Analysis*. Cambridge: Harvard University Press.

Sattath, S., and Tversky, A. 1976. "Unite and Conquer: A Multiplicative Inequality for Choice Probabilities." *Econometrica* 44:79–89.

Savage, L. J. 1954. *The Foundations of Statistics*. New York: Wiley.

Schmalensee, R. 1978. "A Model of Advertising and Product Quality." *Journal of Political Economy* 86:485–504.

Scitovsky, T. 1943. "A Note on Profit Maximization and Its Implications." *Review of Economic Studies* 11:57–60.

1977. *The Joyless Economy*. Oxford University Press.

Seligman, M. E. P. 1975. *Helplessness*. San Francisco: Freeman.

Shubik, M. 1970. "A Curmudgeon's Guide to Microeconomics." *Journal of Economic Literature* 8:405–34.

Siegel, S. 1957. "Level of Aspiration and Decision Making." *Psychological Review* 64:253–62.

Simon, H. A. 1955. "A Behavioral Model of Rational Choice." *Quarterly Journal of Economics* 69:99-118.

1957. *Models of Man*. New York: Wiley.

1959. "Theories of Decision-making in Economics and Behavioral Science." *American Economic Review* 49:253-83.

1965. *Administrative Behavior*, 2nd ed. New York: Free Press.

Skinner, B. F. 1938. *The Behavior of Organisms: An Experimental Analysis*. New York: Appleton-Century-Crofts.

Smallwood, D. E., and Conlisk, J. 1979. "Product Quality in Markets where Consumers Are Imperfectly Informed." *Quarterly Journal of Economics* 93: 1-24.

Smart, D. R. 1973. *Fixed Point Theorems*. Cambridge: Harvard University Press.

Smith, J. M. 1978. "The Evolution of Behavior." *Scientific American* 239: 176-92.

Smith, P. E. 1962. "The Demand for Durable Goods: Permanent or Transitory Income?" *Journal of Political Economy* 70:500-4.

Smith, V. 1981. "Microeconomic Systems as an Experimental Science." Discussion paper 81-32, Department of Economics, College of Business and Public Administration, University of Arizona, Tucson.

Solzhenitsyn, A. 1970. "One Word of Truth." Nobel speech on literature.

State of Michigan. 1974-8. *Bureau of State Lottery Annual Report, 1974-1978*. Box 30023, 6545 Mercantile Way, Lansing, Michigan 48909.

Stigler, G. J. 1961. "The Economics of Information." *Journal of Political Economy* 69:213-25.

Stiglitz, J. E. 1974. "Wage Determination and Unemployment in L.D.C.'s." *Quarterly Journal of Economics* 88:194-227.

Strotz, R. H. 1956. "Myopia and Inconsistency in Dynamic Utility Maximization." *Review of Economic Studies* 23:165-80.

Suppes, P., and Atkinson, R. C. 1960. *Markov Learning Models for Multiperson Interactions*. Stanford University Press.

Suppes, P., and Carlsmith, U. M. 1962. "Experimental Analysis of a Duopoly Situation from the Standpoint of Mathematical Learning Theory." *International Economic Review* 3:60-78.

Thaler, R. 1977. "An Economic Analysis of Property Crime." *Journal of Political Economy* 8:37-51.

Theocharis, R. D. 1962. "On the Stability of the Cournot Solution of the Oligopoly Problem." *Review of Economic Studies* 29:133-4.

Timberlake, W., and Allison, J. 1974. "Response Deprivation: An Empirical Approach to Instrumental Performance." *Psychological Review* 81:146-64.

Todaro, M. P. 1974. "A Model of Labor Migration and Urban Employment in Less Developed Countries." *American Economic Review* 59:139-48.

1976. "Internal Migration in Developing Countries: A Survey." Presented at NBER conference on population and economic change in less developing countries.

Tversky, A., and Kahneman, D. 1974. "Judgement Under Certainty: Heuristics and Biases." *Science* 185:1124-31.

196   References

Tversky, A., and Sattath, S. 1979. "Preference Trees." *Psychological Review* 86: 542–73.

Usher, S. E. 1978. *Consumer Aspirations: A Dynamic Approach.* Ph.D. dissertation, University of Michigan.

Vining, D. R., Jr., and Elwertowski, T. C. 1976. "The Relationship between Relative Prices and the General Price Level." *American Economic Review* 66: 699–708.

Whipple, D. 1973. "A Generalized Theory of Job Search." *Journal of Political Economy* 81:1170–88.

Wilde, L. L., and Schwartz, A. 1979. "Equilibrium Comparison Shopping." *Review of Economic Studies* 46:543–53.

Williamson, O. E. 1963. "Managerial Discretion and Business Behavior." *American Economic Review* 52:1032–57.

Winter, S. G. 1964. "Economic 'Natural Selection' and the Theory of the Firm." *Yale Economic Essays* 4:225–72.

——— 1971. "Satisficing, Selection and the Innovating Remnant." *Quarterly Journal of Economics* 85:237–61.

——— 1975. "Optimization and Evolution in the Theory of the Firm." In *Adaptive Economic Models*, edited by R. H. Day and T. Groves, pp. 73–118. New York: Academic Press.

Zarembka, P. 1970. "Labor Migration and Urban Unemployment: Comment." *American Economic Review* 60:184–8.

Index